HELPING
YOUR TROUBLED
TEEN

HELPING
YOUR TROUBLED
TEEN

CYNTHIA S. KAPLAN, PH.D.

BLAISE A. AGUIRRE, M.D.

MICHAEL RATER, M.D.

FOREWORD BY ROBERT BROOKS, Ph.D.

FAIR WINDS
PRESS
BEVERLY, MASSACHUSETTS

Text © 2007 Cynthia S. Kaplan, Blaise A. Aguirre, and Michael Rater

First published in the USA in 2007 by
Fair Winds Press, a member of
Quayside Publishing Group
100 Cummings Center
Suite 406-L
Beverly, MA 01915-6101

11 10 09 08 07   1 2 3 4 5

ISBN-13: 978-1-59233-262-5
ISBN-10: 1-59233-262-5

Library of Congress Cataloging-in-Publication Data

Helping your troubled teen : learn to recognize, understand, and address the destructive behavior of today's teens / [edited by] Cynthia Kaplan.
     p. cm.
  Includes bibliographical references.
  ISBN 1-59233-262-5 (pbk.)
  1. Adolescence. 2. Teenagers. 3. Adolescent psychology. 4. Behavior disorder in adolescence. I. Kaplan, Cynthia (Cynthia Sue)
  HQ796.H3963 2007
  616.8900835--dc22
                              2007011859

Cover design by Howard Grossman / 12E Design
Book design by Sandra Salamony

Printed and bound in Canada

The information in this book is for educational purposes only. It is not intended to replace the advice of a physician or medical practitioner. Please see your health care provider before beginning any new health program.

Dedication

To our children,
Alex, Nick, Emma, Wes, Olivia, Max, Henry, Sam,
Isabel, Anthony, Lucas, and Gabriel,
who provide each of us with the continued
inspiration to do our daily work.

We also dedicate this book to the countless children and families
who struggle bravely to overcome often-colossal social obstacles
and enormous emotional challenges to live better, healthier lives.

———————

Contents

Foreword

RAISING AND WORKING WITH ADOLESCENTS in today's world is a challenging task, leaving many adults bewildered and confused about the most effective ways to interact with teens. Many parents question how effective they can be in their role, especially given the prominent external influences impinging on their adolescents, including technology and the Internet. The challenge is rendered even more daunting when adolescents display troubling emotions and behaviors such as substance abuse, depression, anxiety, eating disorders, and self-destructive actions, including suicide attempts and cutting themselves.

Helping Your Troubled Teen is an invaluable resource for both parents and professionals in understanding the teens of today, the problems they manifest, and ways to intervene to help them cope more successfully with the struggles they face. The authors are experienced, skilled clinicians who work with many youths who display problematic behaviors. What they have learned from these youths is evident on every page of this remarkable book. Their empathy, their appreciation of what these youths (and their parents) are experiencing, and their clinical expertise in applying innovative treatment approaches are very impressive and will be very helpful to the reader. This is a book I recommend highly to both parents and professionals involved in raising or working with struggling teens. The authors are to be applauded for conveying their ideas in such an informative and caring manner.

Robert Brooks, Ph.D.
Co-author of *Raising Resilient Children*

Introduction

Cynthia S. Kaplan, Ph.D.

THE NUMBER OF TEENAGERS who require psychological help and support has increased dramatically over the past several years. Not only have the numbers of youths and their families seeking professional help swelled, but the range and types of problems they exhibit have also significantly changed.

The same holds true for accounts from communities where complaints abound from parents, school officials, and others who say there are many more teens with problems today than in the past and that they often don't respond to traditional practices and interventions. An example of this shift is exemplified by grievances from school guidance counselors with whom we interact on a daily basis. Many say that a decade ago they worked with approximately 10 percent of their students on non–college-related issues. Today, most school personnel report that closer to 70 percent of students come to the guidance department's attention at some time over issues surrounding divorce, blended families, drugs and alcohol, self-harming behaviors, eating issues, and online offenses. Schools, thus, no longer deal exclusively with educational problems but have also become the landscape upon which many adolescents' social, emotional, and behavioral problems become both apparent and ultimately disruptive.

In the past, adolescents most often sought help for what was traditionally thought of as "mental illness," which included hearing voices, extreme depression, suicidal behaviors, or a lack of functioning and self-preservation. These days, teens are just as likely to seek help for drug problems, promiscuity, legal difficulties, or Internet transgressions as they are for conditions traditionally thought of as mental illness.

In addition, from 1991 to 2003, the percentage of students who exhibited "injurious suicidal attempts" doubled, with the highest incidence among ninth graders, according to the National Center for Health Statistics.[1] *[Note: All footnotes appear in the reference section, starting on page 281.] Further evidence of suicidal and self-injurious behaviors among young people is found in a 2006 study by Cornell and Princeton University researchers, which revealed that 17 percent of college students surveyed reported cutting, burning, carving, or harming themselves in other such ways at some point. Less than 7 percent of these students sought medical help for their injuries. The survey reported that the average age of when these students began harming themselves was between fourteen and fifteen years old.[2]

No longer do the once well-established demarcations between emotional health and sickness hold the same significance. There is no longer an obvious biological presentation or genesis to the majority of mental and behavioral health problems we see. For example, a teenager seeking help may not be hearing voices or experiencing unprovoked mood deregulation but may have been threatening a peer or teacher online or trading drugs in school. These are often problems that either would not have occurred or been possible in the past, or that would have been dealt with in a disciplinary rather than a therapeutic fashion. The problem these days is that many of these behavioral difficulties we see are both manifestations of underlying emotional problems as well as responses to external stress that, if left untreated or simply treated with punishment, will likely worsen.

And while some adolescents undeniably skate through their teenage years without major difficulty, many more fail to manage this transition without encountering trouble. To what can we attribute this change in both prevalence and presentation? And what can parents and concerned adults do to prevent significant emotional problems from developing in a large number of teens?

Higher Stimulation and Lower Supervision

The answers to these questions are not simple or straightforward but must certainly begin with some reflection on the key differences in today's society compared to that of even the past decade. We must look closely at our social environment and community to fully appreciate how much society has changed in a relatively short time and then try and recognize the ways these changes have affected modern adolescents and their families. We need to look at the plethora of choices and information available to today's teens and ask the hard questions: "Is this more than they can handle and if so, what can be done?"

These questions force us to examine how the normal challenges and passages of adolescence have been compounded by such advents as increased drug availability, the expanded information highway, and other technological advancements taken together with widespread changes in both family and community structure. We should ask ourselves how can adolescents, already biologically prone to moodiness, impulsivity, and opposition, possibly handle the high stimulation and lowered supervision of today's world?

The current prevalence of teen troubles compels us to try and account for not only the genesis of the emotional problems but to know when to obtain professional help and how to access this help when needed. Perhaps most importantly, this exploration of the modern adolescent's world also highlights the intertwined and critical issues of early detection and prevention, as well as addressing some of the recent biological discoveries that shed light on how the adolescent brain and the genetics of mental illness work.

This book represents an attempt by a group of seasoned mental health professionals to begin to answer some of these questions. We have tried to construct a guidebook of sorts to the mysteries of adolescent development within the context of today's society and existing scientific knowledge to help youths and parents appreciate, anticipate, and avoid unnecessary emotional and behavioral potholes. Starting with a review of modern-day stresses and an overview of adolescent development, we try to elucidate key problem areas for teens and share our cumulative knowledge about how to limit and treat disorders of mood and behavior.

This information is in no way meant to substitute for real life professional consultation nor does it apply to every individual situation. It is meant to provide an overview, a guide, and potentially some answers and assurances to those struggling with the issues and problems of today's adolescents.

CHAPTER 1

The Modern Adolescent's World

Cynthia S. Kaplan, Ph.D.

There was a time earlier, up until the last ten years in my career as a psychologist, when a majority of the teens I treated were "troubled" in the more traditional, psychiatric sense of the word. By this I mean that they were depressed, hearing voices, or impossibly hyperactive. Their biology was clearly awry and, in turn, they were difficult to manage and hard to shepherd through their adolescence. There were fewer psychiatric medications in existence, multiple times per week spent in therapy, and an emphasis on parent education, in trying to help these adolescents and their families successfully face their inherent challenges.

Now my Mondays usually begin with a startling array of prospective clients, many of whom, in an earlier period of time, would never have come to my attention. These are teens who may have run off with a stranger they met on the Internet, taken OxyContin before football practice, or threatened a teacher in the hallway. They do not know that there once was a time when the same behavior would not have occurred or been possible. Less than a decade ago, there were no chat rooms or blogs, and few prescription medications flowed through the *halls of public high schools. Teen threats were met with detention or an exasperated "kids will be kids" response. But now, in our post–9/11, post–Columbine, Internet-wired world, our adolescents are just not as safe anymore. So what is specifically going wrong and what can we do to ward off this blight of destructive teenage behavior?*

———————

SOCIETY IS DEFINED as "a community, nation, or broad grouping of people having common traditions, institutions, and collective activities and interests," according to *Merriam-Webster's Collegiate Dictionary*. As such, societies constantly evolve and change, presenting unique challenges as they advance to those living within specific periods of time. While adult members of a given society have some power to shape the societal foundation on which they live, the same is not true for children and adolescents. Children and adolescents inherit their environment, both the individual family they inhabit, as well as the society at large in which they grow.

As minors, children and adolescents have relatively little ability to affect or change the world around them and often must work hard to both understand and adequately cope with their daily lives as they exist, not as they might want them to be. Thus before adolescents can effectively make the transition to adulthood, they need to learn how to handle the challenges that face them in their teens.

For each new generation, these particular forces change and adolescents must respond by finding adjustments that enhance their survival and well-being. Although past generations have been plagued by economic and physical hurdles greater than those facing adolescents today, it is hard to identify a prior period during which society has changed so dramatically from one generation to the next, leaving adolescents today with less adult guidance readily available.

With the decline of the nuclear family, increasing prevalence of the two-parent working family, advent of computer technology, and multiple other factors that are hallmarks of recent times, today's adolescent has been left with less supervision and more choice than ever before. For some teens, this modern psychosocial environment presents a potentially dangerous context in which to grow up and from which to try and safely enter adulthood. The net result of the current backdrop for many is that adolescence has become an arena of quicksand in which our youth attempt to respond to a plethora of complex stimuli which are often poorly understood by their own parents, who themselves grew up during such strikingly different times.

Faced with the current generation gap, today's adolescents are often left more on their own than is ideal to solve life's daily, complex problems. Given this, their responses are often replete with coping strategies that are insufficient or inadequate to the task or choice at hand, and this can end with teens making decisions that are ultimately self-destructive, self-defeating, and enduring in terms of negative consequences.

Furthermore, because adults today frequently do not have an adequate understanding of the unique challenges facing their teens, they often miss the early warning signs of impending problems. Armed with a better understanding of modern societal forces, they can enhance their ability to both prevent and predict self-destructiveness before it is too late. An important first step in prevention is learning to understand the world of today's adolescent along with the inherent landmines that need to be recognized and, where possible, avoided.

MODERN RISK FACTORS:
WHAT ARE THEY AND HOW TO AVOID THEM

Teenagers and their families face challenges today that were either unheard of, or certainly occurred less frequently, in previous generations. This changing socio-cultural landscape brings with it both the potential for benefit and harm. Following are descriptions of some of the more recent and significant environmental shifts that affect today's teens in ways that are oftentimes predictable and which can become problematic.

Increasing prevalence of divorce and single-parent homes: Many of the changes in society that have the most effect on today's adolescents stem from the unraveling of the nuclear and extended family system. Since the 1960s, the overall marriage rate has declined, with more couples either living together permanently or delaying marriage because of career issues. Along with this decrease in marriage rates, divorce rates have climbed throughout the 1970s and 1980s, reaching 50 percent by 1980.[1] By 2003, almost one-third of all children lived in single-parent households due to divorce, death of a parent, or other circumstances,[2,3] according to federal data.

The implications of this shift in family structure for the adolescent are wide-ranging. Many social scientists have posited that living in a single-parent family would have a detrimental impact on children due to the consequent lowering of income and supervision as well as the potential increase in family-based stress.

Psychologist and researcher Judith Wallerstein, Ph.D., and her colleagues began a longitudinal study in 1971 designed to assess the effects of divorce on the psychological and behavioral well-being of involved children. They followed 60 divorced families with 131 children over a period of 25 years. The researchers found the group of children from divorced families had "lower rates of educational success, three times the burden of heavy alcohol and drug use, and five times the divorce rate in their own relationships, compared to the control group from intact families."[4] Several other large studies of divorce confirm Wallerstein's results and show children of divorce to be at significantly greater risk for educational, emotional, and social failure.[5,6]

The overall literature points to divorce (and single-parent families in general) as a risk factor that can adversely affect an adolescent's functioning. Although there are certainly children from divorced homes who fare well in life, divorce heightens the risk of children experiencing difficulties with mood, conduct, schoolwork, and peer choice and getting involved with drugs and alcohol. Thus, as the divorce rate rises and more children live in one-parent families, so does the vulnerability of the adolescent population, making it more likely for them to adopt coping mechanisms that can be inefficient at best and self-destructive at worst.

Decreased parental supervision: Although there is less empirical data available about the impact on children of living in two-parent working families, the issues of childcare and supervision are at least anecdotally factors that appear important and need to be considered carefully. The concept of the "latchkey kid" became popularized several years ago with the writings of psychologist Mara Berkley, Ph.D., and others who observed that an increasingly large number of children were returning home after school to empty houses and no direct parental supervision.[7] Clinicians began to see problems emanating from this circumstance, such as unfulfilled homework assignments, difficulties in monitoring children's whereabouts, the engagement of teens in illegal or disallowed activities, the illegal use of parental vehicles left home, and so on.

This mounting list of complaints spoke to the lack of structure provided in an empty household and the need for parents to consider how to provide alternative structure. Approximately one out of every ten children in grades four through twelve is or has been a latchkey kid,[8] according to the U.S. Department of Health and Human Services. The average amount of time a child is home alone either before or after school currently averages two to three hours per day.

Although adolescent difficulties are based at least partly on temperamental vulnerability and biological stage of development (see chapter 2), opportunity also plays a role in observed problems with teens today. The two-parent working family is an advent of the late twentieth century that, again, while positive economically, provides for gaps in adult supervision of teens that did not exist in prior generations. These gaps, in turn, make it possible for teens to make choices and confront challenges without the benefit of parental input or interference. This latchkey circumstance is an integral part of how modern teens can so easily head down a path toward eventual involvement in problematic behaviors and activities.

Increased availability of drugs and alcohol: Most teenagers, by definition, are risk takers. Adolescence is a period characterized by decreased cautiousness, increased feelings of invincibility, and often a profound sense of alienation from adults. This penchant for independence and autonomy, when added to the mix of factors listed above, can lead teens to be at heightened risk for drug and alcohol use. The combination of decreased adult supervision and adolescent daring has become of particular worry in that the array and availability of illegal substances has increased over the past decade.

We live in a time when the cultural message is that if there is a problem, then there is a chemical or drug that can help. Television, the Internet, and the print media are replete with advertisements that suggest a quick fix for almost any difficulty, be it physical or mental. Although adolescents for generations have had to make decisions about whether to experiment with drugs and alcohol, recent surveys by the National Institute on Drug Abuse indicated that by the mid-1990s, two-thirds of twelfth graders felt that they had to make a conscious choice about whether to use drugs. This statistic is significantly higher than in past generations when teenagers were often not exposed to large quantities of alcohol or a plethora of street drugs during their middle and high school years.

Today most estimates indicate that 50 percent of young teens have used an illicit drug during high school by the time they reach twelfth grade.[9] In addition, among youths ages twelve to seventeen, more than one million meet the criteria for substance dependence and more than one million receive treatment for alcohol dependence.[10] In addition to the drinking rate among high school teens, which has remained at about 75 percent for twelfth graders over the past several years, there has been a steady increase in recent years in the use of marijuana, Ecstasy, prescription drugs (such as stimulants and painkillers), and inhalants.

The untoward outcomes related to drug and alcohol use by teens are well publicized, but parents are often uneducated about the scope of this problem and unaware of the early warning signs. We will review this information in depth in chapter 5.

Development of the information superhighway and technological advances: Perhaps more than any other factor previously mentioned, the advent of the personal computer and Internet has changed the landscape upon which the modern adolescent's development unfolds.

Most adults today clearly remember an era when there were typewriters instead of word processors, stationary phones, and no answering machines, DVD players, VCRs, or personal computers. Those were the days when, if you happened to be out and missed a phone call, you needed to actually return home in order to retrieve a message. Today's teenagers are dumbfounded when reminded of the historical recentness of these technological inventions, which they take for granted, and simply cannot fathom a world in which these devices do not exist. In parallel fashion, it is hard for the average adult to comprehend the amount and rapidity of stimulation with which a teen today must contend. The capacity for instant connectivity has both advantages and some serious disadvantages for today's youth (see chapter 8).

Until the late 1960s, no real vision of a global network of computers existed. The early version of the Internet was designed to connect research facilities to each other to facilitate the sharing of data. There were no home or office personal computers in those days, and computers at that time were very complex tools. It was not until the mid-1980s that universities and libraries branched out and began the process of connecting to one another. Because the Internet was originally limited to research, education, and government uses, the government funded it. Commercial use was limited to research and education.

In 1995, the National Science Foundation ended its support of the Internet, whose management was then taken over by commercial and educational institutions. Browsers such as Netscape and AOL were developed to facilitate use of the Internet. With the advent of Microsoft Windows in 1998, the personal computer started to become a household fixture along with access to information and other people in ways that were unanticipated and potentially dangerous for the teenage user.[11] Less than a decade later, we are faced with Internet chat rooms, online blogs, pornography websites, etc.—all of which present both potential pitfalls for adolescents and supervisory nightmares for parents.

The same holds true for the development of technology beyond the Internet. Cellular phones have made it possible for instantaneous contact, allowing for dialogue and planning among teens to reach a frenzied height. No longer does being away from home mean missing a phone call or party, and parents are largely unsure of the whereabouts of their adolescent even though they may "check in" from cellular phones. School days are punctuated by text messages and clandestine communications, and it takes only minutes for the average teen to let dozens of peers know the location of an unsupervised gathering. Add to this the cacophony of stimulation from iPods and video games, and we have a world with few respites and little solitude.

This interconnectivity and reliance on technology for fun and communication is many times more than the adolescent brain can manage and has been shown to contribute to poor decision-making, potential increases in aggressive behavior, and increased teen exposure to both inappropriate people and prurient material.

At a time when nuclear family solidarity and adult supervision are at their nadir, stimulation and the demand for spontaneous communication and decision-making are at their zenith. For many teenagers, this combination can spell disaster. There are no longer the same checks and balances that once existed with one-phone homes, phones that parents could disable or lock, and the expectation that parents would likely be privy to conversations that occur in public areas. There are no longer enforced periods where teens must wait until the next day to talk with someone they are angry with or take the time to compose a note or letter. There are no longer easy ways for parents to control the material their children listen to, watch, and experiment with in the form of computer games and video stations. All of this makes up the world of today's adolescent, which can be difficult and hazardous to negotiate because of the pervasive existence of instant interconnectivity.

Changing social and sexual mores: Along with the technological advances and societal shifts discussed above, the values and sexual mores of our youth have changed. Which of these advents came first, and which led to what, continues to be a matter of urgent speculation by educators, clinicians, and parents alike. Whether the advent of the Internet and television has exposed our youth to more inappropriate material, blended families have subjected our youth to less potentially stable relationships, or that women in the workforce have set different examples of gender roles: The net effect remains the same. The youth of today are not bound by the same sense of traditionalism and conservatism as in the past, and this can be both liberating and destabilizing during the teenage years.

In their 2005 review of 530 studies in this area, San Diego State University researchers showed that "young people's sexual attitudes and behavior have changed substantially between 1943 and 1999, with the largest shifts occurring among girls and young women."[12]

As measured by events such as the age of first intercourse and percentage of sexually active teens by age, both attitudes and behavior toward premarital sexual experiences have become more lenient over the past several decades. As the societal and moral imperatives among teenagers against early sexual activity decrease, it is also safe to say that the likelihood of these encounters becoming destructive and/or dangerous increases. Here again, with a profound schism existing between the mores of the parents' and teenager's generations, the opportunity for misunderstanding, misperception, and missed supervision is more likely than in the past.

While there has always been a cycle between generations toward increased physical and emotional liberation, at no time in the recent past have standards changed so dramatically that what is commonplace sexual behavior now was scandalous behavior just several years back. Again, parents cannot call on either their own experiences or their own past personal rebellions to help set rules and expectations. They are not just mildly shocked by their teenager's behaviors and attitudes in this arena but often confused, ashamed, and unable to differentiate experimentation from true recklessness and self-destruction. How and when to intervene becomes another Pandora's box, with no precedent and few apparent clearcut solutions.

Here, as in other areas reviewed, it is not just the intergenerational differences in behavior that are noteworthy, but the pervasiveness and extent of these differences. During the 1960s and 1970s, for example, the Vietnam protest movement, escapades of the hippie generation, and the sex, drugs, and rock-and-roll mentality was certainly shocking to adults as images of tie-dyed youngsters, seemingly high on drugs, flashed across television screens from Woodstock and similar gatherings.

The difference between then and now, however, is that a relatively small percentage of American youths were actually involved in the more reckless behavior of that era, with vast numbers of teenagers remaining essentially unchanged by what was a largely coastal revolution. The majority of teens at that time had not taken acid, did not march on Washington, and was not influenced in their daily behaviors by images of protesting youths portrayed in the media. In fact, that was still an era when most teens remained sheltered by their communities and were effectively censored by their families from knowing completely what was going on in the "outside world."

Today, however, the advances in information technology and accessibility of most youths to personal computers, iPods, and the like have made it so that cultural images of reckless youths and songs jam-packed with protest and sexuality no longer need to be purchased in a store or condoned by a parent. There is no easy way, in fact, to censor what teens are exposed to in terms of either timing or content. Often, if one teen does not have personal access to certain information, another peer will be glad to provide it.

An example of the negative impact of the widespread increase in unrestricted cultural and technological exposure on today's teens appeared in an article in the journal *Pediatrics* in August 2006, which found a correlation between listening to "dirty lyrics" and precocious sexual behaviors.[13] Specifically, teens who listened to popular music that featured degrading sexual messages were more likely to have intercourse and engage in other promiscuous behaviors than their non-listening peers.

An added problematic impact of our changed sexual and social mores is the overlapping effect between precocious experimentation in different spheres of functioning. For example, early drug use has been tied to earlier first sexual experiences and vice versa. These interrelationships between high-risk adolescent behaviors have been investigated by many researchers including Denise Hallfors, Ph.D., a researcher at the Pacific Institute for Research and Evaluation, who found in her 2004 research that "Teens who engage in high-risk behaviors involving sex and drugs have significantly higher odds of depression, suicidal thoughts, and suicide attempts than teens who say no to sex and drugs." Hallfors's findings not only highlight the dangerousness of increased high-risk behaviors by teens but also help explain the finding that suicide rates in our country doubled from 1960 to 2001. Abstainers, in this study, had the lowest levels of depression, suicidal thoughts, and suicide attempts, while teens with multiple sexual partners who engaged in heavy illegal drug use had the highest levels of self-destructive behaviors.[14]

Increasing competition—the increased pressures of higher education: Historically the United States, like many other places, operated on a cultural system where teens were often groomed to enter the family business once they attained adulthood. This apprentice mentality existed until quite recently, with the option of working within a kinship arrangement was still a viable alternative. This meant that having no education or only a high school diploma was not necessarily a handicap to future economic success.

This ability to survive well with limited education is no longer a reality in the United States. Census statistics reveal that the earnings differentials between high school and college graduates have steadily increased over the past twenty-five years. Not only has the earning capacity of college-educated individuals increased relative to their less-educated peers, but the percentage of American adults achieving more than a high school education has also increased dramatically. In 1970, only 21 percent of adults over the age of twenty-five had completed *any* college education. By 2003, that number jumped to a whopping 53 percent.[15] The implication of this increase is that the pressure on adolescents to both stay in school and do well has also risen significantly.

Without the contingency of a family- or apprenticeship-based future, adolescents today need to compete and succeed academically at much higher levels than before to ensure their long-term economic futures. This situation translates into increased pressures during the high school years, even for teens who are emotionally and/or cognitively less equipped than others for the rigors of higher education. This pressure to perform and do well in school is additionally hazardous during the adolescent years when other competing social, biological, and family forces can make it difficult for adolescents to focus and concentrate in school. This intensified emphasis on education is further aggravated by added technological advances, which in some cases only serve to only further distract and overstimulate teens, thereby diverting them from established educational goals.

There is no easy answer to this dilemma, as increased education will likely become even more desirable and advantageous in the future. It is, thus, one more factor added to the list of pressures and choices that make the adolescent journey so much more precarious today than in the past. It is again an area where parents and involved adults need to help adolescents chart a course that will work for, rather than against, their ultimate well-being. Both too much and too little academic pressure can be problematic, and school-based stress and failure have been clearly linked to increases in teen violence and self-destructiveness.

Trauma and the changing world around us: In many parts of the world, young children and teens are subjected to unimaginable loss, turmoil, and physical trauma, dealing with issues such as poverty, war, and forced labor. This ongoing exposure to profound and potentially life-threatening individual hardship does not, however, negate the emotional harm to our own youth from a potentially dangerous array of environmental and societal dilemmas and stresses, including the recent and ongoing threat of terrorism. On the personal end of the spectrum, many of the societal factors enumerated above have contributed to an increase in both the incidence and prevalence of sexual and physical assaults during adolescence. Most significant among these factors seems to be the dwindling numbers of intact families, the lessening of parental supervision, and the exposure at earlier ages to aggression and sexuality.

Recent investigation shows that one out of every four girls in the United States reports having experienced some form of molestation before they reach adulthood.[16] This statistic encompasses everything from boundary violations committed by biologically unrelated individuals—more commonly than before—living in the same household to the increased availability and use of "date rape" drugs employed to prey on unwilling victims. Boys, too, experience sexual abuse and molestation, but at significantly lower rates than girls.

Moreover, as a society we are exposed to a continual barrage of media and music that glorifies aggression, desensitizes the audience to its peril, and simultaneously promotes and exalts sexuality and the use of alcohol and other chemical substances. Though movie ratings, legislation, Internet censoring equipment, and so on, have all been implemented in an attempt to control this deluge of often-inappropriate information and stimulation to our youth, the floodgates have not been closed. The reality is that teens, and even preteens, today know more about and have personally seen more sexually and aggressively explicit material than in the past. They are exposed to these materials often with little explanation or direction, and they are affected by these materials in ways that are not yet fully understood.

Outside of our homes, the climate has changed as well. Again, while there has always been peril at every age and stage of mankind, the pervasive and invasive threat of terrorism has never before been as real for teens in this country as it is today. It has been centuries since Americans have had battles fought on our shores; armed conflict has always been far off and not of an immediate nature. Only the brief threat of nuclear war during the 1960s was comparable, when students practiced air-raid drills under their desks and feared on a daily basis for their physical safety.

Following 9/11 and the upsurge in global terrorism, though, the threat of aggression and loss again seems pervasive, real, and persistent. There is always the lingering question about "how safe are we really" and tunnels, airports, bridges, water supplies, and so on have all become possible targets of terrorism from the outside world. There is no longer one identifiable enemy (e.g., communism), nor one route of outside attack, such as nuclear assault. Facing a nameless, faceless enemy, willing to sacrifice themselves for a "higher cause," danger seems to lurk everywhere. The net result of this age of global terror is that both parents and teens are left with an increased sense of anxiety and insecurity that adds to an overriding feeling of desperation and further aggravates the adolescent's precarious stance toward the outside world.

This pervasive loss of a sense of safety and security in terms of the world at large has been further shaken by domestic acts of terrorism that occur on an all-too-regular basis. School shootings and violence are certainly dramatic and frightening occurrences to both teens as well as the adults that care for them. Additionally, daily news stories of kidnappings, predatory behaviors by adults in authority, as well as rampant misconduct of celebrities and public figures, leave teens with a high level of stress and sense of unpredictability that is not conducive to emotional well-being.

LOOKING TO THE FUTURE

It used to be that one generation followed the other in a somewhat orderly pattern. In that context, teenage rebelliousness was fairly predictable, and more often than not restricted to understandable, if not acceptable, behaviors. Parents exchanged adages such as "kids will be kids" in an effort to reassure one another that, whatever their child's particular lapse in conduct, it was not anomalous, would likely pass, and was not cause for undue concern. Unfortunately, for this generation of parents, these assurances are hard to come by.

Faced with an array of attitudes, activities, and behaviors so vastly different from their own generation, parents find themselves unprepared and uneducated, often responding too late to an unrecognizable and unfamiliar problem. Lost in a swirl of voice mail, street drugs, instant messages, and video games, parents cannot read the warning signs that now exist in a new, mystifying, and essentially foreign language. In this fast-paced melee of communication and action, informed consent evaporates as parents fail to even understand at times the options to which they are agreeing. Left without a better roadmap, it ultimately becomes difficult if not impossible to distinguish normal from destructive behaviors.

To begin to make sense of what is happening with our adolescents, we have to not only consider the ways society has changed and its influence on today's teen, but also how cultural influences intersect with the unchanging developmental trademarks that have always been specific to the teenage years. For example, how might this added external stimulation and excess of new dangers to which the modern teen is exposed contribute to their already inflated sense of invincibility, increased moodiness, and determined defiance? Has modern society become a cauldron of overexposure and overstimulation, leading almost inevitably to increased emotional and behavioral problems during the delicate period of life between childhood and adulthood?

Fortunately, the answer is that with the new problems have also come much newfound knowledge and many novel solutions. We now know more than ever before about how these stages of teenage development correspond to the unfolding neurological activity of the adolescent brain. We also are more advanced in the fields of psychology and psychiatry in terms of both detection and diagnosis of emotional and behavioral problems, as well as possessing a more sophisticated array of therapeutic interventions. Thus along with the increased perils of modern adolescence stands an impressive array of advances in both the biological and psychosocial realms of treatments that, in turn, lead to enhanced screening devices and potential remedies for today's assemblage of troubled teens.

CHAPTER 2

An Overview of Adolescent Development

Roya Ostovar, Ph.D.

I have worked in the mental health care field for about sixteen years, and most of that time has been spent working with children, adolescents, and their families. I chose to focus my studies and efforts on child and adolescent development because this period is perhaps the most critical and influential time in one's life. Childhood experiences, positive or negative, can significantly affect many aspects of our later years as adults. Adolescence is the time when a step in the right direction—even a small intervention—can make a world of difference.

During my career, I have served both "typically" developing children as well as those with developmental and psychiatric challenges. To this day, I am still profoundly touched and amazed by the children and adolescents whom I see in my practice. I am impressed most by their always challenging presentation: their innocence combined with sophistication, their simplicity and yet their complication, their certainty fused often with pure confusion, and their independence and simultaneous need for intense attachment. More than anything, however, I am always amazed by every child's resilience, potential for learning, and ability to live in the moment, to so fully and completely appreciate and take in what is happening in their lives right there and then. Anyone who has seen an adolescent look at something from a new perspective, and feel with certainty that he or she can improve on what has come before, knows exactly what I am talking about.

———————

ALL, YES ALL, CHILDREN begin their preadolescent years wanting to do well and please the adults around them. And when they don't, we as the adults in their lives need to determine why they are not. There is no secondary gain, as is sometimes proposed, that makes not doing well worthwhile for an adolescent. As you will see later in this chapter, I will talk about how almost every teen behavior is actually some form of communication. Through their behavior, both preteens and teens try to communicate to others what they may be unwilling or unable to communicate verbally.

People who work in the mental health field do not, in general, ascribe to the idea of random or "out-of-nowhere" behaviors, except in select cases, such as those patients with serious psychiatric and neurological abnormalities or deficits. The "presenting problems," in other words the behavioral difficulties and symptoms that a teen may exhibit, are more often than not indicative of other underlying or unrecognized issues that need attention. They're a cry for help, not a bid for attention. These behaviors are an indication that something is going wrong and that the teen may be trying to cope with more than he or she can handle alone. To focus just on the behavior—believing that it appeared out of nowhere—without addressing the core and contributing circumstances is to fix only part of the problem. Suppose, for example, that a table leg breaks because of a heavy weight placed on it. If we keep fixing the broken leg without changing what we put on the table, chances are the leg will keep breaking.

Today's teens, with their easy access to the Internet and other media, are well aware of and concerned about a plethora of external issues. In working with children and adolescents, we must always consider potentially personal relevant stresses such as siblings, parents, divorce, moving, peers, school, family matters, and other issues. However, even larger societal issues such as the economy, job market, availability of resources, cultural/ethnic issues, violence in the community, war, and terrorism play significant roles in how our adolescents feel and behave.

These are exciting and challenging times to be involved in the field of child and adolescent mental health. New research and information on adolescent behavior, psychology, and brain development emerges every day and adds to our understanding of "normal adolescent development."

This chapter will present an overview of adolescent development and what parents can expect to see during this phase of their child's life. It also touches on worrisome symptoms and behaviors that may require additional attention and support from professionals in the field.

STANDARD QUESTIONS
RAISED BY PARENTS OF TEENAGERS

"Is my child's behavior normal?" "How does my child compare to other teens?" "How do you distinguish between normal adolescent behaviors and challenges and those that may require outside help?" These are questions almost every parent asks at some point during those long years when they are raising an adolescent. "Is this normal?" asks the mother of a teenage girl with great confusion, frustration, and a perplexed facial expression. Her daughter is a sixteen-year-old high school junior who has, over the past two years, "changed so much" that her mother "doesn't know who she is anymore." The mother is not alone.

Wondering whether the behavior of an adolescent is normal is a common question and dilemma for many parents. For many families it almost feels as though the drastic changes in their previously cooperative, naive, and innocent child take place overnight. And where they just recently put to bed a sweet, more often than not cooperative child, they wake up trying to manage a "new" individual, one who seems to struggle with wanting to be an adult and yet acts like a child. This new child in transition vacillates between acting responsibly and regressing into behaviors of a much younger child.

The feeling of being torn between two worlds and experiencing conflicting needs is, in fact, the major hallmark of adolescent development, both for the teens themselves as well as their parents. Adolescents often feel caught between wanting the comfort and familiarity of what they knew as young children and simultaneously feeling pressure to be separate and independent. Thus, adolescents frequently seem confused and inconsistent about what their wishes are and how people, other than their peers, can be helpful and supportive of them. For an adolescent, this is an unsettling feeling. "Everything has changed . . . I mean literally," states the sixteen-year-old described above.

An analogy might be that of moving from your small home of a dozen years to a bigger, unfamiliar new house. By far, the hardest times during this period are those few days or weeks of going back and forth between the two locations. This transition encompasses both the feeling that you haven't yet completely left the old house and yet haven't settled into the new, unfamiliar place. The inner emotional tug-of-war that accompanies this transition can be most disruptive, and it captures the essence of the turmoil inherent to the adolescent years. For teenagers, this developmental transition involves significant changes in their bodies, thoughts, feelings, and family and peer relationships, as well as significantly increased academic demands.

CASE STUDY

Jenny—What Is Happening to My Child?

JENNY IS A SIXTEEN-YEAR-OLD who lives with her mother, stepfather, and half brother. Her parents divorced when she was two years old and both parents remarried. Jenny visits her father and his wife regularly on weekends. Her mother reports that although this has been the arrangement for many years, it has recently presented a problem for Jenny. According to her parents, Jenny has not been getting along with either of them or their spouses since she began high school. Her father, who is more permissive, is the only adult she sometimes listens to, her mother states. Jenny has been having frequent arguments with her mother, stepfather, and younger brother. She no longer joins the family at dinnertime, refuses to discuss school matters, and is disrespectful to her parents. She spends most of her time in her room, on the computer, or on the phone with her friends. Her mother reports a drop in Jenny's grades since middle school and a lack of interest and motivation in school.

In addition, Jenny is no longer interested in sports, individual or team, and she has gained weight. This is a significant concern for Jenny's parents because they see this as not only a health issue, but as something that is tied directly into Jenny's self-esteem.

"We don't talk anymore. The only communication is by fighting," reports Jenny's mother. "We are just hoping she will grow out of this phase soon."

DISCUSSION

Unfortunately, Jenny's struggles and her family's sense of helplessness are neither unique nor unusual. Many families are at a loss about how to help their teens and scared of what may go wrong. How much should they push their children? What can they do to help without making things worse? Do others struggle with similar problems? Should they get help from a professional about this issue? These and other related questions are what we hope to shed some light on in this and the following chapters.

Many typically developing adolescents like Jenny will, in fact, "grow out of this phase" and repair their relationships with their families. However, to ensure a favorable outcome, early intervention is the key. For example, an important early step for Jenny was for all the adults in her life to come together as soon as their concerns were noted. This may be more difficult in divorced, blended, or long-distance families. In particular, families that have not yet clearly defined and agreed upon an effective decision-making process when it comes to the children will be forced to do so by this type of adolescent crisis. In times of escalating teenage difficulties, the adults in a child's life must deal with the problem as a united front and put aside conflicts among themselves. Once Jenny's parents and stepparents all sat down together to develop mutually agreed-upon rules and expectations, Jenny began to act out less and communicate more.

THE BRAIN BIOLOGY BEHIND TEEN BEHAVIOR

We have already reviewed the ways in which adolescence is a transitional period in development, a time between childhood and adulthood. This period includes the behavioral and emotional transitions we have discussed as well as the evolution and development of the adolescent brain—a brain that as it turns out, is significantly different from that of either a child or an adult. The adolescent brain undergoes anatomical changes that, in turn, affect mood, impulse control, motivation, judgment, and the ability to think about behavioral consequences.

Thus, while teens have historically displayed much of the same volatility and variability outlined above, there has always been the presumption on the part of adults that, in most cases, the troubled teen just needed to "straighten up." Misbehavior was frequently seen as willful and volitional, and there was a tacit, but globally held, assumption that a good dose of discipline and consequences would most likely solve the problem at hand.

More recently, however, a benefit of our advancing technology has been that we now have had our first real look inside the adolescent brain. As it turns out, the adolescent brain is a structure in motion—motion that often parallels the behavioral and emotional groundswells we directly observe. Much of adolescent behavior appears tied to this evolving brain structure and function and may not, in many cases, be under the adolescent's control.

To better understand this brain–behavior connection, let's quickly review a few brain structures that we now know play a critical role in the behavior of adolescents. These structures are important to be aware of because new scientific technology allows us to better understand how the adolescent's behavior is inextricably connected to brain development within these structures; development that unfolds right "beneath the surface."

The brain consists of two sides, or hemispheres: the right and the left. A dense body of neurons, made of individual brain cells, called the corpus callosum, connects the two sides. This dense body of cells facilitates communication between the two sides of the brain. Individuals with an underdeveloped corpus callosum tend to perform tasks at a slower pace.[1] These tasks involve inter-hemispheric information transfer (such as emotional and conceptual information that depends on language) and complex visuospatial/perceptual tasks (such as copying a complex geometric shape).

In general, the left side of the brain is referred to as the "analyzer" while the right side is thought of as the "synthesizer." The left side analyzes the parts that make the whole and the right side puts together the parts to give the big picture and the ability to make inferences based on past experiences.

AREAS OF CHANGE DURING ADOLESCENCE

Adolescence is a time when significant changes occur, both internally and externally. Here is a brief summary of these changes.

Physical: During this stage of development, teens become biologically capable of reproduction and experience a major growth spurt, changes in height and body shape, and the maturation of the reproductive organs stimulated by hormones. Some girls may start menstruating at this time.

Emotional and psychological: Adolescence is a time of significant emotional and psychological transition, when childhood is left behind in preparation for entering adulthood.

Children face increased academic and personal responsibilities starting in middle school, which are then amplified by the unfolding developmental tasks of identity formation and discovering oneself.

Cognitive: Brain maturation and changes affect the overall functioning of adolescents.

According to Swiss psychologist Jean Piaget, this is the *formal operation* stage of development—a time when adolescents are more capable of abstract thinking and making inferences.[2] Cognitive development changes and challenges of this stage include planning, inhibitory control, problem solving, and assessing the consequences of one's actions.[3]

Social: The most significant social change that occurs during this part of development is establishing closer relationships with peers and having more intense and involved friendships.

Teens are less connected to their family, share less with family members, and often feel that only their friends can understand them.

Of great significance as well is a developing interest in dating and thinking about romantic relationships.

Moral: Cognitively, adolescents are expected to become capable of considering moral and ethical dilemmas, distinguishing right from wrong, assessing how one's behavior affects others, and in general, thinking more globally about moral issues.

For example, the ability to put together the fact that you become irritable when you don't eat at a certain time; to scan a specific event and see whether it is similar to any past situations; to assess what responses have and have not worked in the past; and to put the information together and choose the most adaptive and effective response is getting the big picture. While a map of the brain may show the two hemispheres as separate, in practice the two sides of the brain work together in nearly all functions.

Three Parts of the Brain and What They Do

For the purposes of this chapter, let us consider three major anatomical brain structures and their functions: the hindbrain, the midbrain, and the forebrain.

The hindbrain is responsible for basic and life-maintaining physiological functions such as breathing, heartbeat, and blood pressure. The midbrain is involved in auditory and visual system processing and contains sensory and motor correlation centers. The forebrain, the most forward part of the brain, is most relevant to the discussion at hand. Knowledge about certain structures within the forebrain, such as the limbic system and the prefrontal cortex, is critical to understanding certain typical adolescent behaviors.

More recent scientific research and studies have referred to the adolescent brain as a work in progress. This phase of development involves progressive changes in the brain structure and various, corresponding cognitive functions. New imaging studies suggest that brain development extends well into the teen years and that differences exist between the sexes.[4] Studies show that the volume of gray matter—simply put, the thinking part of the brain—increases during childhood.[5] In the first of such studies, reported in 1999, a second wave of overproduction of gray matter in the brain was found just prior to puberty.

Current work by Deborah Yurgelun-Todd, Ph.D., and her colleagues at the Cognitive Neuroimaging Laboratory of the Brain Imaging Center at McLean Hospital sheds further light on this topic. Numerous studies by this group, using functional magnetic resonance imaging (MRI) scans, have looked at how teens process emotional stimuli.[6,7,8] Functional MRIs differ from traditional MRIs in that they can measure how the brain performs tasks and show which parts of the brain "light up" or get activated when performing a task.

In one study, younger teens activated the amygdala, a part of the brain that processes emotions, more than the frontal lobe, when viewing various faces on a computer screen and identifying the facial expressions, such as one expressing fear. However, in older teens, the brain activity during this task shifts more to the frontal lobe, leading to clearer and more reasoned perceptions.[9] The following section provides additional information on the brain structures most relevant to adolescent behavior.

The Limbic System within the Brain

The limbic system, as mentioned above, is part of the forebrain and plays a crucial role in the regulation of emotions, motivation, and memory. The parts of the brain that form the limbic system are those that are responsible for the adolescent's emotional responses: intense anger and rage and oversensitivity to social interactions. We now know that a small, almond-shaped structure within the limbic system, the amygdala, plays an important part in learning, social language, detecting fear, modulating attention, and emotional processing.[10,11] The cingulate cortex, another part of the limbic system, is involved in emotional behavior, attention, and response selection. The functions of these structures of the brain are important in regulating behavior.

Within the limbic system, the hippocampus also plays a key role in learning, encoding new memories, and retaining information. The hypothalamus is involved in regulating such important functions as sexual arousal, thirst, hunger, and hormone functions. The hypothalamus also governs mood states and behavior patterns such as anger and fear. Clearly, the use of drugs and alcohol can affect the functioning of this area of the brain significantly. This is also the area involved with one's sex drive, sexual behavior, and the hormonal changes that lead to intense emotional responses.

The Prefrontal Cortex

The prefrontal cortex is one of the most important brain structures when it comes to understanding adolescents. This area, located just behind the forehead, is where all components of behavior are linked, or integrated, together. This area is necessary for significant cognitive functions such as planning, foresight, organization, reasoning, problem solving, impulse control, assessing long-term consequences, motivation, attention, and responsiveness. Individuals with prefrontal impairment often display difficulty with practical and social judgment across disparate areas of functioning—as shown through the five categories below.[12]

The prefrontal cortex is responsible for behavioral matters that can be divided into five categories:

1. Initiative and ambition, or "problems of starting." In adolescents, this may be the reason why they appear "lazy and unmotivated" and lack initiative.

2. Flexibility of shifting attention, behavior, and attitude. An example of difficulty in this area may be an inability to see others' perspectives and points of view.

3. The control or breaking of ongoing behavior, delaying gratification, impulsivity, overreactivity, disinhibition, or holding back in responding. These problems of stopping are what are considered most problematic in adolescents. Aggression, rage, or out-of-control behaviors are all typically associated with the prefrontal cortex as well.

4. The simultaneous ability to evaluate various social situations, integrate information effectively, and make appropriate inferences and decisions while maintaining empathy for others. Parents of adolescents often report feeling hurt by their son's or daughter's words and are surprised by the lack of empathy from them.

5. The ability to think with flexibility and keeping a perspective. Included here are planning, performing goal-directed activities, and weighing consequences of a given behavior.[13]

What is now obvious to this generation of parents was not possible to glean in the past—that adolescents are as much victims of their own physiology as they are protagonists. Well-meaning at 6 a.m., they can be monsters by 6 p.m. the same day. Have their brains changed in that twelve-hour period? The answer is obviously not. But adolescents display swings in behavior and mood that we now know are somewhat outside their control, requiring help from adults, and making the teenager uniquely vulnerable to the very outside forces and stimulation that they are so drawn to.

THE ADOLESCENT'S EXPERIENCE

It may help to frequently remind yourself that your adolescent is going through a difficult time. While it may look like fun, capricious rebelliousness, and chaotic irresponsibility from the outside, bear in mind that adolescence is a developmental period marked by heightened turmoil, anxiety, and desperation for the youngster.

Though adults may feel like helpless spectators and victims of the teen's erratic and irrational behaviors, they are just bearing witness to their teenager's distress at having to make such an enormous emotional, social, and behavioral transition in what is really a relatively short period of time.

Following are some of the ubiquitous issues with which teens cope.

Increased peer importance: During this stage, there is a pulling away from family, a heightened need for autonomy, and a greater need for approval from peers. Adolescents feel that peers understand them better, yet at the same time need to know that their families are still there for them. There is great peer pressure and demands to conform to what others around the teen are doing. Rejection and/or social embarrassment can become emotionally disastrous for the more vulnerable teen.

Increased romantic interest: This interest begins toward the end of middle school, more as a group event at first and then slowly progressing toward one-on-one dating in high school. Both parents and teens should have clear limits, rules, and behavioral expectations regarding this issue. It is also important to bear in mind that with the increased social and technological stimulation surrounding today's teen, in addition to the changing mores and decreased adult control characteristic of today's world, adolescents can easily become confused and impulsive in their romantic and sexual lives.

Increased high-risk choices: Many teenagers need to test their limits, challenge authority, and find out what they can and cannot do, as well as take risks. During this period, they may get involved in high-risk behaviors and experiment with new activities. These behaviors may include using drugs, drinking and driving, having unprotected sex, displaying antisocial or delinquent behaviors, getting involved with gangs, or shoplifting.

While not condoning these actions by the adolescent, parents and involved adults must examine each individual episode to determine whether the teen is "just experimenting," being pressured by peers, or showing signs of developing a more problematic pattern of behavior.

Increased mood volatility: Increased moodiness and behavioral unpredictability can surface during the teenage years as the role of the brain and hormonal changes integral to aggressiveness and emotionality are unfolding rapidly. Parents should carefully assess the seriousness of volatile moods and behaviors and take appropriate steps to address these issues on a case-by-case basis.

On the one hand, parents must be open and consider involving professionals in resolving these situations when they are persistent or serious in nature. This does not mean, however, that every slammed door or yelling episode is necessarily reason to be alarmed. Adolescents are physiologically more deregulated than children or adults, often veering from one emotional state to another. This is also difficult for the adolescents themselves who still wish to be able to be and feel more stable.

Increased financial responsibility: Many adolescents will consider getting a job for the first time. By this point in their lives, hopefully, children have learned about the cost of various goods and basic money management skills. This is a good time to revisit such matters as allowance, financial responsibility, and developing healthy, financially responsible habits. This emphasis on self-support and enhanced responsibility can at times, however, place additional stress on the growing teen.

Again, the typical adolescent wants a certain monetary autonomy but does not always have the skills, means, time, or motivation to assume this additional responsibility. Prolonged dependence on adults in this arena can both work to maintain parental authority while also leading to increased conflict over what are reasonable expenditures.

A fluctuating sense of identity: The main task of adolescence is developing a clear and solid sense of identity as opposed to an unhealthy emergence of identity confusion or diffusion. Teens establish a stronger sense of personal individuality as they continue to detach from their parents.

This search for self, however, is marked often by periods of opposition, rebellion, and alternative or unconventional choices. Although adolescents must experiment to "find themselves," this can be difficult for both the teens as well as for their parents.

Feelings of invincibility: At this stage, teens frequently feel immortal, as though nothing bad could ever happen to them. This is evident in their behaviors and attitudes and explains their increased risk-taking behaviors. An example of this mentality would be a teen's driving while drunk, speeding, driving without a license, and other illegal activities. From the teen's perspective, they will never get caught; "it will never happen" to them. This perceived sense of invincibility, an enduring hallmark of adolescent development, has become increasingly problematic in modern times.

Specifically, the opportunity for trouble stemming from increased drug availability, the Internet, decreased adult supervision, and so on has increased exponentially. For example, teens no longer have to wait until the next time they see their peers to tell them they are mad; they don't even have to wait until their home phone is free. For today's youth, expressing anger or behaving impulsively is only a text message or keystroke away. This heightened connectivity makes it more difficult for adolescents to think before they act. Again, feeling relatively unrealistic about the possibility of bad outcomes only places the impulse-prone and opportunity-laden teen at even greater risk for problems.

Increased pressure to achieve: Never before have academic and other pressures to succeed been so unrelenting and severe. Adolescents these days compete with a cohort of peers, many of whom are overachievers by our generation's standards. This current generation of teens has been involved with sports, taken music lessons, frequently has had home tutoring, and taken part in multiple extracurricular activities. College admissions officers no longer find it impressive, for example, that a high school graduate took ballet and piano for four years. Chances are that in the same high school class, there may be many students who are not only involved in dance and music, but are also great athletes, or can speak a second or third language.

Many parents organize their days around their children's after-school and weekend classes and activities. With more involvement in their children's lives, the additional invested energy, time, effort, and money expended, parental expectations are higher than ever before, and children are very aware of that. The pressure to live up to everyone's expectations and successfully compete with one's classmates can be enormous.

It is also important not to confuse heightened involvement with increased communication or control. Many times parents who appear and feel involved with the overt, scheduled part of their teen's existence still know relatively little about what their teen is "really up to."

In the flurry of activity on everyone's part, it is easy to lose sight of whom the teen talks to and what he or she is up to on the computer, and busy schedules and carpools begin to substitute for more heartfelt parent–child interaction and conversation.

Increased conflict with parents: At this stage of development, keeping the lines of communication open is the most crucial parental task. At times, this may feel like an impossible task, since many teens appear uninterested in talking to their parents about important issues.

For parents of preteens, it is best to establish these lines of communication earlier on. But no matter how hard a parent tries, it is the teen's task to learn to keep secrets, extol privacy, and make sure they do not reveal peer issues that may result in their own embarrassment or rejection. By definition, adolescence is a period of decreased revelation between child and parent, which is again, a shift that can be profoundly difficult for everyone involved. Especially in this period of time, it takes additional planning and attention for family members to spend time together and maintain some commitment to an exchange of ideas and communal dialogue.

TEN ESSENTIAL COMPONENTS OF EFFECTIVE TEEN PARENTING

Just as teens have a series of developmental steps they must take and challenges that are nearly inevitable, the parents' task is to be as prepared as possible for what is to come. The saying "forewarned is forearmed" comes to mind as the best advice for parents about to or already dealing with teenagers in the home.

Following are suggestions that might help to better weather the storms of adolescence and perhaps even minimize their impact.

Achieve parental consensus: Make sure parental communication is consensual and that privileges, ground rules, expectations, and consequences are clear and presented uniformly to the preteen/adolescent. Given the plethora of divorced and blended families as well as the prevalence of the two-parent working family, many homes no longer ring with the refrain "wait until your father gets home." Kids are often home for periods of time unsupervised, left to correspond with their parents electronically, and frequently allowed or required to move between different households and caretaker configurations. This lack of constancy can be disastrous for teens who are already trying to establish their own rules and rid themselves of their parents' "prehistoric" notions of "right" and "wrong." Communication and consensus between involved adults has, therefore, never been more important than it is now.

Include other adults in the life of your teen: Examples of this may include a teacher, guidance counselor, coach, best friend's parents, or therapist. It is particularly important during adolescence to determine whether any concerning behaviors are limited to a specific place or a specific person, as opposed to being more pervasive and occurring across situations and people. Also, more adults mean more supervision and more support. Parents are no longer around as much as in the past, and the traditional extended family is virtually nonexistent for many teens. It is essential, therefore, to create an active network of trusted adults to be involved with your adolescent.

Be ready for times of crisis: Few adolescents weather their teen years without having a crisis or two. During these times, their behavior may indicate strongly that something is wrong, but you as the parent are the last one they will talk to.

If your child is not opening up to you, decide whom they may choose as an alternative trusted adult—one who can step in at a time of crisis to help open up the lines of communication. This person could be a family friend, an older cousin, or a current or past teacher. Teens in their communications may mention an adult they respect or look up to; parents should pay attention to these references. Sometimes it is more helpful for parents and children to take a break from one another and have a trusted third party facilitate communication. The adolescent needs to feel that the third-party person can approach the problem from a neutral place, without prejudging or taking sides. Also remember that it is usually best to be on the "safe side" and involve a professional sooner rather than later.

Pick your battles: Often noted, but worth repeating, "pick your battles" is a useful adage to practice with your teenager. Clearly, when there is a risk to your child's or someone else's safety, the involvement of high-risk behaviors, destruction of property, and so forth, there is no room for negotiations. However, in other matters, prioritize what is most important to you, important enough that it makes having a fight with your teen, the stress this conflict causes everyone, and the possible damage to the relationship worthwhile.

Teens, while appearing tough and combative, have fragile aspects to their still burgeoning identities, and conflicts with parents can be more harmful than helpful. This in no way means you should avoid setting reasonable limits or holding clear expectations; it only means to prepare yourself for the refrain that "everyone else is allowed to . . . ," and not dismiss these entreaties without due consideration. There are times to stand firm and times to show your teen that you are someone worth negotiating with.

Share your parenting difficulties with others: Parents of adolescents have to realize that they are not alone in their struggles. Just as there is a sense of pride for parents when their children are doing well, there is a sense of shame when children are not. Supportive, trusted, and nonjudgmental family and friends can be of great help during these times. There is no need for parents to go through these difficult times with their teens alone. Keep in mind that there are also many community agencies with wonderful resources for teens and their families. And most important, do not mirror your adolescent's sense of secrecy and pride; remember some of your own adolescent antics and decide who in your life will listen and lend support. More often than not, you will find one or more parents struggling with the same issues that you face.

Monitor and talk about increased sexuality: This is a difficult topic for many parents to discuss with their teens. Some parents may manage to avoid this topic all together, relying on the health curriculum at school or peers of their children to provide answers. However, it is more important today than ever before to begin these conversations early on, and proactively, as appropriate to the child's age.

Discuss risks such as pregnancy, sexually transmitted diseases, and AIDS. Discuss strategies when talking with your teen—always emphasize that they should have the choice as to when and with whom they have sexual contact, and the choice to say no. Do not try to scare your teen; be open to discussion, nonjudgmental, and do not overreact and potentially further push your teen away by not respecting his or her privacy. Talk about all aspects of sexuality and not just sexual intercourse.

As much as things have changed, many aspects of adolescence have stayed the same. Communicate that you understand the dilemmas facing them and that, no matter what your personal position, you are not afraid to communicate openly about the topic of teenage sexuality.

Expect adolescent egocentrism: A hallmark of adolescence, egocentrism refers to adolescents' sense of personal uniqueness as well as their belief that others are as interested in them, and their physical appearance, as they themselves are. There are two social components that make up adolescent egocentrism—imaginary audience and personal fable.[14] During adolescence, teens experience dramatic physiological changes that in turn lead to a heightened preoccupation with their body image. They are highly cognizant of their physical appearance and social status with their peers. A hair out of place or a blemish on the skin, for example, could be quite stressful to a teenager. "Everyone was staring at me," they will report to their parents.

It is often hard to help a teen feel better about these perceived wounds regarding appearance and popularity, but it is essential for adults to remember that this heightened vanity and self-preoccupation is developmentally appropriate.

Be your teen's imaginary audience: Adolescents often behave as though they are "on stage" in front of an imaginary audience; this may involve attention-seeking behaviors as well as a wish to be noticed by others. If you have ever seen an adolescent girl or boy trying to get ready to go out in the evening, you know what this behavior looks like. At this stage of development, teens feel as though they are under the spotlight and all eyes are on them. Their attention to details, when it comes to their appearance, is often mind-boggling and can be exhausting for the parent observer. Stick with them; if they get your attention and approval, they may be less likely to seek it elsewhere.

Accept your teen's "personal fable" as much as possible: Adolescents feel that no one is capable of understanding how they experience the world. They feel isolated and unique in their problems and believe that the only people who can possibly appreciate and understand their experiences are friends or age-mates. Teens, in general, do not find their parents' stories about when they were growing up helpful in almost any regard. They believe that many current experiences are unique to their generation and the present times. As we have repeatedly mentioned, for this generation, they may be much more right than wrong. The advances in technology and communication that have occurred in this past decade already baffle many young adults, only one decade out of adolescence themselves.

So try, whenever possible, to not embarrass your teen with past tales or assume that you fully understand their predicaments. Be empathic without undermining the teenagers' sense that they face unique challenges that you, as an older adult, cannot possibly fathom.

Maintain active communication with your teen: A style that includes criticism, judgment, handing out solutions, interruptions, and comparing the teen to a peer who seems to make better decisions is one that will likely shut down future attempts by the teen to open up to his or her parents. Unless the behavior or incident at hand is one that has to do with drugs, alcohol, hurting themselves or others, destruction of property, or any illegal acts, parents must listen with an open mind and try to be as nonjudgmental as possible. Teens will question rules and parental decisions; again unless there is a safety or legal issue, parents must be willing to negotiate with their teens. The process of respectful consideration of the teen's opinion will set the right example for the child.

Remember that adolescents revere their privacy and are often afraid or ashamed to tell their parents what is going on in their lives. They are also very protective of their peers, whom they do not want to get into trouble. But when given an opportunity, and a calm environment, adolescents can often be persuaded that negotiation is preferable to outright mutiny, that they are more likely to get your cooperation if you have sufficient information. Again, dialogue is just that; no rule or expectation changes should occur without parental consensus.

HOW TO ASSESS WORRISOME BEHAVIORS IN ADOLESCENCE

Although many teens have loving, caring, and mutually respectful relationships with their families, often families experience significant turmoil, stress, and a decline in the quality of their relationship with their teenagers. While teens may only exhibit the more routine rebellious behaviors understood under a rubric of adolescent delinquency or rebelliousness, they may also display frank emotional disturbances. While, again, some behavioral problems are to be expected during these years of development, specific factors need to be looked at in order to determine whether outside help might be needed.

Consider factors such as the frequency, intensity, and adverse affects on various areas of functioning to determine the seriousness of your teen's behavioral problems. For any adolescent these areas of functioning include academic and school, home and family, peer relations and social functioning, as well as vocational performance. Therefore, any time parents observe a significant decline in a child's functioning in any of these areas, special attention and additional help may be required. For example, if an adolescent who may have always been a little argumentative and moody starts to have daily bouts of verbal or physical aggression, isolates himself or herself, has rapid shifts in mood, or does not engage in regular activities, this may be an indication that additional help is warranted.

Try to pinpoint when a behavior problem began. An important question for parents to ponder is "Why are we seeing these changes and behaviors now?" This is a significant question, particularly if the concerning behaviors are new and seem to have appeared out of nowhere. Parents must keep in mind that adolescents, much like younger children, can be affected profoundly by significant individual, familial, and societal events. Issues, from simple to complex—from acne to moving, an older sibling going to college, the loss of a friend, a sick family member, divorce, a parent getting remarried, or violence in the community—may trigger a change in a teen's behavior. Thinking about when these changes began and whether they coincide with other issues can be helpful to parents, teachers, and professionals.

Related to this discussion are ways for parents to try and identify specific cues that may help predict, for their own teens, when a problem behavior might occur. For example, anxiety and nervousness before exams, games, or competitions may be expressed as general irritability. A

THE DOS AND DON'TS
OF EFFECTIVE COMMUNICATION

Following is a list of tips for approaching communication with your teen, which can seem impossible at times, but is vital to maintaining honesty, openness, and trust between parents and their adolescents.

Do respect your teens and what they are capable of doing. They are moving toward adulthood and need to be in mutually respectful relationships. Behaviors such as name calling, talking down to them or about their friends, criticism, and pointing out their shortcomings or weaknesses to prove a point can only damage the relationship.

Do consider your tone as well as your words. A condescending or sarcastic tone is just as hurtful as words and can be problematic. When you condescend to an adolescent, you are asking for, and will likely get, a fight.

Do not make assumptions, reach conclusions, or make accusations before you have had a chance to talk to your teen. Invite teens to present their side of the story without feeling that they have already been prejudged. If you do not give them a chance to tell you their side, as unbelievable as it might be, they will cease to talk with you. You will have reinforced their maladaptive adolescent assumption that adults won't and can't understand their problems.

Do not lecture. Adolescents will typically shut down, tune out, or storm out in response to long lectures about their behavior. Provide ongoing opportunities during a conversation for input from your teens. Listen to their point of view and give their perspective fair consideration. Do not interrupt. Establish rules for everyone to have their turn to speak. Teens need to feel that they have an equal chance to discuss the issue at hand.

Do talk about how you feel about a situation, action, or statement. Use "I" statements. "I am upset because I didn't know where you were." Do not reference what others may think or feel; teens are sharp to point out hypocrisy and insincerity. If you are having a problem with their behavior, then say so. Do not conjure up images of the school, the law, absent parents, and so on; you only confuse them and give them an unclear message about your own expectations.

Do not generalize or use absolute terms. Avoid saying "you never" or "you always," indicating that there have not been any positive actions. Concede on the positive steps and changes, even when they are imperceptible. The teen, naturally feeling misjudged and misunderstood, will be vigilant about your acknowledgment that they are making an effort, no matter how small.

Do not compare your teen to any other child to further illustrate how poorly he or she is doing. Each child is different. This is helpful only if you are trying to normalize a less than desirable outcome. Starting sentences with such words as, " I don't understand why this is not a problem for anyone else in your class" or "Johnny seems to be able to handle school, basketball, and music lessons just fine" is not the way to get your teen's attention.

Do look for cues from teens on when they are ready and need to talk. Be prepared to just listen. Do not immediately offer a solution. Make the finding of a solution a collaborative process. Teach your teen the process of reaching a solution and considering all options at hand. Try to see the problem from their perspective. Making the suggestion of talking to a teacher about a problem, for example, may not be a viable solution from a teen's perspective. It might mean having to tell on a classmate or getting someone else in trouble. Keep in mind, for an adolescent, being a part of their teen community and having peer approval is crucial.

Do communicate your expectations clearly and concisely. State your teen's responsibilities in specific and simple terms. Have an open discussion about how reasonable and doable these expectations are for them. Avoid giving random ultimatums and making threats.

Do practice putting off a discussion until you have cooled off. Try not to pursue a discussion in the heat of the moment. Adolescents are, by nature, volatile. They are prone to action over cognition and will gladly join you in combat if that is all you offer.

Do try to talk to your teen as much as possible, not just when things are not going your way. Talk about light topics and everyday issues and subjects. Include them more and more in various discussions about family plans, siblings, and general concerns. Treat them like a mature participant whenever possible.

Do be patient. Try to remember when you were a teen and going through similar difficulties. The world of a teenager is even more complicated now than it was when you were growing up. Remember, they are dealing with intricacies and a demand for instant connectivity that is unimaginable to most of today's adults. Before you make decisions, find out more about what they are dealing with and the cost–benefit ratio of your rules and decisions.

teen who is not exactly the best athlete in his or her class, the fastest run-
ner, or coordinated physically may be irritable, anxious, depressed, shut
down, or excessively wary and vigilant on Tuesday night, the night before
the weekly physical education class. Does this mean he or she has a
psychiatric illness? The answer is no, although these issues and problems
can be further compounded by additional stresses and/or an underlying
biological vulnerability, as will be discussed in the next chapter.

It is up to the parent, in collaboration with trusted other adults, to decide how to support the teen through these stresses or, alternatively, act
to remove those stresses that appear to be unmanageable. The hallmark
of adolescent problems of greater concern are those where no trigger is
apparent and/or when removing a stressor does not result in behavioral
and/or emotional improvement.

WHAT TO DO WHEN CONCERNING BEHAVIORS PERSIST

Many adolescents will either not be able to recognize the true causes of
their behavior or not openly talk about what is really bothering them.
Some may even deny the parent's observations and suggestions of what
may be happening to them, insisting that you have things "all wrong."
Being able to identify people, situations, settings, and any other variable
that may bring on or influence certain troubling behaviors is nonetheless
helpful. Knowing the signs of a looming problem will empower and assure you as a parent even if you cannot change things in the moment.

Using the knowledge about adolescent development and your own
teen in particular, parents can try to identify and understand the possible trigger for any undesirable behaviors and act as soon as possible to
determine what things cause or escalate the behavior and what strategies
might work to ameliorate the problem. Ideally, the goal is to replace the
maladaptive behaviors with more adaptive and acceptable ones while
obtaining the desired outcome for the teen.

The more serious adolescent behaviors—antisocial, delinquent, and/or
depressed and disorganized behaviors—are clearly indicative of more acute
underlying issues. These behaviors include such things as involvement with
drugs and alcohol, gangs, weapons, and more generalized antisocial behavior as well as extreme, persistent moodiness that impairs functioning. Many
of these more serious problems will be discussed in the following chapters.

Overall, given that it can be hard to distinguish "normal" from more worrisome behaviors, the best strategy in dealing with your adolescent is to be proactive. It is imperative to have established open communication lines and clear family expectations with your teen during the earlier, preteen years. During those earlier years, parents can create healthy communication habits that are more likely to withstand the storms of adolescence.

Of great importance, additionally, is what the teenager has observed in terms of styles of communication between the various members of the family. In particular, the communication style between the adults, namely the parents, is of crucial significance. By nature, children are very observant. They learn very early on, by observing their parents, what works and what doesn't in their families. They know what style of communication is acceptable in the home, what language is used and allowed, and what behaviors will get someone what they want. Parents' behavior in the presence of their children is the most powerful teaching tool during the most formative years of development.

During adolescence, however, even the best attempts at communication and modeling might fail. Again, if communication is impaired along with evidence of persistent emotional and/or behavioral problems, it is probably the time to seek professional help. Even with help on board, however, it is still crucial to try and maintain a dialogue with your teenager.

WHEN CONCERNS INDICATE PSYCHOLOGICAL DISORDERS

In the following chapters, we will present certain psychological disorders to more fully explain when a problem behavior may require additional attention.

For a problem behavior to be considered a psychiatric disorder or pathological, however, it has to meet certain clinical and diagnostic criteria and it has to significantly interfere with the youngster's functioning. These aspects of functioning of potential concern may include academic, family, social, and occupational areas of the teen's life.[15] An example of a psychiatric problem that requires immediate attention is a psychotic disorder such as schizophrenia. Here, the individual is unable to understand reality as expected for his or her age and developmental level. There may be signs of hallucination—for example, hearing voices, having delusions or bizarre beliefs, or thinking illogically.

Normally, patterns of problems or symptoms that are disruptive, potentially dangerous, and persist over the course of several weeks require professional attention and may be the sign of a more serious mental health issue. An example is experimenting with marijuana or alcohol once as opposed to becoming addicted to a drug or alcohol. Additionally, adolescents can exhibit one-time behavior that, because of its magnitude and dangerousness, requires professional intervention, such as cutting themselves.

Once it is clear that your adolescent needs professional help, a full diagnostic evaluation by a qualified professional is necessary. This evaluation will include a diagnosis based on the presenting problems and symptoms and also a treatment plan. For many psychiatric disorders, a treatment plan may involve any number of the following options: individual psychotherapy, group therapy, family therapy, social skills train-

KNOW WHEN TO SEEK PROFESSIONAL HELP

Although there is no simple answer to this dilemma, and each family must make this decision as it sees fit, there are general guidelines that may be helpful. Following are times when a family might wish to consider getting professional help.

- The child has destroyed property, (e.g., in anger, in response to limits set, or with a group of teens in the community).

- There is involvement with drugs, alcohol, or illegal activities.

- The adolescent becomes more noticeably withdrawn and emotionally unresponsive.

- There is a sudden change in the child's behavior and performance at home or school that does not respond to the usual interventions.

- There is a significant change in eating habits, including noticeable weight loss or weight gain.

- The teen has experienced or observed traumatic events such as violent crimes, natural disasters, abuse, or loss.

- The adolescent is dealing with a chronic illness such as a seizure disorder or diabetes, which interferes with his or her ability to fully participate in desired activities.

Please note that these are general guidelines and examples of when teens or their families may decide to seek professional help. These warning, school-based treatment programs, medication, or acute residential treatment and hospitalization. You and your team of mental health care professionals will determine a viable option for your teen's specific need.

SUMMARY AND CONCLUSIONS

It is rather unfortunate that in our culture, for many, the word "teenager" is synonymous with trouble. "Teenagers . . . what are you going to do?" say many adults in response to others' complaints, or when referring to their own teen. If we are going to make strides toward solving our "teen problem," however, we have to start by changing our way of thinking. For it is true that the way in which we perceive a situation makes that situation, at least in part, what it is. If we view adolescents as problems, then our logical thinking dictates that we solve the problem. In thinking about a problem,

ing signs are not necessarily indicative of a more major emotional or behavioral problem, especially if they are short-lived and of mild intensity. But any change in adolescence needs to be observed because waiting too long to intervene is potentially more dangerous than asking questions early, whether of friends, school personnel, your pediatrician, or others.

Families, based on what they know about their children, must determine for themselves when they may benefit from consulting with a professional in the mental health care field.

To reiterate, the task of adolescents is what is referred to as identity formation, that is, trying to figure out "Who am I?" "Where and how do I fit in?" and "What am I going to do with my life?" These are difficult enough issues in themselves, but they have been made more complicated by the intricacies and connectivity of modern life. In addition, while going through all these significant, predictable emotional issues, the adolescent is also experiencing major physical changes as well. If your teen exhibits any of the changes listed above, has experienced a major loss or life stressor, or begins behaving in any way that concerns you, it always better to err on the side of caution and seek professional advice.

any problem, all our senses are aroused and we are likely to go on the offensive. More so when we are personally involved, our capacity for logical, critical, and objective thinking can be compromised. We may, inadvertently, close crucial lines of communication and reach a completely false conclusion, based more on apprehension and assumption than on reality.

We should celebrate adolescence as an important phase in the developmental process. It is an opportunity for connecting with our children on a different and more profound level. It is the time to take a step back and trust your instincts while also maintaining a watchful, active stance. It is a time not to assume the worst but also not to expect the best in terms of your adolescent's level of functioning and resiliency. The nature of your relationship with your children is changing for certain, and you will be playing a different role in their lives.

While perhaps struggling more to maintain a constructive connection with your teens, your role to guide and support them as they make responsible choices has not changed. What has changed is their inherent stability—one day displaying defiant rebelliousness followed the next moment perhaps by obsequious platitudes and pleas for forgiveness. Remember, neither of you is necessarily crazy, but adolescence is a time of great imbalance, unpredictability, and change. And in response to this variability, you must also change, displaying trust when it is earned over time and maintaining your authority and leadership until your teen fully reaches adulthood.

The goal for all parents is to develop and maintain a healthy and responsible parent–child relationship in the early years that will endure the strains of adolescence. A mutually respectful, trusting, and cooperative relationship within which communication is the foundation allows for parent–child roles to become gradually more independent and equivalent over the course of adolescence. Communication, at all times, not just during a crisis, establishes and maintains this connection. Although teens may not want their parents around when their friends are nearby, they take comfort in knowing that parents are "right next door" should they be needed. Parenting an adolescent, particularly in these high-stress, high-stakes times, is a journey that will at times be challenging and difficult, but it can also be an amazing, gratifying, and marvelous phase in the life of a family. The key to surviving and flourishing as the parent of a teen is to maintain interactions, limits, and expectations that accurately reflect your teen's current emotional needs and capabilities.

This is not to say that, in spite of one's best efforts, those things do not sometimes go seriously wrong. When this happens, it is hard for parents not to panic and feel that they are losing the wonderful child they once had. Communication breaks down, symptoms worsen, and an entire family system can become disorganized. When this happens, it is time to accept that your teen's behaviors may be outside the scope of normal developmental variations, and it is then essential to seek professional help.

A first step may be to read about teen development and the types of problems that today's teens are experiencing. A second is to accept that the teen's brain and body are changing rapidly and what might be a problem today may not endure or permanently disrupt either their growth or your relationship. In some instances, however, the problems consolidate and are revealed to be hallmarks of a more serious psychiatric disorder. The following chapters cover ways to identify and address some of the more troubling and pervasive problems of today's teens. We will start by looking at depression, as this is a problem both prevalent in adolescence and often difficult to distinguish from more routine teenage troubles.

CHAPTER 3

Adolescent Depression

Michael Rater, M.D.,
and Ken Sklar, Ed.D., LICSW

Depression in adolescents is not unusual. Approximately 5 to 15 percent of adolescents have symptoms that meet the psychiatric diagnosis of depression.[1] Despite its prevalence, depression is hard to recognize because almost every teen experiences negative moods.

Knowing when an adolescent moves from age-appropriate moodiness to true depression and possibly preoccupations with self-harm is one of the greatest challenges parents of teens face today. This distinction is often hard to discern, even for those of us engaged professionally in treating teenagers with emotional and behavioral difficulties.

Parents of depressed adolescents may feel guilty that they did not notice their adolescent's mood problems sooner, but moods are private, particularly for teenagers. Only the behaviors and often indirect communications that result from depression signal to parents that something may be seriously wrong. When the behavior is to withdraw, or the adolescent becomes irritable and hostile and pushes people away, or the "communication" is to stop communicating, then the depression becomes even harder to recognize. Because many adolescents don't communicate well with adults, it is common to miss the early signs that a teen's moods are worsening.

Often, we will hear concerned parents tell us that their child's depression "just snuck up on us."

In this chapter, we offer parents guidance on how to recognize depression and differentiate it from typical adolescent moodiness, as well as ways they can help their teen, from opening the lines of communication to seeking professional help.

———————

AS WE'VE DISCUSSED in previous chapters, adolescence is a time of growth and change for children—physically, mentally, and emotionally. This period of change is usually accompanied by turmoil and rapidly changing moods, feelings, and sensations. The adolescent's mood can swing from happy to angry to sad and back again within a few minutes. These mood changes are, moreover, easily influenced by external situations, such as schoolwork (a bad test grade), sports issues (being dropped from a team), and social situations (rejection from a romantic interest or a fight with a friend or parent).

In addition, today's generation of adolescents faces unique circumstances, such as the advent of many new technologies and instant communication, the dissolution of the nuclear family, the prevalence of single-parent families, and increased academic competition. All of these factors make adolescence a time of transition that is frequently very difficult for both parents and their teens to deal with.

Typical adolescents tend to spend less time with their parents, often wanting to be alone at home or with friends instead. This behavior is part of adolescent attempts to separate from family and develop an identity that is unique to them—attempts that can result in an exhibition of new and often unpredictable behaviors. Changes in their moods, behavior, and relationships with family can make it difficult to distinguish between adolescents who assert their independence in potentially alarming and alienating ways and those who struggle with symptoms of depression.

Some adolescents are remarkably resilient in the face of these pressures and are able to use internal coping strategies and external support such as family, friends, or teachers to manage these challenges. However, other teenagers are not quite as fortunate and find that the culmination of stressors places them in a position of feeling overwhelmed, anxious, and depressed Sometimes they become desperate and cannot see alternative solutions to their problems.

Before going any further, let's take a look at some of the differences between depression and typical adolescent "blues."

THE KEYS TO SEPARATING NORMAL MOODS FROM DEPRESSION

Frequency, duration, and intensity are the key words that separate clinical depression symptoms from normal adolescent moodiness. The symptoms of "normal adolescence" and "moodiness" are, interestingly, the same as the symptoms of depression. In depression, though, the person is overwhelmed by the symptoms. The symptoms are too frequent, last too long, and are too intense for the teen to manage.

Normally, part of an individual's mind knows that something unpleasant will end, and this knowledge helps us get through the experience—"It will just hurt for one minute." In depression, this knowledge can be lost. It is the awful feeling or the immediate intense sadness or panic that dominates and seems as if it will last forever.

It is normal for motivation, initiative, or drive to come and go. When it goes, it returns after a period of time, especially when we really need it. In depression, however, people lose their drive and motivation more completely and for longer periods. Clinical depression is a condition in which motivation, initiative, and drive are impaired for two weeks or longer. In serious cases, these psychological features can be severely impaired for several months up to one and one-half years. It is difficult for depressed people to concentrate and focus on tasks and even more difficult to persist with what they are doing.

Frequently, one of the first things depressed adolescents lose interest in is school, resulting in falling grades, missed exams, absent days, and so on. They also tend to withdraw from friends and family, spending more time alone. At times, their thinking gets caught in negative loops, resulting in them assuming they are bad and worthless, and these thoughts make them feel even more dreadful and insignificant. These thoughts are called ruminations and can start to interfere with all aspects of a teen's functioning.

Thus, part of the answer to the difference between moodiness and depression is that with depression symptoms are more severe and persis-

THE WARNING SIGNS OF TEEN DEPRESSION

Following is a list of many of the most common warning signs of depression. Again, any one of these lasting for a brief period is not necessarily cause for alarm. As discussed previously, it's when these symptoms persist and become more intense that parents and others need to become concerned and take action. We will outline options that parents can pursue further in this chapter.

- Depressed mood, exhibited by crying, social withdrawal, or irritability.

- Noticeable changes in eating or sleeping habits, either eating or sleeping more or less than usual.

- Intense, persistent withdrawal from friends or family.

- Recent severe stressors, such as difficulties in dealing with sexual orientation, unplanned pregnancy, or significant loss of a parent, friend, sibling, or relationship.

- Impulsive and aggressive behavior and frequent expressions of rage.

- Loss of pleasure or interest in activities that were once enjoyable, such as athletics, hanging out with friends, and going to the movies or mall.

- Unusual neglect of appearance. Not showering or caring about their looks.

- Expression of low self-esteem (statements such as: "I can never do anything right!" or "I am a loser!") on a persistent and pervasive level.

- Difficulty concentrating or making decisions.

- Drug or alcohol abuse.

- Abrupt and/or persistent personality change, such as moodiness, lack of a cheerful countenance, and withdrawal socially.

- Concerns expressed by others, such as teachers or peers, friends, or teammates.

- Unexplained drop in the quality of schoolwork, grades dropping significantly.

- Talk of suicide or death, such as "If I kill myself, everyone will be better off!"

tent, interfering with aspects of routine daily functioning. Rather than interest, enthusiasm, and occasional irritability, the emotional landscape becomes one dominated by fatigue, lethargy, disinterest, and a sense of gloominess about the future. While the degree of depression can vary from mild to severe, the basic symptoms overlap, and we now know are due, at least in part, to imbalances in brain chemistry that disrupt the already fragile biological balance of the adolescent brain.

THE CAUSES BEHIND ADOLESCENT DEPRESSION

Different factors play roles in the causes of adolescent depression. Among them are biology, societal issues, social events, and gender. An adolescent's biological brain chemistry, for example, affects their predisposition to depression.

The "primary sense areas" of the brain—those that record sight, sound, smell, feel, and taste—are established and unchanged by puberty. These "primary sense areas" send "basic information" to other brain regions that combine this information in multiple ways, blending it with memories from the past, mixing in "emotional information" with "factual data" and then using the blended information to plan, organize, and carry out actions. The brain's regions that combine, analyze, and share this primary information are the regions that grow in size and interconnections during adolescence.

Additionally, the brain regions that process emotions are rapidly changing as well, and their connections to the planning, organizing, initiating, and sustaining brain regions grow constantly. Add to this growth changes in the brain regions that regulate social interactions and you have major developments in the brain areas that have to do with the areas of thoughts, feelings, and behaviors—often referred to as the "big three" areas of depression symptoms. The famous teenage angst, with the questions of "Who am I?," "Who are you?," and "What is the meaning of life?" is due, at least in part, to the brain regions that generate these questions exploding with activity.

It is therefore no wonder that the adolescent brain is vulnerable to problems and that problems in brain functioning can, in turn, lead to the syndrome of depression. Because there are so many moving parts within the brain that connect to each other in circular ways, problems in many different areas can all lead to a similar set of symptoms.

Inheriting a Predisposition for Depression

Adolescent depression often results from a family predisposition or biological vulnerability that is then triggered by stress, pressure, and/or adversity. If there is a history of depression or other mood disorders in your family, be on the watch for it in your adolescent. If an adolescent experiences negative life situations, which is inevitably going to happen, then the adolescent with a familial vulnerability will often be at greater risk for developing depression.

An individual teen's biological vulnerability and level of stress exist along a continuum, each contributing to the potential for development of a psychiatric problem such as depression. Someone with a major genetic vulnerability to depression, for instance someone with a mother and/or father with a major depression, is more likely to become depressed when there are negative things that happen in life. A person's brain with a genetic propensity toward depression is more likely to focus on negative aspects of issues, which then can trigger a vicious downward cycle.

Someone with a minor vulnerability—and all people have some vulnerability—may be able to handle life's usual troubles but will have increasing problems with a major loss, like the death of a parent, or with a series of smaller problems that can have a cumulative effect.

The Role of Gender

It is also important to note that depression affects female adolescents twice as often as it does males. Males are more likely to suffer from impulse control disorders, such as substance abuse, criminal behavior, and obsessive-compulsive disorder. Some people attribute these differences to hormonal differences that set in around puberty. Others attribute the differences to social factors, such as society's different expectations for girls and for boys. Both of these explanations are probably true to a degree.

Another area that is of interest is that there are differences in brain development between males and females. The brain regions that are important in controlling impulses develop earlier in females than in males, likely making females less susceptible to impulse control disorders. The brain areas that deal with emotions and their expressions take longer to develop in females, which in part helps to explain the increased female vulnerability to depression.

Beyond Biology: Other Factors and Their Role in Depression

Many of life's hard knocks—such as the death of a loved one, family financial pressures, ill health, demands to succeed, friendship issues, and physical injuries—often contribute to the pressure of the adolescent who is just beginning to learn to how to cope with loss, disappointment, and adversity. Sometimes this pressure is too much, though what is "too much" can be different from one teenager to another.

In addition, the ability to accept not reaching a goal is an important milestone in adolescent development. Learning to accept that you do not always succeed at everything you try and not allowing this to adversely affect your self-image is an important step. Adolescents lack previous experience in understanding that the disappointments or upsets of today will pass and there will be other opportunities to be successful. One of the most critical challenges for adolescents is to maintain their self-image after experiencing rejection, failure, loss, or disappointment. It is appropriate to have feelings related to life's challenges. However, it is equally as important for adolescents to find their way through the crisis without compromising their overall self-image.

Moreover, today's generation of adolescents faces additional challenges stemming from the rapid technological changes in our society. Adolescents today have almost constant access to their friends through cell phones, text messages, instant messaging, and the Internet. Today's world can be just too much too fast for any teen to handle. The amount of stimulation that surrounds us can paralyze even the most well-intentioned adolescent. Being overwhelmed by life's problems, or by the pace of modern life, can itself result in depression. This environmental stress can add additional pressure to the already rapidly developing brain that we have described. Stress can also magnify vulnerabilities in the brain's development and contribute to the development of depression.

Adolescents who suffer a major injury to their self-identity can develop a rapid and potentially dangerous depression, even without any obvious biological predisposition. This is the adolescent who places too much emphasis on school success, for example, and overworks himself. He gets fatigued emotionally as well as physically, and starts thinking irrationally. He believes that a bad result is catastrophic and he acts in sync with this perception and tries to kill himself. This is the lovesick adolescent who feels rejected by her loved one. It might be a literal rejection, just as it might have been a legitimate "bad result" for the adolescent in the previous example, or it might be a perceived rejection, just as it might be a perceived bad result for the previous adolescent, something that objectively speaking is "no big deal." This type of logically wrong, heightened negative perception is called cognitive distortion, and it is a key symptom of depression—first, because this kind of thinking impairs a person's judgment, and second, because it can be specifically targeted by cognitive behavioral therapy, utilizing techniques to help recognize and neutralize cognitive distortions.

WHAT CAN A PARENT DO?

Following are suggestions for parents who suspect their teens may be depressed.

Maintain communication with your adolescent: As outlined previously, you can ask your adolescent whether he or she is depressed, but you can't always rely on what he or she says. You need to ask, though, no matter the response, because maintaining communication is essential for treating depression in adolescents. Breakdowns in communication can be associated with bad outcomes. Maybe the adolescent avoids the parents. Maybe he or she says everything is fine. Maybe he or she is hostile and has worn people down with sharp replies, like "Don't worry about it!" "Leave me alone!" or "I have it handled!"

But regardless of what the adolescent claims, teens require active parenting. These youngsters who are "forming their identity" need frequent interactions with adults to achieve this important goal properly, but they may fight bitterly at times against this involvement. Also, the adolescent can be too wrapped up in his or her own perspective to recognize the compelling need for other people's insight and help.

The adolescent mind, in general, tends to be overly absorbed in its own perspective. The ability to take a step back and see oneself from another's point of view develops later, with evolving maturity. It is the adult who ultimately provides the oversight and sense of continuity that the adolescent desperately needs.

So remember to ask your adolescent regularly how he or she is doing, or, if warranted, whether he or she is depressed. But don't take what your

WHAT SHOULD PARENTS DO
WHEN THEY SUSPECT DEPRESSION?

If an adolescent has some, or many, of the symptoms of depression listed in this chapter that last for a couple of weeks or more, then it is important to seek help. Even one of these symptoms, if worrisome to you, is at least reason to have a conversation with your most likely reluctant adolescent. Do not let his or her reluctance dissuade you; parents often have a good sense about problems with their teens and need to seek information, reassurance, and/or outside help sooner rather than later.

Parents may easily attribute depressed mood and irritability to just "being a teenager" and may not want to meddle or interfere where they are not welcome. In an effort to give their teens "space" and let them become individuals, parents may overlook the beginnings of a more serious depression. The best additional way to assess whether an adolescent is depressed is to gather information from school personnel, your teen's friends, and others whom he or she may confide in or trust, as well as from observing his or her behavior over time.

Today's parents are often under enormous pressure to balance work, endless carpools, and attendance at athletic and/or extracurricular events while also trying to find some time left over for their own relation-ships. The pace for today's family is hectic, filled with pressure, and, at times, overwhelming for parents and teenagers alike. So how do parents begin to recognize whether their teenage sons or daughters are in trouble or just trying to balance all the demands placed on them? There are no easy answers. However, there are signs that parents can look for and specific questions they can ask to get a better handle on separating out normal adolescent behavior from adolescent depression.

Try these suggestions.

• Talk to your teenager. Open communication between parents and their adolescents is essential. Ask them whether they have been depressed. Be willing and ready to listen. Be compassionate and supportive and do not minimize their feelings. Make sure you are in a private area and that both you and your teenager do not have to be somewhere else soon.

• If you are worried or concerned about your teenager, then be honest and let them know. Be specific and tell them exactly what you are seeing that has led you to be concerned.

• Be willing to let your teenager know that you care and are willing to get them whatever help they need.

• Remind your teen that no matter how awful the problem seems, things can, and will get better with help.

• Ask your teen whether there is anything you can do that would be helpful now.

• Try to help balance your adolescent's reaction to an adverse situation by pointing out some of the positive aspects, which can get lost in the present.

• Do not be afraid to ask your teenagers whether they have had thoughts about hurting themselves. Remember, talking about suicide does not put the thought in their head. In fact, getting the word out in the open may make it easier for your teenager to talk about depression and suicide more openly.

• If your teenager acknowledges that he or she has had thoughts about suicide, then ask whether he or she has a plan as to how to do it. If he or she acknowledges a plan and intent, then the risk for suicide is high and you should seek professional help immediately by going to your nearest hospital emergency department.

Parents and teenagers need to remember that there is help available for depression. Medication, therapy, and parental understanding and support are all helpful. Addressing the external life stressors when possible, such as allowing your adolescent to drop a course or a sport, can be helpful. If there is a way to provide your adolescent with a sense of hope that things will get better over time, this can also serve to be helpful.

Remember, parents may have little information to help them understand the meaning behind their adolescent's symptoms and, thus, are apt to see changes in behavior such as alcohol use, a drop in grades, irritability, or lack of interest as willful or disrespectful behavior. Getting information about the causes and symptoms of depression can provide parents with a better understanding of how not to personalize the behavior. Rather than getting angry with your teenagers, provide them with support and understanding, which may well help them feel less alone and better understood. These actions may begin to provide them with a sense of the possibility of improvement. It is essential to take heed of persistent symptoms and try to get help making the critical determination of whether your teen may, in fact, be clinically depressed.

teen says at face value, and remember that the process of working to stay involved is as important as the actual information or responses that you get back.

Assess objective information from alternative spheres: Look at your teen's school performance, friendships, relationships with others, and ability to handle situations when trying to determine whether he or she is depressed. Ask yourself these questions.

- How are they doing in school? How are their grades?
- How are their work habits?
- Do they interact easily or are they difficult to interact with?
- How do they act with peers?
- Do they have a range of friends?
- Are they able to make friends, be disappointed, fall out with people, and then make up?
- Is there is a lot of "drama" in their lives?
- Are they either too absorbed by one relationship or do they lack relationships?
- Are they able to adapt to situations?
- Can they handle frustrations?
- Do they participate in daily activities?
- Can they initiate and motivate themselves to handle structured and unstructured time?

If they can't handle frustration, or if they are not as involved with people as they should be or lack initiative and drive, these are additional possible signs of depression.

Continue to help your adolescent identify the problem: Be direct. Give information. Let your adolescent know when and why you are worried. Let them know you care about them and tell them what you are going to do and what you can do to help. They may not thank you for the above sentiments, but they need to hear you care. Remind them that, no matter how awful their problem, things can and will get better with help. They will not necessarily be able to see the reality of their depression at first and might immediately respond negatively to your concerns, but you must let them know you are worried. Ask whether there is anything you can do to help and explain that depression exists in adolescence and that they may feel better with treatment. With a depressed adolescent, parents have to be more in charge than they normally would be. Depression robs adolescents of some of their executive functioning ability.

Help them problem-solve: As mentioned, depression includes getting stuck in negative brain loops. Trying to help adolescents expand ways to think about solving a problem or managing upsetting events in their lives can be very useful at these times. Try to help balance the adolescents' reaction to an adverse situation by considering with them some of the positives, which can frequently get lost in a deluge of negative emotions. While you cannot spend your time as a perpetual cheerleader, you do need to help your teen see solutions that may not be apparent to him or her.

Seek professional help: There are times when even recognizing and discussing a mood problem with a teen does not help to resolve the trouble. The teen may remain lethargic, unresponsive, and unmotivated. Their functioning, across the board, remains diminished and blind alleys abound. Every day shows deterioration rather than an improvement and talking, fact-finding, supervising, and collaborating only seem to be making matters worse. It is now time to seek professional help. Starting with your pediatrician, school personnel, or mental health professionals, there is help for teens who experience prolonged, significant symptoms of depression. In general, these interventions include adjustments to school schedules, medication, individual counseling, and often family therapy.

If you are thinking about medication or regular therapy, then you already have a strong belief that your son or daughter is depressed, or someone has told you he or she is. Sometimes, the adolescent requests help, but this situation is rare. Getting help will usually be somebody else's idea—the parent, schoolteacher, pediatrician, or counselor.

People have usually thought about and tried to address social factors that cause depression before they consider medication. The symptoms will have often been unnoticed for a while, or you will finally notice something that you "should have seen" but didn't for some period, like increased withdrawal, time spent alone, and maybe self-destructive behavior such as cutting or drug and alcohol use. If the symptoms have developed during the summer, then the school year may lead to an even greater worsening of the warning signs.

Consider the following case study about how depression evolved in one youth and seemed to "sneak up" on his parents.

CASE STUDY

Justin—The Evolution of Depression

JUSTIN WAS FOURTEEN YEARS OLD and going into his freshman year in high school. He knew the school, because his grandmother lived in the town and he had lived there himself a few years ago, but his family had moved to Florida and it was only when his father's job fell through that the family decided to move back to Massachusetts. However, there was a fire in the moving van, and all their belongings were lost.

Thus, there were plenty of reasons for Justin to be upset that summer. He stayed in his grandmother's duplex playing a fantasy adventure computer game into the night. He slept during the day and was awake playing his game at night. His parents were distracted by their own worries and were reassured that Justin wasn't being a "problem." Justin no longer bathed as much, but that was hard to notice, as he had become so isolated. He wasn't getting out. He avoided conversations and activities. He wouldn't go with his mom to the store, and when he did he was quiet, often staring straight ahead listening to his iPod.

School started. By the third day of classes, Justin was at the nurse's office. He was so anxious that he was shaking. He needed to go to the emergency room. He could barely speak. He was diagnosed with depression. What had snuck up on everybody and initially gone unrecognized was suddenly obvious. Justin hung his head and no longer made eye contact. He reported no energy. He felt guilty. He was entirely and utterly slowed down.

By the time school started, Justin showed the classic symptoms of severe depression. The onset had been gradual at first, and then became more sudden. Later we discovered that Justin's father had a history of depression, so this genetic vulnerability became part of the picture. Justin had suffered a number of losses and changes, which we pinpointed as "triggers" so often associated with depression. Justin's mother and father were also less available to him as they struggled individually to get back on their feet after suffering job problems and financial losses. They were focused on their own problems and getting the family settled, and they lost track of Justin to some degree.

Justin's case shows how an adolescent can become withdrawn in ways that can be attributed to normal teen moodiness. His story also demonstrates how the intensity and stress of school can bring out problems that have been developing, more quietly, over a longer period of time. Although Justin was sent to his pediatrician and then to a child psychiatrist, his depressive symptoms worsened over the fall as he refused to take medication or return to school and became increasingly preoccupied with thoughts of death. His depression had advanced too far, and there had been too many shifts in his environment and support structure for Justin to stabilize on an outpatient basis. Justin needed hospitalization to ensure both his safety and treatment compliance.

JUSTIN IN THE HOSPITAL:
TREATING MORE SEVERE DEPRESSION

In the hospital, Justin was prescribed multiple medications. When his doctor saw him a few weeks later for an outpatient follow-up appointment, he was a slow-moving boy who avoided eye contact, dressed sloppily, and had little facial expression. His mother had no idea what to do to help her son. She was bewildered. She had to work. Her husband had to work. Her mother was home watching Justin because he would not go to school and stayed home playing computer games. The doctor suggested that limits needed to be placed on the game playing and Justin glowered. The mother was frightened. Justin had lashed out at her before when she had asked him to get off the computer, so she had stopped asking. The glowering was a positive sign, though. At least he could communicate with his emotion. The doctor was glad at least for something to fight about. Any way you can manage to engage with a depressed adolescent, you take, and so the doctor intentionally did not back down but pushed the point about getting him off the computer game and back into the social and academic world. But Justin's demeanor and irritable responses indicated that he was not yet ready to get the care he needed at home.

Justin still needed urgent attention.

He was next admitted to a residential treatment program that was like a hospital, but with a little more freedom and responsibility for the patient. Justin had to be out of his home and someplace where adults would structure both his sleep and meals. In the residential program, he had "forced" socialization with peers and adults, as socializing is important for mood regulation. Depressed teens especially need to maintain some degree of social interaction to effectively fight their depression, but the illness makes them unable or unwilling to provide this for themselves, so the socialization often needs to be organized on their behalf. Depressed adolescents also have persistent negative ways of thinking about things. They need to be educated as to the ways that depression distorts their thinking. This is active work—encouraging social behaviors, self-care, and balanced thinking.

Justin's depression was quite set in by his admission, and he did not respond immediately to treatment. The medications he was placed on did not initially appear to work. He continued to be withdrawn and was not able to generate his own social activity. But his parents kept at it, setting limits, getting him up and to the day-hospital, as he wasn't yet able to return to school. Even though this process took months, slowly but surely Justin came around. He became brighter. He began seeking out activities on his own. The computer game lost its central position in his life. Justin was finally able to get to school and sustain his workload. Eventually, following a third antidepressant trial plus ongoing structure, parental guidance, and individual therapy, Justin's depression lifted and he began to appear to be what his mom fondly referred to as "the old Justin."

DISCUSSION

Hospitalization can be an important part of treatment for moderately to severely depressed adolescents. The hospital environment keeps them safe from harming themselves, and self-harm is a major risk of adolescent depression. The hospital creates unavoidable social interactions and social demands; it also helps regulate self-care and daily activity level. In Justin's case, this involved getting him away from his computer obsession. Playing endless games on computers is a natural avenue of escape for depressed adolescents, particularly boys. The fact that the game is not "real" and that their own life is stalled while their game life is going on, is lost on these boys. All they experience is relief from the demands of the world and the pleasure of artificial agency, efficacy, and social exchange. Computer and video games are a poor substitute for the "real thing." Too much gaming is bad for mental health, as is the avoidance of school and friends.

The adolescent often cannot perceive his or her own difficulties, however, and the intervention needs to be forceful. Trying to take away any activity from an adolescent can lead to serious fights and sometimes violence. From the way that Justin glowered in the outpatient meeting, it was obvious that he was at risk of getting into a physical struggle with his parents or perhaps becoming suicidal if they set determined limits on his game playing and isolation at home. The same thing can be said for taking away a cell phone for an adolescent who has organized his or her coping mechanisms around social exchanges with friends.

From an outside observer's perspective, such as a parent's, the adolescent's preoccupations and avoidant patterns only seem to lead to more problems, but the adolescent does not see that point of view. Bringing an adolescent into the hospital or brief residential care is one way to forcefully break a destructive cycle of behavior and buy time for a new cycle of more positive behavior to set in.

Justin's case also shows that interventions such as hospitalizations do not necessarily follow the same time course as the actual, underlying condition. They are only one part of what can be a lengthy continuum of care and intervention. Untreated depression, on average, lasts eighteen months or more. Hospitalizations usually last from one to two weeks. Thus, a hospitalization can be thought of as akin to shocking a cardiac patient whose heart has stopped. You hope a more normal rhythm is the result, but you know that you must continue with exercise, diet, medication, and monitoring in an ongoing fashion after the paddles have been removed.

The same was true for Justin. His "arrhythmic" pattern of behavior was eventually broken and he established more healthy interactions, but to achieve this he required a full array of counseling, medication trials, social activities, and eventually, school-based services for months to come to a point where he could both maintain and extend his gains.

Not all adolescents with depression are actively self-destructive or need to be hospitalized. Most depressed teens continue to function in their lives and can receive treatment in the community. Some get better with an adjustment to their school schedule, or with counseling or with a first trial of a medication. This is most often true when teens function well in most aspects of their lives, but begin displaying appetite and/or sleep disturbances, mild to moderate loss of enthusiasm and energy, and feelings of hopelessness around selective areas of the future (such as college admission). These target symptoms, in an otherwise well-functioning teen, can be serious but do not necessarily have a prolonged course, nor do they necessarily require more than intervention on an outpatient level.

CASE STUDY

Nancy—Uncomplicated Depression

NANCY CAME TO THE outpatient clinic with her mother. She was a smart, athletic girl in her sophomore year of high school. She was shy by nature, but with time would show her sense of humor and playfulness. She lived with her mother and father and had friends. Nancy was doing fairly well in school but felt that there was "something wrong." Her mother said she was "dragging." She was tearful a good deal of the time. Nancy reported having a hard time focusing on her classes. She became extremely anxious around people and felt like something was weighing her down. She did not know where these feelings came from.

There was no clear social stress, besides the usual pressures of school, activities, friends, and family. She was busy and life was hectic, but it had always been that way for Nancy. That didn't seem like a good explanation for how she was feeling. She was prescribed a low-dose antidepressant and began to feel and function much better within a few weeks. Nancy became noticeably more social and less anxious in crowds.

She was brighter and less withdrawn.

In about six weeks, Nancy decided that she felt significantly better but she still felt slowed down in her thinking and sadder than she remembered herself being. With an additional small increased dose of medication, her mood continued to improve until she was back to her "normal" self. Entering weekly psychotherapy that focused on understanding how her thinking and expectations contributed to her depression also helped Nancy. The therapy also focused on teaching Nancy to "self-monitor" her moods and thoughts, akin to an emotional calorie-counting technique that helped her judge whether her mood was improving.

DISCUSSION

With Nancy, the process of evaluation was the same as with any other patient showing symptoms of depression. A complete history was taken and a screening was done for the entire range of social, medical, environmental, and genetic factors that are known to play a role in depression. Nancy was diagnosed with depression without a clear trigger for the onset identified. As noted above, for some people depression can simply be a medical condition to which a given individual is more susceptible. Moreover, although there were some qualities of Nancy's temperament that were consistent with her depression, like being somewhat shy and socially anxious, plenty of shy people do not develop depression, so temperament in itself is not a sufficient explanation for depression.

Nancy's case illustrates that sometimes teens do recognize their own depressive tendencies and seek treatment. It also illustrates that seemingly "normal" kids can go through periods in which they develop frank symptoms of clinical depression, although they lack a clear "trigger" or prolonged history of deterioration that precede the time they require professional help. For a significant number of these teens, medication works well without further intervention. The side effects are tolerable, the benefits are notable and robust, and the patient and family are satisfied. It is usually important, however, that medication is not prescribed in a vacuum and that adequate time is spent monitoring and understanding the patient's progress; this often involves the inclusion of psychotherapy on at least a short-term basis as part of the treatment regimen. Understanding the basics of depression, how to identify and intercede with a repeated episode and how to handle any stigma attached to an episode of depression, all need to be reviewed thoroughly with the involved adolescent.

MEDICATION TRIALS IN ADOLESCENT DEPRESSION

Medications are important in treating depression. For some teens, they can be lifesavers. For others, they don't work at all. For most, the results are somewhere in the middle. Medications almost always need to be combined with multiple social interventions. We now know something about the underlying mechanisms of psychotropic medications although there is still much that is unknown.

Parents should know a little about how these medications work, anticipated results, and how effectiveness might best be evaluated. Following is important information on the medications commonly used and the evaluation of individual response. Chapter 12 will discuss in some detail what we have learned empirically, on large numbers of teens, about which treatments work best for specific diagnoses.

Brain Neurotransmitters

There are hundreds of chemicals, or neurotransmitters, at work in the brain. Most we know very little about. We now know a great deal about some, however, and the ways that these are distributed in the brain. These neurotransmitters are manufactured deep within the brain, and nerve cells travel from these subterranean areas all through the extended brain, serving to connect the regions of primary feelings and sensations with regions serving information processing, and the planning and carrying out of activities. Chemical neurotransmitters, thus, play a central role in the development of depression.

The neurotransmitters we know most about that are involved in depression are serotonin, norepinephrine, dopamine, and acetylcholine. These chemicals work together to connect and regulate the brain regions responsible for generating our moods and for producing the constellation of symptoms that, as discussed, are collectively known as depression.

The Effects of Antidepressants on Nerve Transmitter Systems

No one knows exactly how antidepressants work. People talk about a "chemical imbalance." But even though we know that a specific antidepressant medication affects the serotonin or the dopamine system, for example, the actual antidepressant effect takes a couple of weeks to become significant or visible. Why is this? There is no definite answer. This is an area of very active research, and a much better understanding will come over the next decade. A recent theory is that antidepressant medications stimulate cell growth, and this is thought to lead to their eventual antidepressant effect. It is only within the past ten years that we have learned how much change the adolescent brain undergoes. This knowledge has generated clues about the biological causes of depression and about how antidepressants might work.

Expectations for Antidepressants

To date, there is no way to tell which antidepressant is going to work for which person.

Antidepressants work very effectively one-third of the time with adolescents. They work modestly one-third of the time, and one-third of the time they don't help and may cause problems of their own.

Some doctors look for clues in selecting a medication, like whether a parent became better on a medication. Many doctors, however, prescribe antidepressants based on their own experiences with patients. Chapter 12 will discuss which medications have robust scientific evidence to support their use with children and teens and how health care practitioners make specific prescribing and treatment decisions.

Potential Side Effects of Antidepressants

Some anecdotal and scientific data suggests that antidepressants may increase the risk of suicide attempts or suicidal thinking and self-injurious behaviors in certain adolescents. In a U.S. Food and Drug Administration review, no completed suicides occurred among nearly 2,200 children treated with selective serotonin reuptake inhibitors (SSRI) medications such as fluoxetine (Prozac). However, the rate of suicidal thinking or behavior, including actual suicidal attempts, was 4 percent for those on SSRI medications, which was twice the rate of those on inert placebo pills (2 percent). Antidepressants can also lead to states of poor insight and judgment for some adolescents.[2] The good news is that the completed suicide rate has declined over the past decade, during the period when SSRI medications have been in widespread use.

CASE STUDY

Michael—When Antidepressants Don't Work

MICHAEL WAS DIABETIC. Adolescents with diabetes and other chronic medical conditions are prone to depression. They struggle to comply with necessary medical care and often refuse to acknowledge that their medical conditions are related to their depression. In addition to his diabetes, Michael drank heavily and had become suicidal. He needed to be hospitalized and watched carefully.

During Michael's hospitalization, he was started on an antidepressant but did not show signs of getting better. Over the next week in the hospital, in fact, his behavior and mood began to worsen. He became more quarrelsome. His logic did not make sense. He argued with his mother and father, which he typically did, but not as severely as he was doing now. He shouted in meetings and erupted in anger almost continuously. His antidepressant was stopped and his symptoms of aggression and agitation decreased within twenty-four hours.

DISCUSSION

With Michael it was clear that his diabetes chipped away at his psychological well-being, which compelled him into actions that were a desperate attempt to escape his difficult reality. Everyone wished Michael would acknowledge his grief vis-à-vis his medical condition so that he could come to terms with it. According to common wisdom in the field, we have to acknowledge vulnerabilities before we can reconcile and learn to cope with them.

In Michael's case, his level of depression made it worthwhile to attempt a trial of antidepressants. Because of Michael's agitation, however, the trial of medication was stopped. The most helpful "work" that was done with Michael was undertaking a course of psycho-education to help him accept and cope with his illness. This "work" was less about treating the specific symptoms of his depression than engaging him in the real-life issues that mattered most and developing everyday coping strategies and a more optimistic outlook regarding his prognosis.

Thus, although Michael initially said that he wanted to die and didn't care, the talk and educational therapies he engaged in appeared to ultimately make the most significant difference. His depression was not necessarily due to a suspected imbalance of neurotransmitters but rather to maladaptive coping strategies he had developed in response to a chronic medical stressor. In Michael's case, antidepressants only served to further accelerate and confuse his already distorted thinking about himself, his current status, and future possibilities.

BIPOLAR DISORDER

It is said that Eskimos have 500 words for snow. Psychiatry, however, has only two words for mood disorders, despite the fact that moods are so variable. Mental health professionals call mood disorders depression or bipolar disorder, or some variation of these two.

Bipolar disorder, formerly called manic-depressive illness, is a condition that in its classic form affects less than 1 percent of the adolescent population. It is a dramatic and serious illness involving alternate states of mania and depression. During the manic, or "up" episodes, individuals display an intense, elevated, or irritable mood, feelings of grandiosity, racing thoughts, pressured speech, increased energy, and a decreased need for sleep. The "down" part of a bipolar illness is characterized by depression, with disheartened mood, lethargy, suicidal thoughts, lack of interest in activities, and guilty, hopeless thinking.

What can be confusing is that it is also common for adolescents to have simple depression, which can include periods of intense irritability, major mood swings, hyperactivity, and reactive outbursts. Sometimes

CHOICES OF ANTIDEPRESSANT MEDICATIONS

Following are descriptions of antidepressant medications and how they work to alleviate the disorder, in addition to potential side effects.

Selective serotonin reuptake inhibitors (SSRIs). The first medications usually tried with adolescent depression are SSRIs. These medications affect the serotonin system in the brain, leading to an increase of serotonin, which is thought in turn to alleviate depression. The SSRIs include fluoxetine (Prozac), sertraline (Zoloft), paroxetine (Paxil), citalopram (Celexa), L-citalopram (Lexapro), and fluvoxamine (Luvox). These are all different medications and although they may be marketed differently (for example, Paxil is marketed for social anxiety), many psychiatrists use them interchangeably.

Norepinephrine medications and mixed serotonin/norepinephrine medications. A group of older antidepressant medications can affect the norepinephrine system. These are still used, but not as often, because they have significantly greater side effects than the SSRIs, such as weight gain and dry mouth, and they can be more dangerous if used in an overdose attempt. Some newer derivatives with norepinephrine activity are also used. These are the "mixed" antidepressants, such as venlafaxine (Effexor) and duloxetine (Cymbalta). This class of medications is usually tried after several SSRI trials, but some psychiatrists prefer them and use them first because they affect two separate neurotransmitters thought to be important in adolescent depression.

Dopamine medications. The neurochemical mechanism of the antidepressant effect of bupropion (Wellbutrin) is not exactly known, although it is thought in part to increase dopamine (a chemical associated with attention, impulse control, and pleasure seeking). Sometimes this medication is used first in adolescents because it has added effectiveness for attention deficit hyperactivity disorder (ADHD), and many teens have both ADHD and depression, or their depression has serious concentration and attention problems associated with it.

these mood swings are present right from the beginning of the adolescent's troubles. Other times, the agitation develops as the depression sets in over a period of months. The variable mood states, if extreme, cyclical, and persistent, can be diagnosed as bipolar disorder and are then treated with mood stabilizer medications.

Antidepressants and Bipolar Disorder

Actively treating depression in any form includes considering the role of psychotropic medications. Occasionally, however, antidepressants can make the individual feel worse by leading to agitation. In these cases, the natural salt lithium, anticonvulsants such as valproate (Depakote), lamotrigine (Lamictal), oxcarbazepine (Trileptal), and carbamazepine (Tegretol), or the antipsychotics such as aripiprazole (Abilify), olanzapine (Zyprexa), or quetiapine (Seroquel), are used to achieve mood stabilization. None of these medications are primarily antidepressants, though lithium and Lamictal are effective against depression.

These medications are used when bipolar disorder is suspected, when trials of antidepressant medications have failed or worsened an adolescent's moods, or when a depression carries extreme impulsiveness and mood instability. The most commonly used antipsychotics are risperidone (Risperdal), aripiprazole, quetiapine, ziprasidone (Geodon), and olanzapine. These help sedate, calm, and decrease aggression in people with bipolar illness.

SIDE EFFECTS OF MEDICATIONS
FOR ADOLESCENT BIPOLAR DISORDER

Mood stabilizers and antipsychotic medications have potentially much more serious physical side effects than antidepressants, and they are therefore used with great caution. Antidepressants, on the other hand, have more serious behavioral side effects, with the potential for self-injurious behaviors and/or suicidal thinking. The anticonvulsants, mood stabilizers, and antipsychotics can cause weight gain and sedation. They also each have particular side effects that are unique to a single medication or class and can be serious in a given individual. Lithium, for example, can affect the thyroid gland and also leads to increased urination, fluid retention, tremors, weight gain, acne, and psoriasis.

The anticonvulsants can affect the blood cells, the liver, and slow the "thinking" parts of the brain, as well as in some cases lead to a life-threatening skin rash. The antipsychotics can in some cases cause serious metabolic problems like glucose intolerance, which can lead to diabetes, weight gain, and a worsening cholesterol profile. The antipsychotics can also cause painful muscle contractions and other problems with control of the motor system, including tardive dyskinesia, or repetitive, involuntary movements of the facial, trunk, and extremity muscles. Tardive dyskinesia is a side effect that is rare, particularly with the antipsychotic medications that health care practitioners currently use, but may occur with prolonged use of antipsychotic medications—generally use that lasts longer than one year, though the condition may be seen after several months. The lower the dose of medication, the less likely the condition is to develop. Once the condition is detected, the medication should be stopped. The condition may then persist for a number of months or it may even be permanent. There have been reports that SSRIs can cause this side effect, too.

Thus, although all these medications have a role in treating more serious disturbances of mood and behavior in teens, they can be a mixed blessing and must be scrupulously prescribed and managed. Teens have enough self-image issues without having to worry about weight gain and acne as well. A parent has to weigh the risks and the benefits when psychotropic medication is prescribed to their children. While medication may have an essential role, it can only be used by well-trained professionals and has to be used in the context of thorough evaluation, diagnosis, sustained monitoring, and adjunctive treatment.

SUICIDE IN TEENS

The most serious problem associated with depression is suicide. A Centers for Disease Control and Prevention (CDC) report from the U.S. Surgeon General in 1999 states that "major depressive disorders account for about 20 to 35 percent of all deaths by suicide." [3] Adolescents are also at increased risk to kill themselves because of reckless decision making, either through an accident such as a motor vehicle accident or an overdose on drugs, as well as through an intentional act of suicide. Parents, family, and friends often blame themselves after a child commits suicide.

While often there are signs of depression preceding a suicide attempt, sometimes no one can anticipate the adolescent's action.

Girls threaten to commit suicide more than boys, though boys complete suicide more frequently. Alcohol and drug use are major risk factors in depression and for suicide. The judgment that is made worse by depression is made increasingly worse by drugs and alcohol, and these substances can have sudden and intense negative effects on mood.

Communication is critical to suicide prevention. Adolescents who lose the ability to communicate with their peers and parents are at increased risk.

The U.S. statistics are daunting: [4]

• Suicide was the third leading cause of death among young people 15 to 24 years of age, following unintentional injuries and homicide. The rate was 10 deaths for every 100,000 people ages 15 to 24 or .01 percent.

• The suicide rate among children ages 10 to 14 was 1.3/100,000 or 272 deaths among 20,910,440 children in this age group. The gender ratio for this age group was 3:1 (males: females).

• The suicide rate among adolescents aged 15 to 19 was 7.9/100,000 or 1,611 deaths among 20,271,312 adolescents in this age group. The gender ratio for this age group was 5:1 (males: females).

• Among young people 20 to 24 years of age, the suicide rate was 12/100,000 or 2,360 deaths among 19,711,423 people in this age group. The gender ratio for this age group was 7:1 (males: females).

CASE STUDY

Carolyn—A Suicide Attempt

CAROLYN BECAME INCREASINGLY DEPRESSED through middle school. She let her hair hang over her eyes. She only wore black. She felt intensely self-conscious. A friend of her brother, two years older, was staying with the family for a few months and Carolyn developed a crush on him. They kissed and engaged in sexual activities just short of intercourse. She didn't tell anyone about this, not even when the boy became rejecting and mean toward her.

She started cutting herself on her arms and legs. Nobody knew any of this. Her parents only knew that her grades were dropping and her early adolescent moodiness was giving way to more hostility and bursts of anger. They put her in counseling. The depression was gaining momentum. The counselor was trying to get to know her, but it was always during a time of crisis—an argument with her parents or siblings or a bad grade in school. Carolyn didn't tell anyone about the cutting or the rejection from the older boy, so there was a secret and shame involved, further impairing communications. One physician tried her on a few medications, but nothing worked.

Carolyn relied on her small group of friends for help and support. She thought her friends really "understood her," although she did not tell them important things, like her cutting or that she thought about dying sometimes. Typically, Carolyn would get involved in conversations and then become frustrated when people didn't respond the way she thought they should. Her perceptions of people shifted quickly. The people she thought "really understood her" one day, she thought "hated her" the next day. All of this was going on inside her head without an outlet because she had shut off communication with her family and her communications with her friends were no longer successful. She sent out an instant message saying goodbye to her friends and took an overdose of sleeping medication. Her friends called her parents, who found her unconscious in her room.

The doctor in the emergency room reported an incredible disquiet when he interviewed Carolyn and her parents. Her parents were in the waiting room while Carolyn was in the treatment bay. The depression and attempted suicide had stunned the family into paralysis. "You can't even put the pieces together," as they put it, "because you don't know what is broken."

The emergency room doctor blamed the parents. How could they sit there, fifty yards away, while their daughter was in an emergency room bay, just having tried to kill herself? The outpatient doctor, too, thought the parents did not understand how to reach out to this girl. The girl, however, wasn't making it easy. She lashed out at her parents. She sat with her arms folded, angry at the world.

Carolyn was started on an antidepressant. Within twenty-four hours, she was crouching in her bedroom, hysterical, talking about how her parents were hiding in the bushes, ready to catch her. She came into the kitchen, throwing plates. She was irrational and out of control. The medication was stopped, and the exacerbated symptoms went away.

Her cutting did not go away, though. Neither did her irritability. The next four years were filled with stops and starts, ups and downs. She would develop a crush on a boy, or a friendship with a girl. The friend would let her down, or the boy would break up with her. She would ruminate over the relationship. She took scissors and carved "I'm sorry" into her leg.

Slowly but surely, however, she began to get better. Over time almost every intervention was tried: hospitalizations, medications, different kinds of therapies, different school placements. Summers home. Summers away. Often you can understand what part of an adolescent may be "broken," surround them with a cast, and pray that healing begins to happen. It did with Carolyn. Dialectical behavior therapy—described in the "discussion" section—was recommended. Carolyn gradually learned to manage her emotions and interact more effectively with others. Eventually she even graduated from college, her hardheadedness and irritability of early adolescence transformed into the shrewdness and strong work ethic of a healthier young adult.

DISCUSSION

Dialectical behavior therapy, or DBT, is a cognitive-behavioral treatment approach that teaches the skills of mindfulness, interpersonal effectiveness, emotion regulation, and distress tolerance. DBT is a subset of cognitive behavioral therapy, which has been shown scientifically to be the treatment of choice, either alone or in combination with medication, for a number of the psychiatric illnesses that affect teens.

Mindfulness refers to the practice of paying attention, on purpose, non-judgmentally, to what is happening in the moment. This practice underlies all the other skills taught. The interpersonal effectiveness skills that are taught focus on effective ways of achieving your objectives with other people: to ask effectively for what you want, to say no and have it seriously, to maintain relationships and self-esteem in interactions other people. Emotion modulation skills are ways of changing disng emotional states, and distress tolerance skills include techniques tting up with these emotional states if they cannot be changed for the time being.

Depression, in Carolyn's case, revolved around a very injured sense of self. The depressed person can become self-absorbed and think and act differently and much less reciprocally than would be age-appropriate. Hospitalization, medications, and other forms of treatment can all help to push a teen's inward thinking to move outward. All these interventions can be necessary when there are biological, social, and psychological imbalances that are long-standing, interwoven with one another, and cause the adolescent to become chronically self-injurious and even suicidal. Parents, when dealing with teens with chronic depression, can also become isolated and self-absorbed, assuming no one else can understand their plight.

In the emergency ward, Carolyn's parents were about as internally preoccupied as they could be. We see in this situation the pervasive individual and family communication breakdown that can occur in depression. People cannot reach out to each other because they have become absorbed in themselves, their pain, and hopelessness—in other words, in the fog of their own cognition.

Depending on biological vulnerabilities, historical traumas and losses, recent stresses, and more, it can be a long haul for adolescents to recover from depression and chronic self-injury, and to do so without causing themselves any permanent, serious self-harm.

DEPRESSION AND DRUGS AND ALCOHOL

Parents often assume that teens try alcohol and drugs to rebel or fit in with their peer group. However, teens with undiagnosed emotional or behavioral problems often use drugs and alcohol to relieve their frustrations. A depressed teen may self-medicate with marijuana or alcohol to escape a terrible, underlying sense of hopelessness. Unfortunately, alcohol and marijuana only exacerbate these symptoms.

Drugs like Ecstasy and other club-drug uppers may even make some depressed adolescents feel "normal" when for weeks they have felt miserable. The effect of such drugs on chemicals in the brain that regulate mood (serotonin, dopamine, and endorphins) can be devastating for children and adolescents. The damage they do to receptors in the brain can make the road back from depression even harder.

While some teens self-medicate to treat depression, others end up with a serious mental disorder due to the abuse of drugs or alcohol. Abusive drinking or drug use can seriously undermine your child's physical, emotional, and psychological health. Some drugs, such as methamphetamines, can seriously and sometimes irreversibly affect the neurotransmitters, which we now know are the "messengers of the brain." Recent studies suggest this damage can be long-lasting, even permanent.

Many teens have the mistaken notion that alcohol, marijuana, and club drugs are benign. In fact, while they might feel good while taking them, they can make it difficult for the child to feel good naturally for a long time to come. The longer children use these drugs, the more difficult treatment becomes and the higher the rate of relapse because of their inability to feel good or even "normal" due to the damage to their neurotransmitters.

CASE STUDY

Paul—Depression and Substances

PAUL WAS A SIXTEEN-YEAR-OLD from the suburbs. He was smart and athletic, the star of his football team. He also had been using drugs heavily for nearly one year. Cigarettes, marijuana, and alcohol had become part of his daily habit

Paul had smoked marijuana daily for several months by the time his school and family problems had progressed to the point where his family sought professional help. He was getting more irritable, his insight was distorted, and he insisted adamantly that the marijuana was helping him calm down. He was taking illegal prescription pills. They were making him more irritable, too, but he didn't see or acknowledge this. His world became bleaker and bleaker. When a girl he liked broke up with him, he began to feel suicidal. Paul claimed that he hated the girl and that he hated his friends. He thought no one seemed to understand him and that they all would finally get the message when he crashed his car on the freeway.

Paul survived the car wreck and was lucky enough to successfully go through the painful individual and social recovery from this desperate suicide attempt. He had to confront his substance use. He had to confront how isolated he felt and learn to communicate with others. Medications played a role. Counseling played a role. Depression, here again, required a full-court-press approach and included addressing the substance abuse issues that were now intertwined with Paul's depression.

DISCUSSION

Paul was "unlikable," as one counselor who worked with him put it. He was spiteful, arrogant, and demeaning. He was bleak. Nothing anyone could say at the outset would penetrate his conviction that life was horrible and nobody understood him. He was only happy, or so he claimed, when he was high.

Paul gradually accepted the reality that he had not succeeded in killing himself and that his counselors and parents would not abandon him to his own devices, no matter how hard he tried to push them away. The conversation of recovery continued. He wrote poetry, which was initially bleak and relentless. But at least his writings gave the adults trying to save him something to talk with him about. The trick was to engage him somehow, to be honest with him about the drug use, and to try and connect with him in a way that cut through his ruminations and articulations about how bitter he was. Slowly, Paul's denial and avoidance abated and he started to get better.

Family work was essential. Often parents approach the issue of drug and alcohol use as simply a discipline issue for a child who is "bad." However, in many cases, the adolescents may be depressed. They may be unable to express exactly how they feel but are, in reality, medicating themselves to feel better. If a child is self-medicating to treat depression, anxiety, or other emotional or behavioral disorders, simply applying more discipline and creating more rules will not affect the underlying problem that led to the substance abuse in the first place. Families need to understand this and work with their clinicians in a unified treatment approach that addresses the cycle of depression leading to drug use, which again only worsens the depression.

Anthony—Depression and Sexual Orientation

ANTHONY WAS A SEVENTEEN-YEAR-OLD, good-looking son in an Italian family. He was the eldest of three children. His sisters were aged fifteen and twelve. He was a good student, popular among his peer group, and reasonably athletic.

Anthony's parents were first-generation Italians living in a relatively affluent suburb. His mother worked part-time as a nurse, and his father owned a successful landscaping company. During the summer, Anthony worked for his father's company.

Anthony was well liked and always tried to please his family, friends, and teachers. He was aware of his sexual interest in some of his male friends but kept these thoughts and feelings a secret from everyone. Anthony's father was concerned that he had many girls *as friends* but had never had a *girlfriend*. His father was uncomfortable with some of his son's interests, which included painting and listening to classical music. He encouraged his son to play sports and get a girlfriend. Anthony began to feel like he was a disappointment to his father, whom he idealized.

He had heard his dad make disparaging comments about "queers" on many occasions. Anthony developed a close relationship with one of his friends who shared his interest in art. One evening they both had too much to drink and began to kiss and touch one another in a sexual manner. The following day, Anthony felt guilty, angry with himself, depressed, and fearful that his parents would discover what he had done. He began to withdraw from his friends, had difficulty concentrating in school, and although he felt terrible about what had happened, he began to have romantic feelings toward his friend and frequently had masturbatory fantasies about having sex with him.

Anthony felt incredibly alone with his feelings of shame and confusion and began to have thoughts about suicide as he felt that there was no other way out of his dilemma. He had tried to stop his feelings of attraction to his friend but without any success. One evening when his parents were out, he ingested a bunch of pills. He went to his bedroom and then broke down in tears, as he didn't really want to die. He called his parents on their cell phone and told them what he had done. They called 911 and the paramedics took him to a local emergency room. His parents were totally shocked that he had made a suicide attempt.

After Anthony recovered physically, he was put in an observation bed overnight. The next morning he was seen by a psychiatrist. Anthony told him about his sexual behavior and fantasies and worried that he might be bisexual or gay. He also said that he could not bear telling his parents why he had tried to kill himself as he felt so ashamed and was worried his dad would disown him.

Anthony felt a sense of relief that he had finally shared his secret with someone. The psychiatrist was warm, accepting, and supportive and assured him that he was not the only seventeen-year-old who had concerns about his sexual orientation. Although he informed Anthony that he could not predict his father's response, he encouraged Anthony to share his feelings with his parents in a family meeting.

Although his parents were surprised and upset, they assured Anthony that their love was unconditional and they would all get through this. Anthony promised that he would not hurt himself again and the family agreed to outpatient counseling.

DISCUSSION

The onset of Anthony's depression was directly related to his awareness of his same-sex attraction to his friend and his ongoing unsuccessful attempts to suppress and deny these feelings. Anthony's situation demonstrates how a relatively healthy looking adolescent can begin to develop depressive symptomatology as the result of crisis around sexual identity.

Anthony began to develop feelings of self-hate, guilt, and shame related to his feelings of same-sex attraction. He became fearful of what his family, especially his father, and friends would think of him if they knew the truth about his feelings and thus he felt a sense of extreme isolation because there was no one he could talk to.

For gay or lesbian adolescents growing up, even before they are totally aware of their feelings of attraction to members of the same sex, they often feel different from their peers and feel badly about these feelings.

These adolescents often feel a need to keep their feelings secret from everyone for fear of rejection. The emotional cost of keeping the secret over time can be devastating and lead to low self-esteem, shame, depression, anxiety, and possible suicidal thoughts or behavior. Often these adolescents deny these feelings and compensate by overachievement in academics, sports, or hobbies. On the flip side, their ability to cope can become compromised, leading to depression, which affects their ability to function with peers and family. Their academic performance can suffer and suicide can begin to feel like the only solution.

THE TREATMENT OF CHOICE

The evaluating emergency room psychiatrist recommended family and individual counseling. Anthony saw an individual therapist for several years, with whom he openly discussed his uncertainty about his sexual identity.

His therapist was fully accepting and supportive of Anthony's attempts to understand the meaning of his same-gender attraction. The therapist helped Anthony understand that adolescents may have occasional homosexual fantasies and this may, or may not, mean that he was gay. He reassured Anthony that his true sexual orientation would likely become clearer during his early adulthood. He also assured Anthony that whether he was straight, gay, or bisexual, he could have an emotionally healthy life, which could include a partner and children if he desired.

Anthony was not comfortable discussing his same-sex feelings with his peers. However, he did find it helpful to get involved with the gay/straight alliance in his school as well as occasionally attending a group for adolescents who experience sexual identity confusion. Anthony and his parents also participated in family counseling. The focus was to educate his parents about sexual identity and help them acknowledge their unconditional love for their son.

Anthony's parents also attended meetings with the family therapist to address their own feelings of homophobia as well as addressing issues related to self-blame and concerns about his safety. The parents attended a few Parents and Friends of Lesbians and Gays meetings, which provided them with much-needed support from other parents who were struggling to understand and accept their children's sexual identities. They learned to accept the uncertainty of Anthony's sexual identity and come to terms with the acceptance of whatever the future held regarding his true sexual identity.

CONCLUSION

Studies have reported that up to 2.5 percent of children and up to 8.3 percent of adolescents in the United States suffer from depression. A National Institutes of Mental Health–sponsored study of nine- to seventeen-year-olds estimates that the prevalence of any depression is more than 6 percent in a six-month period, with 4.9 percent having major depression. In addition, research indicates that depression onset occurs earlier in life today than in past decades. A recently published longitudinal prospective study found that early-onset depression (in adolescence) often persists, recurs, and continues into adulthood, and the study indicates that depression in youth may also predict more severe illness in adult life.[5] Depression in young people often occurs with other mental disorders—most commonly anxiety, disruptive behavior, or substance abuse disorders—and with physical illnesses, such as diabetes.

Depression in children and adolescents is further associated with an increased risk of suicidal behaviors. This risk may rise, particularly among adolescent boys, if the depression is accompanied by conduct disorder and alcohol or other substance abuse. Among adolescents who develop major depressive disorder, as many as 7 percent may commit suicide in the young adult years. Consequently, it is important for doctors and parents to take all threats of suicide seriously.

Although we know more than ever before about the adolescent brain and have a plethora of new medications and treatments at our disposal, why is the situation not improving more dramatically? The answer most certainly lies in the documented simultaneous increase in psychosocial stressors that place our adolescents at increased risk for depression and despair and concomitant forms of maladaptive coping. We must recognize that this era of high stimulation and low supervision places a greater burden on those youngsters who are already predisposed to depression. The task, therefore, is to identify the triggers, decrease the stress and stimulation, increase supervision and structure, and learn to recognize and treat the early warning signs of this potentially lethal syndrome.

As importantly, we must also identify and treat the array of destructive strategies and behaviors that teens use to escape from a potentially developing depression and/or cope with the higher and more rapid-fire environmental demands that they experience on a daily basis. Anxious about their present status, their achievement and self-sufficiency, and the world around them, teens are now turning in higher numbers and at earlier ages to the use of drugs and alcohol, and many other self-destructive behaviors: cutting, dangerous eating behaviors, and delinquent behaviors in greater numbers and of a more serious nature than in the past. These discrete disorders, while almost always related to mood disturbances and underlying anxiety in adolescence, are each different in their etiology, presentation, and treatment. We will turn now to these disorders in adolescence and examine them in greater depth.

CHAPTER 4

When Your Teen Cuts

Michael Hollander, Ph.D.

Raising children is hard work, and *while each developmental stage has its own difficulties, adolescence is certainly one of the hardest for parents to negotiate. And in this modern world, the stakes have become even greater. While self-destructiveness has always been an aspect of adolescence, never before has it been so pervasive or invasive. Self-injury, often initiated by a teen to gain control or feel temporarily better, has now been glamorized and popularized through the mass media. Once started, it can be a difficult behavior to stop and one that literally can drive parents crazy as they are forced to bear witness to their child's self-mutilation.*

———

SELF-INJURY

The journey through adolescence becomes especially difficult if a child begins to have emotional difficulties. It is all too easy for parents to get lost in the emotional storms and breakdowns that overwhelm our kids. This understandable worry about our children's emotional states sometimes makes clear thinking impossible. Additionally, our health care system can appear to be designed to prevent children from getting the help they need to get better.

When kids purposely hurt themselves, parents often become frightened and confused, and sometimes angry. It can seem that whatever you try to do to help your child only boomerangs and makes the situation worse. Frequently, a parent's personal frustration leads to further tension with his or her parenting partner, who can have different ideas about how to manage the situation. When you can't seem to agree with your partner, or if you are a single parent, your frustration can increase and leave you feeling alone and helpless.

The purpose of this chapter is to offer you a route to understanding self-injury and, more important, give you ideas about how you can effectively get the help your child needs. I also provide you with tips about how to help your child and take care of yourself to tolerate what can be a very bumpy and uncomfortable ride.

I am going to start with two examples from my practice to help you see that you are not alone on this journey. While these examples typify two of the most frequent kinds of adolescents I see, there are, of course, many variations on this theme.

CASE STUDY

Sara—Failing to Progress

SARA, AGE FIFTEEN, and her parents enter my office for their first consultation. Sara is nicely dressed in jeans and a pretty blue blouse. She has an easy manner and appears quite comfortable in this situation. Her father had called earlier and requested the consultation on the advice of Sara's therapist. During the phone call, he reported that Sara's therapist, Dr. Jones, wasn't sure they were making any real progress. Her father also told me that he thought that Sara had a good relationship with her therapist and that Sara said she liked to meet with Dr. Jones, but was still cutting. Sara's dad went on to reassure me that the cutting was superficial and never required medical attention. He told me that Sara is a good student who has many friends but often doubts her own abilities.

Very soon into the visit, it is clear that Sara is a bright and personable young woman. She tells me that she has been self-injuring since middle school and that she engages in the behavior two to three times a week—sometimes less, and in times of stress, more frequently. When I ask her what she means by "stress," she describes feeling emotionally overwhelmed, like she wants to "jump out of her skin." When asked when her parents learned of her behavior, Sara's mom says that she learned of it only eight months ago when the school nurse called her and told her that she had noticed superficial cuts on Sara's shoulders. She becomes visibly sad at this point and Sara's dad quickly asserts that as soon as this came to their attention they found Dr. Jones and set up an appointment for Sara.

I turn to Sara and ask her about her work with Dr. Jones. She tells me that she likes Dr. Jones very much and finds her very easy to talk to. I ask what kind of things she and her therapist speak about. She tells me "all kinds of stuff, like school stuff and friend issues."

"Do you speak about your cutting?" I ask.

"No, not very often," she replies, "but I know Dr. Jones doesn't want me to do it. We are trying to understand why I do it—you know, to figure out what it means."

I ask Sara whether she feels a sense of relief from stress after she cuts. She replies that she does feel better, calmer, after she self-injures. I ask her if she wants to stop cutting and she assures me that she does.

"Why?" I ask.

She tells me that she knows it is unhealthy, that it worries her parents, and that she doesn't want scars on her body. I tell her that these are good reasons to stop cutting, but in my experience, they rarely have been sufficient for someone to stop. I ask her in more detail about the experience of being emotionally overwhelmed. She describes feeling "sort of crazy on the inside like I am about to get out of control." She lets on that cutting has been the only thing that has helped her calm down in these situations.

"How long does the relief last?" I inquire. "And what happens when the relief is gone?"

"It depends," she replies. "Sometimes a few days and sometimes only a couple of minutes. Afterwards I feel kind of guilty. I used to tell myself I won't ever do that again, but I don't do that anymore. I know when I get into that state I don't have any control over myself."

"So cutting really works at helping you manage really powerful emotions. It is a simple, relatively easy thing to do. Are you sure you want to stop?" I ask. "Suppose I could convince your parents not to worry about the cutting and reassure you that in the future cosmetic surgery will probably be able to take care of the scars. Would you still want to stop?"

A faint smile appears on Sara's face as she says, "No, in fact, I really don't want to stop."

DISCUSSION

Sara's admission that she is not so sure she wants to stop cutting clearly surprised her parents. It is often the case, however, those adolescents who self-injure have come to realize the effectiveness of the behavior in helping them to soothe themselves. It is not at all unusual for them to have mixed feelings about giving it up.

The example highlights two important themes. First, self-injury usually is in the service of helping kids calm down from an intense emotional state. Second, sometimes really good therapists, the kind who really know how to relate to teenagers and are helpful in most ways, can miss the boat on self-injury. This can happen when the therapist concentrates the therapy on discovering the meaning cutting has for the teenager rather than how it functions to help regulate the child's emotional state. Insight can be very useful in psychotherapy, but it often leads into a blind alley when the issue is self-injury.

The Facts About Teens Who Cut

Self-injury, or what clinicians call non-suicidal self-injurious behavior (NSSIB), affects an estimated 14 percent to 39 percent of the general adolescent population.[1] That means more than one teenager in ten, and as many as one in three teenagers, have engaged at least once in this behavior. There is evidence that in the general teen population there are an equal percentage of boys and girls who self-injure. In research samples of children who come to clinics, however, girls are much more likely to be in treatment for self-injury.[2]

Deliberate self-harm can be done in a variety of ways. Cutting, scratching, and burning are the most common, but skin picking and head banging can also be part of the picture. For most kids the type is self-injury is less important than its function, which is mostly to relieve intense emotional stress.

For some adolescents, cutting is something they try once or twice. For others, it becomes a stable way of managing painful emotions or to escape an awful feeling of numbness and emptiness.

———

Interestingly enough, self-injury does not usually occur in the context of a teenager abusing substances or alcohol, nor does the adolescent feel pain at the moment of injury.

———

For parents, it is worrisome, frightening, and terribly confusing to have a child who engages in self-injury.

This chapter is intended to help you understand what self-injury is all about, what kind of help is out there, and what you can do to help your child and yourself. The goal is to give you the information you need to cope with the inevitable worry that comes with having a child who is struggling, and to help you to develop skills that will enable you to tolerate your distress.

CASE STUDY

Marie—Cutting and Suicide

WHEN MARIE AND HER PARENTS came for their initial consultation, it was immediately clear that Marie was here under protest. Unlike Sara, on the surface at least, Marie was not at all interested in pleasing her parents. Slumping into the chair, she stared at me with an expression of contempt and disinterest. I knew immediately that my day had just become harder.

"It looks like you are thrilled to be here," I say.

"I hate shrinks," she replies.

Marie is an attractive young lady with purple hair and several face piercings. She is seventeen years old and has a long history of failed psychological treatments. She has had six inpatient admissions at local hospitals for cutting and two for overdosing on pills. She has had seven therapists in the last four years. In addition, Marie spent nine months in one of the best long-term residential placements in the country. When she left residential placement, she and her parents were hopeful about the progress she had made. She had stopped cutting and no longer felt that suicide was an option in her life. The gains she made when living away from home, however, quickly disappeared upon her return. Clearly everybody was disappointed that Marie seemed to be back to where she had started.

Marie's last therapist described her as "unwilling to get better," and as someone who appeared to like the role of being a patient. He referred her to me but was clear in the referral packet that he felt she just wasn't ready to engage in therapy. It was not too hard for me to imagine that Marie could be pretty stubborn. The therapist suggested that Marie's cutting was about letting people see how awful she felt about herself and that self-injury had the added benefit of helping her receive attention from her friends.

"So why did you come today?"

With a scowl on her face she grumbles, "They made me."

"And you do everything they tell you?" I ask innocently.

At this point Marie's father interjects that if Marie doesn't start to get "her act together," he is going to send her back to the long-term residential placement where she had done so much better. While clearly he is fed up and at his wit's end, it also seems that he would be willing to do whatever it takes to help his daughter. His statement was not so much a threat as an expression of his ongoing concern and, perhaps, an indication of how fearful he felt about his daughter's future. Unfortunately, Marie only heard it as a threat and slumped further into her chair.

I ask Marie's dad how he understands her problems. Without missing a beat and with a clear sense of certitude, he tells me that her problem is that she keeps trying to get attention. He understands that her early trauma of being sexually molested by a baby sitter may be a factor in how she feels about herself, but if she just had a little more will power about putting the past behind her she wouldn't let herself suffer so much. Marie's mother chimes in that her daughter has always been rather "dramatic" and too sensitive, and while in some ways they are alike in that regard, she has done everything she could do for her daughter and is running out of energy. She exclaims that she has no idea about what is going on with her child and bursts into tears. Marie begins to express her annoyance at having come to this appointment and threatens to leave.

I ask Marie whether she could stay for just a few more minutes as I have a couple of questions to ask her. She reluctantly agrees.

I am really relieved that Marie agrees to stay because there are important questions that I need to get answers to right up front. The first is about her experience of cutting and overdosing. I want to determine whether cutting and overdosing have similar or different ways of helping her cope. I tell her that I am going to ask her a few questions that call for her opinion about herself.

"When you cut yourself, is your goal to die?"

"No!" she replies without hesitation and a hint of annoyance.

"I didn't think so," I respond. "What about when you overdosed; did you intend to die then?"

"Yes," she mumbles. "I couldn't stand it anymore."

"So, for you, cutting serves a different purpose than overdosing. Is that right? Cutting solves the problem of how you feel in the moment, and overdosing is about ending it all."

"Yeah, that's right."

"Okay Marie, just a few more questions. When you think about yourself compared to others, do you think that you are more sensitive than most people?"

"Definitely," she says.

"Do you think that it takes longer for you to get over an emotional situation than other people? Do people tend to tell you things like, 'Get over it already, you're stewing over something that happened days ago?'" The briefest of smiles and the beginning of curiosity cross her face as she responds, "Yes."

"And finally, do you respond really quickly to emotional situations? That is, you know what you feel about something almost immediately and if you can't name the feeling you still know you feel something very strongly?"

"Totally, but sometimes I don't feel anything at all. I just feel numb and empty," she replies.

I ask her when she was feeling numb and empty if cutting made her feel alive again. In other words, does it seem to bring her feelings back?

"Yes!" she replies.

DISCUSSION

Marie's story highlights two important points about self-injury. First, teenagers often have a different intention when they deliberately self-injure than when their intention is suicide. It is critical that a mental health professional conduct a thorough suicide assessment whenever self-injury is part of the picture. It is equally important that self-injury not get mixed up with suicide because in some important ways each requires a different treatment approach. For more about the treatment of depression and suicide, see chapter 3.

The second issue is whether self-injury is a deliberate attempt by the adolescent to get attention. In my experience, this is one of the most frequent misconceptions about self-injury. Parents and therapists alike hold to this misunderstanding as they struggle to understand this worrisome and perplexing behavior.

Here is how this misunderstanding comes about: When we are emotionally involved with someone, it is difficult for us if we can't make sense of his or her behavior. Furthermore, it is especially hard to think clearly when our emotions run high. In these moments, we are prone to confuse a person's intention with the effect their behavior has on us.

For example, when I've told my fifteen-year-old son to get to his homework for the hundredth time as he continues to play video games, I find myself becoming annoyed. Sometimes it seems as if he is purposefully ignoring me just to get a rise out of me. As my emotions mount, I begin to get locked into thinking that he is intentionally trying to drive me nuts. When I can step back from the situation, however, it becomes clear to me that he would much rather play electronic games than do his homework and that his choice to do this has little to do with me. My annoyance arises from the effect his behavior has on me rather than because of his intention.

A similar pattern can occur when parents and therapists try to understand a teenager's self-injury. Self-injury is a perplexing behavior that engenders powerful emotions in the people who take care of the adolescent. Frequently it seems that the behavior is intended specifically to get those very same people to notice the teenager's distress, and of course it often does. From here it is just a short jump to concluding that the adolescents' intention is to get the adults around them to pay attention.

Here is the problem: Self-injurious behavior often starts weeks, months, or even years before any adult is aware that it is happening.[3] Think about it: If you wanted to get someone's attention, would you deliberately hide the very thing that would catch the attention you so desperately wanted? The majority of adolescents who self-injure are represented in the two case studies described earlier in this chapter as well as typical parental responses.

Reasons for Self-Injury in Teens

The two most common reasons why children self-injure are either to help them control the extremely painful and frightening experience of overwhelming emotions or to help them escape from an awful feeling of being numb and empty. These children are extremely sensitive to loss and rejection and consequently a real or perceived loss of a friend, a change in school, or divorce are all examples of the kinds of things that are difficult for them to manage.[4] Some teens experience both of these emotional states.

Parents who struggle to understand their children can sometimes underplay the seriousness of the behavior or become so emotionally overwhelmed that they have trouble keeping perspective. What most parents share is helplessness and profound worry.

The paradox of self-injury is that what usually brings pain in most situations brings immediate emotional relief. The key concept in understanding self-injury for the vast majority of teens is that it is an emotional coping strategy. Furthermore, as a short-term strategy to manage awful emotional experiences, it can be very effective.

It's true that some adolescents self-injure for other reasons. Some of these teens feel completely unnoticed, socially invisible to the important people around them. When this awful feeling becomes unbearable, these children can resort to a number of behaviors that will get them noticed—

self-injury being one of them. Other children who self-injure do so to avoid situations that raise their anxiety to an intolerable level. These kids become so worried about a future situation that they resort to desperate measures as an avoidance strategy.

There are two other groups of children who can resort to self-injurious behavior. Children who have a psychotic illness can have "command" hallucinations that "tell" them to hurt themselves. These are usually auditory hallucinations that seem very real and frightening to the child. The second group consists of children with obsessive-compulsive disorder who pick at their skin. Once these children start picking, they seem to get stuck in the behavior.

It is obviously essential when seeking help and designing an intervention to first assess which of the above groups the teen most closely belongs to. While sometimes there is overlap, or a teen who initially cuts for emotion regulation ends up getting secondary gains from additional attention, the vast majority of kids who cut do so as a coping strategy. They need to learn new skills to manage their emotions and interpersonal relationships to stop their self-injurious behavior.

Common Misconceptions about Self-Injurious Behavior

Misconceptions about self-injury can lead to therapies that move in the wrong direction, leaving even the most competent therapist, the struggling adolescent, and the most dedicated parent feeling hopeless and frustrated. Usually these errors are made because of an inadequate assessment about the function that self-injury has for the child. An all too common error in psychotherapy is to begin to problem-solve before an adequate assessment of the problem has been conducted. This error is made more likely when the situation is jam-packed with high levels of emotion on the adult side and by an adolescent who gives his or her parents and therapist little information about the situation.

To complicate matters even more, people are often not very good at knowing why they do the things they do. Psychologists who study something called attribution theory found that the reasons people often gave for why they did the things they did and what actually motivated their behavior were not always the same thing. This is true in as diverse areas as consumer buying patterns to clinical psychology issues. I am not implying that people are fundamentally dishonest, rather that when we try to understand our own complicated behavior patterns, we sometimes become swayed by our own beliefs about why we did something rather than why we actually did it.

Why Certain Teens Resort to Cutting

Understanding your child's worrisome behavior will help you in two important ways. First, it will help decrease your anxiety. When we understand something, our fear and worry usually decrease. Don't expect to become calm about your child's trouble, but odds are, once you understand it, you won't panic as much. Second, knowing why helps you locate appropriate treatment and better able to assess whether your teen is making progress.

So we know that teens who cut themselves are trying to manage their emotional experience. What is it about their experience that leads them to this drastic behavior? These teens feel like they are swept away by a tsunami of emotions, and it knocks them off kilter. Teenagers often describe this experience as feeling like they are going crazy or that they want to jump out of their skins. To the outside observer, it sometimes seems that these teens are being overly dramatic, throwing a tantrum, or making an emotional mountain out of an inconsequential molehill. Psychologists refer to this phenomenon as affective dysregulation, which is the state of being overwhelmed by an avalanche of feeling.[5]

Being affectively dysregulated generally takes two forms. The first and most common is the sense of being emotionally out of control; you are pushed and pulled by feelings so powerful that you fear you are going crazy. The second is that of being numb and empty of all feelings. Often parents know that something is deeply troubling their child but when questioned all they get is a bland denial or the classic, "I don't want to talk about it." When we don't know what we feel, we lose an important data stream to help guide our actions.

In short, you can become dysregulated by being overwhelmed by emotions or by not having your emotions available to you. This can have an impact on every aspect of an adolescent's life, from friendships to a sense of identity, to what is sometimes described as "impulsive" behavior.

Adolescents who cut, or deliberately self-injure in other ways, lack the skills necessary to manage their feelings. Furthermore, their emotional systems are more high-powered than most peoples'. They don't just feel things; they *feel things very deeply*. These kids, as may be obvious, would have more difficulty responding to the plethora of stimuli and spontaneous decision-making that faces today's teen in particular.

Self-injury is a way for these overwhelmed and internally dysregulated youngsters to regain emotional balance; it is a solution to the extremely disturbing emotional problem of feeling out of control. An important twist to keep in mind is that cutting really works. In a way, it is an effective emotional regulation strategy. The biggest problem with cutting is that it is an effective short-term solution. It relieves the immediate emotional distress, but it hinders kids from learning how to solve the problems that got them distressed in the first place.

One of the ways to think about self-injury is what I call the "aspirin analogy." What do you do when you get a headache? You take an aspirin. What happens? Your headache goes away. How much time do you spend after the relief actually thinking about why you got a headache in the first place? For most people the answer is not too much time. It seems to be human nature to solve a problem, but not spend much time thinking about why it occurred. The same is true for self-injurers. Once they solve the problem (the overwhelming emotion or devastating numbness triggered by external or internal stimuli), they go on with their lives. All too often they don't bring the necessary attention needed to understand what events or issues set them off or develop the skills needed to solve the initial problem. In short, self-injury is the solution to the problem of emotional dysregulation; it solves the problem of how you feel in the moment.

We are just learning more scientifically about the biological and environmental factors that might cause a child to resort to this behavior. It appears that these children's emotional systems are hard-wired to be extremely sensitive to emotional stimuli. In other words, they feel things more deeply than most other people, their response to emotional events is immediate, and once stimulated they take longer to return to a calm state. There are, however, any number of very sensitive people who *don't* resort to deliberate self-harm as a way to regain emotional balance.

Here is where the biological factors and the environmental influences can interact in a way that might lead a child to self-injury. Imagine that you are a child who has an extremely reactive emotional system. Life's twists and turns seem to affect you more intensely than other members of your family. In fact, your parents often can't understand why you get upset so easily. In response to your emotions, they often try to reassure you that whatever is bothering you isn't so bad after all and you should just calm down. Though your parent's intent was to be helpful, you most likely feel misunderstood. The misunderstanding is rooted in the disconnect that takes place between the intensity of your feelings and your parents' communication that you are somehow misreading the situation in the first place. Kids describe this experience of being emotionally vulnerable as akin to going crazy on the inside. They discover that if they cut themselves they will experience an immediate sense of emotional relief.

DIALECTICAL BEHAVIOR THERAPY

Dialectical behavior therapy (DBT), developed by Marsha Linehan, Ph.D., at the University of Washington, is a cognitive behavioral treatment that has shown real promise in helping kids who self-injure. The therapy focuses on two primary areas. The first is in helping the child know and anticipate the kinds of events—both psychological and external—that are likely to trigger deliberate self-harming behaviors and the second is about teaching and having the child practice the skills necessary to avoid self-injury.

A central hypothesis in DBT is that adolescents who self-injure do so as a way to manage the painful feeling of being emotionally overwhelmed. In DBT, the therapist assumes that her patient either doesn't possess the skills necessary to manage these emotions or for some reason cannot access them in the moment of greatest need.

The treatment has four components:

• Individual DBT therapy. In this component, the therapist and patient examine the situations that seem to precipitate self-injury with an eye toward coming up with more effective solutions.

• DBT skills training group. These groups, which are more like seminars than traditional group therapy, teach the four DBT skill sets of mindfulness, interpersonal effectiveness, emotion regulation, and distress tolerance. Mindfulness is the capacity to focus our attention and/or broaden our awareness of the moment and to do so without being judgmental. Mindfulness helps

Treatments for Teens Who Self-Injure

The good news is that there are effective treatments available for kids who deliberately injure themselves.

Therapy, for example, is crucial to helping these teens. What is most important in finding a therapist is to ascertain his or her level of experience with self-harm and specifically how he or she is going to address the behavior. Therapists who lean toward seeing self-injury as a communication of the child's distress or think they need to find the meaning behind the behavior are, in my opinion, less likely to be effective. On the other hand, therapists who actively work at teaching kids how to manage their emotions with specific skills are more likely to be effective in a shorter period of time.

us experience our situations with a sense of clarity. Interpersonal effectiveness skills focus on learning how to ask for what you need, repairing relationships, and setting limits while retaining your self-respect. Emotion regulation skills involve techniques for decreasing your vulnerabilities to negative emotions and decreasing the duration and intensity of negative emotions. Skills are also taught to increase the likelihood of more positive emotions. Finally, distress tolerance skills are used when we come across a problem that we cannot solve and have to bear the distress. These skill sets are thought to be central in helping kids stop cutting as they all directly or indirectly target emotional dysregulation.

• Between-session skills coaching. The DBT therapist is on call for skills coaching regardless of the day or the hour. It is important to note that this is not therapy over the phone but rather a focused coaching session (usually only ten or fifteen minutes) with the goal of helping the child access more skillful behavior in dealing with the specific situation at hand.

• Therapist consultation team. The last component involves a therapist consultation team that aids the therapists in staying on track.

To date, DBT has been shown to be the most effective therapy for kids who harm themselves.

In addition, a relatively new treatment called dialectical behavioral therapy (DBT) has been shown to effectively reduce self-harm behaviors. See more about DBT in the sidebar on page 96.

What Parents Can Do for Themselves and Their Children

Things for parents to avoid doing are concluding that the self-injury is a bid for attention, that self-injury is just a manipulation strategy, or that the child could do better if he or she just wanted to. These teens are really suffering, though they may want you to believe that it really doesn't matter to them. In my experience, they are troubled by their behavior, so don't be fooled by their apparent lack of concern.

———

The sad fact is that there is not a whole lot that parents can do to help their children when it comes to deliberate self-harm, but an enormous amount they can do to make the situation worse.

———

Parents who understand the function of self-injury are in a better position to weather the storms that come with having an adolescent who is struggling with psychiatric difficulties. Parents who are not harsh or critical when their child self-injures but at the same time expect their child to work this behavior out in therapy generally set the ideal climate for change. Parents need to seek out professionals who are trained to deal specifically with teens who struggle with heightened emotionality and chronic self-destructiveness and in the forms of cognitive behavioral therapy that have been shown to be most effective with these types of problems.

In addition, I encourage parents to seek either a skills-focused parent therapy or a supportive treatment to help them through these very stressful times. When parents are able to take care of themselves, they create a climate that will support their child's growth away from deliberate self-harm.

Your teen doesn't need be in this situation. Parents must also learn to understand their child's problems and the skills that will eventually form the foundation of the solution.

CHAPTER 5

Teens and Substances

Richard L. Falzone, M.D.

Many of the drug-abusing adolescents I work with come into treatment thinking they know more about the chemistry and effects of various substances than I do. Sometimes they are right. It's hard to keep up. Pro-drug websites provide detailed instructions on how much over-the-counter cough medicine is needed to "trip" (reach a state of hallucinatory psychosis) or which brand of decongestant provides the best "rush." The Drug Enforcement Agency sent out an alert in 2006 about a new trend among high school students: mixing cough syrup and "power drinks" to get high. And high school students come seeking prescriptions for Ritalin or Adderall, having already tried samples given or sold to them by their classmates.

The situation can be even more frustrating for parents. What do our children know—or think they know—about substance abuse? What are the real risks of tobacco, alcohol, illegal drugs, over-the-counter medications and supplements, and prescription medications? How can we help keep our children out of trouble? How do we know if they're in trouble? Sometimes we feel like we want to keep them in their rooms for their own protection until they turn eighteen (or thirty!). Or maybe we don't want to talk to them at all. After all, if we ignore the problem, it may just go away.

THE NATIONAL INSTITUTE ON DRUG ABUSE (NIDA) and the Substance Abuse and Mental Health Services Administration (SAMHSA) report overall declines in the rates of tobacco, alcohol, and some illicit drug use by school-age children. Yet the use of other substances, like prescription medications and Ecstasy, are on the rise.

Although there is good news, statistics alone provide little information about actual degree of use. It's sort of like discussing the average weather conditions across the country. It does not mean much that "on average" the nation is partly sunny and warm when there are tornadoes in your neighborhood tearing homes apart. The National Center on Addiction and Substance Abuse at Columbia University in New York is sounding the alarm that too many parents underestimate or are not aware of the dangers teenagers face, and that inadequate supervision contributes to the drug problem in our country.

Parents who are informed and determined to stay involved in their children's lives are more likely to prevent or delay initiation of substance use. As we will see, some risk-taking behavior is normal—and even necessary for healthy development—but research shows that delaying the use of drugs and alcohol is associated with better outcomes. Older teenagers have more information, a more solidly developed sense of themselves, and are better equipped to decide what is and is not in their best interest.

CHALLENGING AUTHORITY, TESTING LIMITS

Understanding the tasks of adolescence—what teenagers must accomplish to become adults—provides a context for differentiating between normal and worrisome behavior and highlights the ways substance use can derail healthy development. The intellectual and emotional transformations of adolescence are at least as profound as the physical changes of puberty. Young children think in simple, concrete terms: Things are right or wrong, good or bad. Around age ten or eleven, they begin to consider "what if" as their thinking becomes more complex.

Armed with a developing capacity for abstract thought, the adolescent is able to view situations from multiple perspectives, perceive shades of gray, and appreciate paradox. Conflicting and shifting emotions are confusing for parent and child alike. The moody adolescent demands to be treated as an adult, yet longs to be taken care of. Some parents see this period of transition as "the terrible teens," but unlike the simple "no!" repeated at age two, this wave of defiance is backed by reasoned conviction. The rebel is searching for a cause. Challenging authority, testing limits, and exploring a wider intellectual, emotional, and geographic space are all part of becoming a healthy, independent adult. Much of my work with families involves reminding (or convincing) parents and adolescents that they share the same ultimate goal: development of the adolescent into a psychologically and physically healthy, independent adult.

Parents cannot inoculate their children with the wisdom and judgment to guarantee safe passage to adulthood. Teens pretty much have to figure it out as they go along. And whether or not children admit it, they rely on their parents as models for adult behavior.

Parents underestimate their influence on their teen's behavior and desire to become a healthy adult. When I encounter parents who have lost faith in their child's inner drive for mastery, I ask them how they taught their child to walk. They look at me quizzically and say something like, "We didn't teach her to walk, we just stayed close by making sure she didn't bang her head on the coffee table, and she eventually figured it out." Exactly. Let's look at this example of development more closely. Once the child achieved the necessary physical strength and neurological maturity, she naturally copied the behavior she saw modeled around her. The parents provided encouragement and a safe arena. As every parent knows, the arena becomes larger and harder to monitor the older the child gets.

Adolescence is a time for figuring out how relationships work. Teenagers develop mature social relationships based on reciprocity and trust. They explore and come to accept their bodies. Sexual curiosity and gradual exploration are normal as teenagers discover (and decide) what being a man or a woman means for them in terms of behaviors, attitudes, and values and learn what makes people attractive to one another. Teenagers strive to achieve emotional independence from their parents and develop their own guiding system of values and ethics as they prepare for family and career. The vast majority of children adopt the values of their parents, underscoring the importance of modeling.

WARNING SIGNS OF TROUBLE

Defining "normal" during adolescence is challenging, but certain warning signs should alert you that your child may be getting off track. A significant change in appearance, style of dress, or makeup or a change in self-care should get your attention. Keep in mind that trying on different images is normal, so this can be a tough call. (For parents considering whether to allow their teenager to get a tattoo or piercing, keep in mind that holes close over, but ink is hard to get off.) Marked changes in behavior also warrant investigation. Examples include a normally upbeat and interactive child who begins to isolate himself in his room or away from home, or a talkative child who stops communicating and begins to avoid contact with family members.

Parents often report that they first became concerned when their child dropped out of organized after-school activities. Many of the teenagers I work with in the adolescent substance abuse group were active and successful in sports until they started using drugs and decided sports was a waste of time. Later, many admit that they became less competitive because of the time spent using drugs rather than practicing or playing and due to the toll drugs, alcohol, and tobacco took on their bodies.

Perhaps the biggest red flag is a change in your child's peer group. Do not allow your children to be vague about where they are going and with whom they are hanging out. If you notice kids hanging around who are not interested in meeting you, or in your knowing their parents, it is time to get scared. You should know every one of your child's friend's first and last names, and you should have established some contact with their parents.

SUBSTANCE ABUSE AND BRAIN CHEMISTRY

Contrary to what was previously believed—that the brain was basically mature by the end of puberty—we now know that significant structural brain development continues into a person's twenties. There are trillions of connections between the billions of neurons that make up our brains. Neurotransmitters are chemical molecules that allow brain cells to communicate with each other. We've previously mentioned the neurotransmitters serotonin, dopamine, and norepinephrine, which are associated with mood regulation. Less well known, but equally important, are gluta-

ASK YOUR TEEN ABOUT SUBSTANCE ABUSE

Clinicians like simple, reliable screening tools. A great example of this is the CRAFFT questionnaire. It's a popular, research-validated, six-item test that was developed by noted pediatrician and adolescent substance-use expert, John Knight, M.D., and colleagues at Children's Hospital in Boston.[1] There is no reason why parents shouldn't ask the same questions.

1. Have you ever ridden in a **C**ar driven by someone who was using drugs or alcohol?

2. Do you ever use drugs or alcohol to **R**elax?

3. Do you ever use these substances when you are **A**lone?

4. Do you ever **F**orget things you did while you were using drugs or intoxicated?

5. Do **F**amily/**F**riends tell you that you should cut down on your use?

6. Have you ever gotten into **T**rouble while using drugs or alcohol?

A single "yes" indicates a 30 percent chance that someone has an alcohol or drug disorder. The probability increases to 50 percent for two positive responses and to more than 80 percent for four positive responses. Communication, which includes using tools like this one, is your most effective tool for steering your teenager away from trouble. You can access it at www.childrenshospital.org.

mate, an excitatory neurotransmitter involved in learning and memory, and gamma amino butyric acid (GABA), an inhibitory neurotransmitter critical for maintaining balance in brain activity.

Mental actions such as remembering a telephone number and physical actions such as moving your eyes across this page involve a balance between stimulation and inhibition of different brain areas. The synapse is the point of contact, where one neuron releases neurotransmitter molecules that bind to receptors on a neighboring neuron. Balance within and between the many neurotransmitters' signaling systems is vital for normal functioning and development.

Neurons in the brain are conveniently grouped into functional areas, which communicate with each other via neuron tracts. Roughly speaking, higher-level brain functioning happens at the surface. The prefrontal cortex (discussed at length in chapter 2) is involved in executive functioning—planning and judgment, execution of tasks, and anticipation of consequences. The limbic system contains structures that are important for emotional processing, motivation, and memory formation. Our most basic functions—hunger, thirst, regulation of heart rate, and breathing—are carried out deep in the brainstem. These functional areas are highly interconnected with and influence each other. For example, seeing a tiger generates certain thoughts ("I better run"), feelings (terror), and physiologic responses (increased heart rate and respiration).

Experience Changes Brain Structure

At the most basic level, learning and memory are the result of new physical connections (synapses) between neurons. This process of forming and remodeling connections is dynamic and ongoing.

Our experiences literally change our brains. Emotionally charged experiences, like a first kiss or first traffic ticket, tend to be remembered more than routine or trivial experiences. Brain pathways that are used frequently become stronger, and those that are not tend to get pruned away. In other words, use it or lose it. This is how we learned our multiplication tables: After some repetition, it became hard-wired that 9 x 6 = 54 (I think that's correct). This is also why chronic drug abuse is much, much harder to treat.

Like walking and speaking, executive functioning develops at different rates for different people. Parents asking "What were you thinking?" are responding to a situation in which their teenager's imperfectly developed executive functioning was revealed.

But who becomes addicted, and to what? It's a fact that certain substances are more addictive than others, and that certain people are more vulnerable to substance use disorders than others. Why? Part of the answer relates to the way substances of abuse affect the three key brain areas collectively known as the "reward center." When we do certain things—such as hear an entertaining joke, eat chocolate, or snort cocaine—our reward center releases some of the chemical dopamine and we feel pleasure. We are hard-wired to repeat things that bring us pleasure. But with experience, we learn when to say enough. For example, after eating a certain amount of ice cream, abdominal discomfort (consequence) outweighs pleasure (reward). Learning to control urges and impulses is part of becoming mature.

However, addicting substances, such as nicotine and cocaine, act as "super-stimuli," activating the reward center more intensely, releasing larger amounts of dopamine. Just how addictive are these substances? Pharmaceutical companies commonly use rats to test the "abuse potential" of medications in development. For substances like cocaine, laboratory rats will choose to press a lever to receive a dose of cocaine and ignore food and water until they die.

A key point is that the drugs themselves do not directly cause the pleasurable sensation—rather it is the release of our brain's own stores of dopamine that make us feel good. In normal situations, our brains maintain a balance, regenerating and recycling dopamine as it is released. But there is a limit to how fast our brains can restore balance after the massive release of dopamine caused by drug use. We experience the depletion of dopamine as the opposite of pleasure. A benign example of this is the lull experienced by coffee drinkers after the initial lift. The more dopamine released, the more extreme the highs and lows.

During the "crash" following cocaine or Ecstasy use, the individual feels lethargic, irritable, and depressed, which leads many to seek out more drugs. A vicious cycle ensues. With repeated drug use, tolerance develops as the reward center gets desensitized (through a decrease in the number of dopamine receptors expressed on the surface of neurons). The user needs higher and higher doses of the substance to achieve the same effect. Eventually, high doses are needed just to feel "normal." Pleasurable experiences—a good movie or a beautiful sunset—become boring. Executive functioning, in other words the ability to anticipate consequences and change behavior accordingly, becomes progressively more impaired. The ability to regulate emotions erodes. Drug use becomes compulsive as the brain struggles to function under the altered chemical equilibrium. These consequences help explain why addicts continue to use long after their pleasure pathway stops giving pleasure.

Why Certain Teens Can Limit Substance Use

Keep in mind that by high school graduation, about half of teenagers have not used drugs. For those who have, curiosity and a desire for closeness and shared experiences with peers were often behind the decision to try a substance for the first time. Most of these teens are careful to limit their "recreational" use of substances and are able to avoid significant negative consequences. For some, however, the motivation to continue using substances differs from what got them started.

Psychiatrict Lance Dodes, M.D., an expert on addictive behaviors, and former director of the substance abuse treatment program at McLean Hospital in Belmont, Massachusetts, looks at the problem from a psychological perspective. In his book, *The Heart of Addiction*, Dodes convincingly argues that emotional distress is behind the drive to repeat addictive behavior.[2] It does not matter whether the focus of addiction is chemical (drugs and alcohol) or behavioral (gambling, shopping, Internet gaming, or pornography). From this perspective, the decision to repeat a behavior in spite of harmful consequences represents an attempt to regain control over an intolerable feeling.

In the adolescent substance recovery group that I conduct at McLean Hospital, each group member is challenged to identify the feeling states they find intolerable. Boredom is the most commonly reported intolerable emotion, followed by anger and sadness.

Understanding how drugs and alcohol interfere with brain development tells us why preventing (or delaying) substance use is so important. Understanding what drives addictive behavior clarifies a major parenting task—making sure your child has the skills and tools to deal with painful emotions.

Reduce Risks and Enhance Protective Factors

Prevention research has identified factors at the level of the individual, the family, the community, and the world at large that influence the chances someone will get into trouble with drugs and alcohol. International factors such as the explosion of heroin production in the Middle East in the wake of war in Iraq and Afghanistan are beyond the influence of most families. But parents can change what goes on in their household and influence what happens in their communities.

Individual factors are largely biological and often evident from very early in life. Children with difficult temperaments, those who are highly impulsive, have learning disabilities, and have difficulty forming trusting attachments to caregivers are at higher than average risk for developing substance use problems later in life. Extreme shyness or aggressive behavior is often apparent before a child reaches school age and may indicate an underlying mood or anxiety disorder. Family members, other parents, and teachers can provide feedback and guidance. If there is significant concern, formal evaluation by a child psychiatrist or child psychologist is indicated. Early intervention and parent training can be life changing, even life-saving. Children can learn self-control, emotional awareness, and social problem-solving skills. Untreated, these children can become marginalized from the mainstream, leading to the development of a negative self-image. By late elementary school or middle school, they may begin to associate with similarly troubled or unsupervised children. For many, experimentation with substances follows.

Family factors include parenting style, communication patterns in the household, and level of supervision. A family history of drug or alcohol problems has both biological and behavioral aspects. Parental substance abuse and untreated mental illness in the family increase the chances a child will use drugs and alcohol. Parental attitudes toward drug use are a powerful determinant of risk. Children whose parents strongly disapprove of marijuana are less likely to use drugs and alcohol, or they begin using later in life, which reduces the chances they will develop a substance use disorder.

Parenting style is highly correlated with child well-being in terms of social and emotional development, school performance, and proneness toward problem behaviors, including substance abuse.[3] One style of parents, uninvolved parents, do not respond to, or demand much from, their children. Lacking guidance or responsibility, these children learn to fend for themselves and resent attempts by other adults to set limits on them. They tend to get into trouble starting at an early age, perform poorly in school, have low self-esteem, and experience higher levels of depression and substance abuse later in life.

Another style of parents, indulgent parents, are highly responsive to the needs of their children but do not demand much from them. Entitled and demanding, these children tend to get into trouble and perform poorly in school, though they tend to have better social skills and higher self-esteem. Many of the teenagers I treat for substance use disorders report that they had "too much money and freedom, and nothing to do."

A third style of parents, authoritarian parents, are highly directive and demanding, but not very responsive to their children. Children of authoritarian parents tend to stay out of trouble and do moderately well in school. But having been treated as though their needs did not matter, their capacity for empathy is impaired and they have poorer social skills. They also have lower self-esteem and suffer higher rates of depression later in life.

The parenting style that is associated with the best outcomes is authoritative parenting, according to the accumulated data in the field. I call this the nurturer-consultant-enforcer stance. These parents respond to their children's needs and hold their children to high standards of behavior. They also teach by example, modeling the way mature adults can disagree strongly but remain respectful of each other. Emotional and psychological autonomy are valued. Children are encouraged to develop their own opinions and ideas, even if they are different from the parent's ideas. Limit setting (curfews, screen time) is thoughtful and reasonably consistent. Children are allowed to make certain choices, but this is not a democracy. The parent retains full veto power. These parents recognize and rely on the power of their own authority as parents.

For the modern and mobile adolescent, peer and community influences become more important. Poverty is a risk factor, but it is a mistake to think that more affluent areas are less drug-infested than poorer neighborhoods. I get as many referrals from highly affluent towns as I do from working-class neighborhoods. Almost every day I hear from my young patients that parents are clueless about what goes on at teen parties. Or worse, that parents have an idea what goes on but do nothing to intervene. I have had to contact the department of social services on several occasions because parents were supplying alcohol and marijuana to their children and their friends.

As mentioned earlier in several chapters, unsupervised use of increased technology and interconnectivity are also newer, profound risk factors for substance use and abuse. Not only do teenagers exchange war stories of substance use via text messages and the like, but they can find illegal drugs online. The Internet is an endless source of communication and glorification of both drug and alcohol use during adolescence.

THE SUBSTANCES: WHAT EXACTLY IS MY TEEN USING?

Parents are surprised to learn that inhalant use often starts in elementary school, and that it is among the most dangerous forms of drug abuse. There is truth to the "gateway hypothesis" that minor experimentation can lead to major problems down the road. I have yet to meet a heroin addict who knew the first time he smoked a cigarette that he would one day stick a needle in his arm. No one plans to get hooked, especially adolescents who think that nothing bad will ever happen to them.

Inhalants

Johnny is eight years old and struggling in third grade. He sees his dad every other weekend, unless his dad is out of town. Johnny has to go to his friend's house after school until his mother gets home from work. Sometimes they play basketball, but sometimes they go into the garage and smell the gasoline in the snowblower. It smells good, and it makes Johnny feel silly and warm inside. After a few deep breaths, it sounds like helicopters in his head. And Johnny's friend laughs when Johnny falls over and bangs his head on the ground. And Johnny laughs too because it doesn't even hurt.

Inhalant abuse, also known as "huffing" or "bagging," starts early and can cause permanent brain damage. It may start when young children discover they like the smell of gasoline and the warm, dizzy feeling they get when sniffing it deeply. Commonly abused items include volatile solvents such as paint thinner, shoe polish, gasoline, and glue; office supplies such as correction fluid, computer dust-off, and certain felt-tip markers; and gases such as butane, propane, and nitrous oxide. Nitrous oxide comes in several grades. Industrial grade, used as race car fuel, is the cheapest and dirtiest; foodservice grade, used in whipped cream containers, is the easiest available; medical grade, such as laughing gas, is the purest and most expensive.

Inhalant abuse peaks between the seventh and ninth grades.[4] According to the Monitoring the Future study, inhalant abuse is declining among tenth and twelfth graders, but it has increased significantly among eighth graders for the past two years. In 2002, there were about one million new inhalant abusers; 80 percent of them were under the age of eighteen and roughly split evenly between boys and girls.

Inhalant intoxication mimics drunkenness. After a brief period of euphoria, during which the user feels dizzy and may act silly, comes drowsiness and loss of coordination. Users may lurch around or fall down, increasing the risk of injury. Speech becomes slurred and lethargy sets in, followed by agitation, confusion, or loss of consciousness. Headache, nausea, and vomiting are common. The most dangerous short-term risks are asphyxiation (suffocation) as oxygen is displaced in the lungs, convulsions, and coma. "Sudden sniffing death" syndrome results from irregular heart rhythms and can occur during the first use of inhalants. Some experts estimate that of all inhalant-related deaths, 40 percent occurred the first time the user abused inhalants, probably due to some biological vulnerability to abnormal heart rhythms.

Solvents dissolve grease and fats, also called lipids, which is what our bodies and brains are made of. Chronic inhalant abuse is among the most difficult of all addictions to treat due to permanent damage these solvents cause throughout the brain. MRI brain scans of chronic inhalant abusers show loss of brain tissue volume and changes in brain structure. A 2002 study compared chronic solvent abusers with cocaine abusers and found that the solvent abusers had far more severe brain abnormalities and cognitive impairments.[5] Cognitive testing shows marked impairments in problem solving, memory, concentration, and other areas of thinking among inhalant abusers, and it has been shown that after stopping all inhalant use, only about two-thirds of lost cognitive functioning returns. Other permanent consequences include hearing loss, limb spasms, and damage to the liver, kidneys, and bone marrow.

Evidence of inhalant abuse may be pretty obvious: paint stains on face and hands, chemical odors on breath and clothing, red eyes, and runny nose. But because the intoxication is so brief, children are often able to hide what they are doing. It may take only five minutes to sneak into the garage, become intoxicated on gasoline in the snowblower, and recover. Be alert for clues such as finding unusual substances in your child's room or drippy whipped cream spray cans. (By spraying them in the upright position the nitrous oxide propellant is released while the whipped cream remains in the canister.)

It would be impractical to rid your home of all abusable substances, but it is important to store chemicals safely. Parents should begin talking with children very early about product safety, poison control, and things that do and do not belong in your body. Parents should avoid using terms like "getting high" which sounds attractive and may have the unintended negative consequence of stimulating curiosity.

———————

A fourteen-year-old girl in my teen recovery group described using a store gift certificate to purchase her first can of computer dust-off so she could get high like the girls portrayed in the movie Thirteen.

———————

She had just seen the movie with her mother, who hoped it would scare her away from problem behavior. Another example of bad modeling is inhaling helium from balloons to do the "munchkin voice." Even though helium is not dangerous, it is not something that belongs in our bodies and sends the wrong message to children.

Tobacco

Despite his freckled boyish face and spiky red hair, Marc tries hard to look and sound like a gangster wearing flashy, oversized clothing and a baseball cap turned askew. Life at home was a chaos of yelling and slamming doors. After his parents divorced, Marc discovered he could disappear for hours to hang out with his friends without being missed. Emboldened by a lack of limits and consequences, he began to skip school and came home late at night, sometimes drunk and high. When Marc was thirteen, his parents obtained a court order to try and re-establish some control over his rebellious behavior. After several months, Marc began to appreciate that his parents cared about his whereabouts and what he was doing. He began taking school more seriously and asked me how to cut down on his two-pack-a-day smoking habit.

The good news is that from 1995 to 2005, the rate of cigarette smoking decreased by half among eighth and tenth graders, and by one-third among twelfth graders.[6] More sobering is that the rates of smoking are higher for teenagers than for adults—about half of children have tried cigarettes by twelfth grade. In addition to peer influences, adolescents may be more vulnerable to nicotine addiction due to biological changes they are going through. The American Cancer Society puts it succinctly: "Nearly all first use of tobacco occurs before high school graduation . . . for the most part, people who do not start using tobacco when they are teens never start using it."[7] Another startling fact is that only three out of 100 high school smokers think they will still smoke in five years, but studies show that sixty out of 100 will smoke seven to nine years later. This explains why tobacco companies work so hard to get young people to try their products.

Both cigarettes and chewing tobacco efficiently deliver nicotine to the brain. Each of those deliveries activates the brain's reward center, as described earlier. Twenty puffs per cigarette multiplied by 20 cigarettes amounts to 400 activations of the reward center, which is a major reason why the cigarette is an ideal vehicle for addicting young people. Before the first puff is exhaled, releases of dopamine and adrenaline cause a brief period of increased focus and well-being, followed by lethargy and a desire for more nicotine.

Cigarette smoke contains more than 4,000 chemicals, including carbon monoxide. Smoking is linked to 90 percent of lung cancers, which is the number one cancer killer in both men and women. Smoking worsens asthma in children and adults, and it is associated with cancers of the mouth, pharynx, larynx, esophagus, stomach, pancreas, cervix, and urinary tract. The rates of cancer death are twice as high in smokers as in non-smokers, and they're four times as high in heavy smokers.

Prevention starts by establishing a non-smoking household. If you smoke, quit. Or keep trying to quit. Practically every child knows that smoking is dangerous, but they tend to mimic behaviors they see around them. Your child's knowing that you are trying to stop can be a deterrent to his or her starting. Stay aware of your child's activities. Neglected or unsupervised children are four times likelier to smoke and abuse drugs and alcohol than children living with parents who are regularly present and mandate a structure lifestyle.

It's pretty easy to tell if your teen is smoking. Be alert for odors on your child's breath and clothing and evidence such as butts and wrappers in the car or around the house.

Alcohol

Luke is a moderately overweight seventeen-year-old who takes pride in his unkempt, "drifter-anarchist" appearance and attitude. His long, unbrushed, slightly oily hair is held to his head by a rolled-up bandana, and he wears a green army jacket. Socially awkward and with significant learning disabilities, Luke felt isolated and stupid. Rather than suffer the pain of rejection, he rejected mainstream values and began to associate with similarly marginalized peers. He continued to deny he had a problem with alcohol until waking up for the third time in an emergency room with no idea how he got there. During Luke's stay in acute residential treatment, he began to realize that he, like both his parents, was dependent on alcohol.

Alcohol is the drug of choice among young people.[8] By eighth grade, half of students have tried alcohol and more than 20 percent say they have been drunk.[9] Twenty percent of eighth graders and half of twelfth graders have used alcohol within the past 30 days. One-third of high school seniors report binge drinking—consuming five or more drinks on one occasion—in the past two weeks. Alcohol use is particularly dangerous for young people whose judgment and impulse control are in the early stages of development.

To make matters worse, too young to go to bars, many teens drink while driving or while parked in their cars. Teenagers need to know that cars are lethal weapons. Motor vehicle accidents are the leading cause of death of fifteen- to twenty-year-olds.[10] Alcohol also increases the risk of being a perpetrator or victim of sexual assault, and engaging in high-risk sexual activity with the attendant risks of pregnancy and contracting sexually transmitted diseases. Alcohol worsens depression, reduces inhibition, and increases the risk of suicide.

Long-term, heavy alcohol use can lead to a state of physical dependence that requires medical treatment. Suppression of the brain's natural inhibitory mechanisms by alcohol markedly increases the person's vulnerability to seizures, even death, if alcohol is suddenly stopped. This is why medically supervised detoxification using anticonvulsants or benzodiazepines, which work through the same pathway as alcohol, is required once a person has reached the point of physical dependence.

The most reliable predictor of an adolescent's drinking is the behavior of his or her friends, which underscores the importance of knowing your child's friends, and those friend's parents. You do not need to be best friends with the other parents, but you should have established lines of communication. Talk to the parents of teenagers who will be hosting a party. Make sure that there will be adult supervision and that alcohol will not be served or allowed. And make sure the parents are clued in to the fact that some partygoers may try to sneak in substances so they need to be on the lookout for any signs of use or intoxication. Hold your children to a reasonable curfew and check in with them when they arrive home.

Teenagers also need to know whether there is a history of alcohol-related problems in their families since substance use disorders commonly run in families, putting them at increased risk for getting into trouble with substances compared with peers without a family history.

Too many parents consider underage drinking as normal, and even support the use of alcohol by teenagers in their homes ("I'd rather they drink here where it's safe"). This is a cop-out. Parents need to be clear that any drinking (or drug use) is unacceptable. Teenagers need to socialize, and given the constraints on healthy social interaction during the day due to school and homework, they hold parties at night and on the weekends. Indeed, the term "partying" has become synonymous with using drugs and alcohol. Teen parties are awash in alcohol and drugs.

An August 2006 survey by the National Center on Addiction and Substance Abuse provides the following sobering data about the prevalence of substance use at teen parties and the alarmingly lax attitudes of many adults toward underage drinking.[11]

• One-third of teenagers report attending parties where teenagers used alcohol, marijuana, cocaine, Ecstasy, or prescription drugs while a parent was present. Yet 99 percent of parents say they would never serve alcohol at their teenagers' parties.

• When parents are not present at parties, the likelihood that alcohol is available is 16 times higher, that an illegal drug is available is 15 times higher, and that marijuana is available is 29 times higher than when parents are present.

Marijuana

Sam is an exceptionally bright seventeen-year-old sophomore in the public high school of a wealthy town near Boston. He began smoking marijuana two years ago and was able to maintain straight A's despite a pattern of drug use that progressed to daily smoking before, during, and after school. His parents confronted him, but they gave in to his defiance, feeling that they had no grounds to set firm limits since he was maintaining his grades, was not depressed or otherwise emotionally disturbed, and was socially popular. Sam's parents finally sought treatment in hopes of lessening the legal consequences when he was arrested and charged as an adult for possession with intent to distribute when he was caught with marijuana, scales, and baggies.

Attitudes toward marijuana, the most common illegal drug in the United States, are alarming. Today's teenagers, and many of their parents, think of marijuana as safe. Teens or parents often omit marijuana when I ask about drug use because they do not consider pot a "real drug." Parents seeking help for their child's cocaine or heroin problem say they wish their child were "just smoking pot, like a normal kid."

Working one afternoon in the clinic I was not sure whether to laugh or scream when a father indignantly complained to me that his child had gotten into his (the father's) stash of marijuana. Sensing my thinly controlled outrage, the father tried to justify his attitude toward pot by engaging me in a philosophical discussion about how marijuana was safer than alcohol. Rather than argue with him and risk losing the chance to positively influence his and his son's decisions about future drug use, I focused on the ways in which mind-altering substances complicate the already daunting challenges of growing up. On an intellectual level, the father could understand the neurochemical explanation for why substance use was particularly risky for the developing adolescent mind.

Once the father trusted that I was not interested in shaming him, he was gradually able to reflect on the ways marijuana (and alcohol) had delayed his own emotional development. He eventually admitted feeling some shame that his son knew about his drug use. Over the course of several family therapy sessions, father and son talked about the role drugs and alcohol had played in their lives, and together they agreed that they would both stop using any substances for six months.

This casual acceptance of marijuana as a normal stage in adolescent development has profound consequences. As previously mentioned, pot is the most common illegal drug in the United States, and today's pot is up to five times more potent than it was a few decades ago. In the past fifteen years, the rates of marijuana use have increased by about 50 percent among middle and high school students. About half of high school seniors report smoking pot at least once, and about a third of those who have tried marijuana report regular use.

Research has shown that marijuana affects the brain for several days after a single use, impairing memory, concentration, and judgment. Repeated use saps motivation and ambition and derails emotional development. Depression, anxiety, and even paranoia and personality disturbances are associated with long-term use.

Controversy over whether marijuana is addictive boils down to semantics. From a physiological standpoint, withdrawal effects are relatively mild and not medically dangerous. Emotional volatility, irritability, sleeplessness, and anxiety typically resolve within a few weeks of stopping. However, psychological factors can take much longer to address. Former pot smokers commonly report intense cravings for weeks to months after quitting. A skilled therapist or drug abuse counselor can help the teenager identify and manage the intolerable feelings that bring on the cravings to use. Family therapy can help parents and siblings understand and correct dysfunctional communication patterns.

Cocaine and Stimulants

Cocaine and stimulants such as methamphetamine are powerfully addictive and deadlier than most teenagers realize. In 2005, 4 percent of eighth graders, 5 percent of tenth graders, and 8 percent of twelfth graders reported use of cocaine at some point in their lives. Half of these teenagers reported smoking crack, a cheap, concentrated derivative of cocaine, at least once in their lives.[12] Methamphetamine is more prevalent in the western and southwestern United States, but it is becoming more popular in the East. In 2004, 6.2 percent of twelfth graders reported using methamphetamine at some point in their lives.[13]

Stimulants and cocaine work by blocking the reuptake of dopamine, which then floods the brain's reward center. Tolerance develops quickly since neurons cannot replace dopamine quickly enough to maintain balance. Users experience a brief, intense euphoria, and then they crave more. Physical effects include increased heart rate and blood pressure due to constriction of blood vessels. Cocaine in particular can also cause sudden cardiac death by the closing of the arteries that feed the heart and by stroke due to constriction of blood vessels in the brain.

Pharming

Annette is a fifteen-year-old sophomore in an affluent boarding school. She had heard that OxyContin was expensive so she was thrilled when a friend gave her a 40 milligram tablet for free. Ten minutes after taking it, she complained that she wasn't feeling anything from the drug, so her friend gave her another 40 milligram tablet. Twenty minutes later she became delirious, then unarousable. Some of her friends got scared and ran away. Luckily, someone called for help and Annette was taken to a local emergency room and revived. She recovered but it is not clear whether she suffered any permanent brain damage.

The term "pharming" refers to a relatively recent trend among middle and high school students. They raid medicine cabinets and pharmacy shelves to collect whatever medications they can get their hands on. Teens then hold "pharming parties" where they swap and trade pills, often not even knowing what they are taking under the assumption that medications must be safe.

More frightening are the cases where nothing is done. Sometimes victims get lucky and sleep off whatever medication they ingested. But I have firsthand knowledge of dozens of bad outcomes. One stands out for me: a boyfriend and girlfriend, both seniors at a private high school near Boston, experimented with what turned out to be Valium and OxyContin at a party in a local town. They were both relatively "med-naive," meaning they had not used either substance regularly, so neither had developed a physical tolerance for the drug, nor did they know anything about whether the dose was high or low. Both were found in the back seat of the boy's car in the morning. He was dead, having stopped breathing hours earlier due to respiratory depression. She awoke from a coma five weeks later with significant cognitive loss due to cerebral hypoxia and ongoing physical rehabilitation because of the damage to her nervous system.

Club Drugs

Parents need to know about a number of substances popular among young partygoers. Keep your eyes and ears open for substances like Ecstasy; Ketamine or "special-K"; gamma hydroxybutyrate, also called liquid ecstasy or GHB; and Rohypnol or "roofies." The chances your child will be offered substances increases sharply between the ages of thirteen and fourteen.

Methylenedioxymethamphetamine (MDMA), otherwise known as Ecstasy, causes euphoria and increased energy because of its effect on multiple neurotransmitter systems. Teens are unaware that Ecstasy inhibits their metabolism and can quickly rise to toxic levels, leading to hyperthermia and multiple organ failure. Users can become dehydrated and succumb to cardiovascular collapse. Repeated use of Ecstasy has been shown to cause permanent damage to the serotonin system, leading to a state of permanent depression.

Ketamine is a human and animal anesthetic classified as a narcotic. Users experience hallucinations and dissociation—a feeling of being outside their bodies. Dangers of ketamine include delirium and accidents, increased blood pressure, and respiratory depression.

GHB is a central nervous system depressant taken for its euphoric and anabolic (body-building) effects. It is also commonly used as a date-rape drug. Use of GHB has been associated with seizures, coma, and deaths from overdose.

Rohypnol or "roofies" is a benzodiazepine (like Valium or Klonopin) that is used as a date-rape drug. Particularly when combined with alcohol, this and related substances can cause "anterograde amnesia" during which the user cannot remember events following ingestion of the drug.

CONCLUSION

While there are no easy answers or guarantees that your child will avoid the dangers of substance use, there is plenty of room for optimism. Sometimes circumstances get in the way, but kids want to grow up healthy.

The bottom line is that communication is your most effective tool. Your attitude toward substance use and the behavior you model are the biggest determinants of your child's risk of getting into trouble with drugs and alcohol. If you make a big deal out of cigarette use, for example, your child is less likely to smoke, and less likely to move on to more dangerous substances. Appeal to reason and remain consistent and firm in your efforts to convince your teen that substance abuse is foolish and dangerous and not something you, the parent, will back away from confronting.

If your child has begun to experiment, you have not failed. Many teenagers with highly competent, loving, and involved parents still choose to experiment with substances. This is not an all-or-none situation. Too many parents give in or give up once they learn that their child is using. Giving up on the problem is failing your child. You will decrease the chances that experimentation will progress to problem use if you maintain your position that substance use is not acceptable.

You are not alone if you have made any of the following correctable parenting errors.

• "I did it and I turned out okay." This error is usually based on shame or embarrassment, and not on the heartfelt conviction that substance abuse is a right every teenager should enjoy. It is not your kids' fault that you got away with something dangerous or that your parents could not keep as close an eye on you as they should have. Maybe you got lucky or maybe substance use cost you more than you are comfortable admitting. In any case, do not perpetuate the error by having a lax attitude toward substance use by your children.

• "If I don't see (or smell) anything, there must not be a problem." This error is usually based on denial or fear. As addiction psychiatrist Henry David Abraham, M.D., put it, "Turn on your parents' radar . . . choose heads-up rather than head-in-the-sand parenting." Build a family culture of talking to each other. Maintain an interest in your children's activities, music, and video games. Hug them often.

• "Do as I say, not as I do." This is surprisingly common and probably the most challenging parenting error because it is based on the parents' inability or unwillingness to change their own behavior. If you know you have a problem with drugs or alcohol, you need to get help and demonstrate that you are working hard to recover. Even if you do not have a substance use problem, but your child is getting into trouble, you should eliminate substances from the house. You wouldn't smoke in the same room as someone suffering from pneumonia, right? Sadly, many parents consider unreasonable the suggestion that they cannot keep alcohol in

DRUG SCREENING FOR YOUR TEEN

I encourage urine toxicology screening—drug testing—for teenagers suspected of using drugs. Yes, they will argue about how this invades their privacy, but bottom line, their health is at stake. For example, if I were treating my child for diabetes I would not simply take their word that they were eating properly and taking their insulin; I would routinely monitor their blood sugar and hemoglobin A1C, a marker for long-term blood sugar control.

The level of intervention and scrutiny should be in line with the severity of the problem. I do not recommend testing "just to check" whether there is no indication of a problem. But if your child has been caught using or you suspect has been high, ask him or her to provide a urine sample at the pediatrician's office. For a teen who has been repeatedly caught using drugs, I suggest weekly urine screening either at the family's pediatrician's office or at a local laboratory. Toxicology testing can be quite expensive. The laboratory that I use charges more than $200 per test, though insurance usually covers the fee. While home tests are available at pharmacies, laboratory testing is more sensitive and accurate.

For many teens, the simple threat of random testing by their parents is enough to convince them that using drugs is simply not worth the hassle. Yet, don't expect an impaired mind to make healthy decisions. Parents still have the responsibility for keeping their teenagers safe and on track.

Should your child receive a positive result, avoid an extreme response—such as ignoring the result or threatening to ground the child for life. These responses generally do more harm than good. Like any other medical test, a positive result should result in further investigation, increased scrutiny, and appropriate intervention. Punishments, such as being grounded, tend not to be effective because they don't teach anything. Frame consequences in terms that appropriately reflect parental concern and caring. For example, a car is as close to a lethal weapon as most teenagers will possess. Loss of driving privileges is completely reasonable until parents are satisfied that their teenager is no longer using any intoxicating substances.

the house just because their teenager has gotten into trouble drinking. It's not fair, but parents are burdened with the responsibility for modeling mature behavior. I will ask these parents to take a hard look at their own use of alcohol. Is it so important that they maintain a handy supply? Parenting involves sacrifices. Make a commitment to abstain from use at least until your teenager is out of trouble.

If you are concerned your teen is abusing substances, get your concerns out in the open. In addition to talking with your child directly, have a frank discussion about substance abuse with your pediatrician, the child's school counselor, and any other adults your child regularly sees. Hold a neighborhood meeting with other parents and their teenage children. If you *know* your child is using substances, get professional help. Some of my most rewarding work involves brief consultation with families who need help reopening the lines of communication with their teenager.

You will need to step up your efforts if your teenager continues to use or refuses to follow limits you have set. Evaluation by a child and adolescent psychiatrist or psychologist may uncover mood or anxiety problems that need to be properly addressed with therapy and possibly medications. Recall that people with social phobia and other anxiety disorders are at much higher risk for developing alcohol problems because of "self-medication."

For aggressively defiant teenagers, or teenagers so impaired they are unable to curtail their use, residential treatment or hospitalization with detoxification can be life-saving. Most of the teens in my recovery group are referred from McLean's acute residential treatment program. For kids at this stage of use, there is not time to wait and try to talk them out of using. Many kids I work with say they would not have stopped using if they had not been taken out of their environment and restricted from access to drugs for several months. This shows the degree of impairment in executive functioning that substances cause in the adolescent brain. The good news is that many of the most hardcore drug users can recover fully and get back on track. But it takes months or years, not days or weeks. Start soon.

CHAPTER 6

When Your Teen's Eating Becomes a Problem

Thomas J. Weigel, M.D.

While some teens are able to handle today's adolescent pressures by finding a sensible balance, others use food to cope with these stresses. This use of food can manifest itself in consuming too much or not enough—a reflection of a culture that, while in the midst of an obesity epidemic, is also seeing a rise in the popularity of eating disorders.

Youths with eating disorders have found one area of their life they can fully control. Their parents, on the other hand, face the challenge of helping their children while also controlling their children's exposure to websites that feed their obsession, a celebrity culture that embraces unrealistic body images, and even competition with like-minded peers.

One goal of treatment is to give kids suffering from disordered eating a stronger sense of effectiveness and control over other aspects of their lives so they can slowly give up the stranglehold that food has on them. This is what we try to accomplish on the eating disorders unit where I work as an attending psychiatrist.

Little evidence exists of eating disorders in the distant past. In the hunter-gatherer society, there was often insufficient food, thus death by *involuntary starvation was only too common. There was likely little or no social pressure to be thin.*

With the surge in availability of low-cost fast food and pre-made packaged food in the 1980s, obesity rates swelled, particularly in Western populations with low socioeconomic status.[1] Images of obesity became associated with poorer populations, while Hollywood promoted the value of thinness and its relationship to beauty, popularity, and success.[2] These cultural images, in turn, spread like wildfire via the technology superhighway, leading to an emphasis among teens in particular on thinness as the standard for beauty and, subsequently, peer popularity.

The numbers of people with eating disorders are thought to be on the rise. There has been nearly a threefold increase of anorexia over the past 40 years among women in their twenties and thirties, and the risk of bulimia and binge eating disorders is also increasing. The rate for anorexia in teens has remained stable, though there may be factors in the teen years that influence the increase seen after age 20.[3, 4]

This may be due to the worsening childhood obesity crisis and increased, countervailing societal pressure to be thin, especially among teens and young adults. Many fashion designers take advantage of this desire to be thin and size their clothing to match their target audience. For some companies, what is known now as a size 4 was formerly designated as a size 16 before the 1960s. Hollywood and the media (e.g., TV, magazines, etc.) also play a large role in societal ideals. If you look at the magazine rack at the supermarket, you will see some covers that promote dieting next to others that portray waif-like, ultrathin actresses and models.

By writing this chapter, I hope to educate parents about eating disorders, so they can recognize them in their children. This chapter will provide guidance for the confusing and often traumatic experience of having a family member with an eating disorder. I also hope to raise awareness about these debilitating and, at times, deadly illnesses.

Becky

BECKY CAME FROM A FAMILY where overeating and dieting was common. Her mother was morbidly obese, although she was always trying some new diet from an entertainment magazine. Becky's father was closer to a healthy weight, but that was due to his focus on exercise rather than culinary restraint.

At age twelve, Becky was often teased at school for being overweight. At home, her uncle referred to her as "pudgy" rather than by her real name. At one point, Becky saw herself in a family holiday photograph, taken in Bermuda, and felt disgusted with her appearance.

Becky started to skip breakfast each morning before school in an effort to lose weight. She set her alarm clock for later and told her mother she did not have time to eat. After a month of this behavior, Becky noticed she had lost a few pounds.

Her initial weight loss encouraged Becky to make further decreases in her diet. She started skipping lunch in addition to breakfast and stopped indulging in junk food, such as potato chips and candy. As a result, she lost even more weight the next month, and kids at school began complimenting her on her appearance.

Though Becky soon began feeling like her dieting was getting out of control, she enjoyed the positive feedback she was receiving about her new look. Fearful of drawing attention to her eating habits, she did not eat with her friends at school, or with her family at home. She worried that others would force her to eat, making her "fat" once again.

Becky continued her food restriction for a third month, dropping additional weight and losing her menstrual period. Her parents became concerned by her appearance and took Becky to her pediatrician, who was alarmed at the speed of weight loss and made referrals to a nutritionist and therapist. The pediatrician made a diagnosis of anorexia nervosa and scheduled weekly appointments to monitor Becky's weight and vital signs and perform laboratory tests.

Becky has an eating disorder, along with at least 5 percent of American females and possibly 1 percent of American males. Becky worked with the nutritionist to develop a daily meal plan so that she would stop losing weight and start making modest weight gains. Although Becky was initially reluctant to follow the meal plan, support from her family and friends added motivation to make the necessary changes.

Through therapy, Becky was able to challenge the automatic negative thoughts she was having about her body image, food, and self-esteem. She learned more about the origins of her low self-esteem and began to understand how that developed into an eating disorder. After a year of treatment, Becky's weight stabilized within a healthy range, giving her more time to spend with family and friends, rather than with doctors and specialists.

TYPES OF EATING DISORDERS

Becky's diagnosis—anorexia nervosa—is the refusal to keep one's weight at or above a normal place. Most definitions of anorexia list a criterion weight less than 85 percent of that expected for one's age and height. Anorexia involves an intense fear of gaining weight, even though the individual is, in reality, underweight. Anorexics typically think they are overweight or that their bodies are fat despite their starved state, and they deny the seriousness of their low physical weight. Self-worth becomes overly determined by their body image. Females lose their menstrual cycles or never start menstruating in the first place. Some people with anorexia rely on restricting their food intake, while others also binge eat and purge.

Bulimia nervosa, in contrast to anorexia, involves recurrent episodes of binge eating. An episode of binging is characterized by consuming an amount of food that is much larger than what most people would eat under similar circumstances in a short period of time (for example, two hours). A binge episode also involves a sense of lack of control over one's eating during the actual episode. This may include a feeling that they cannot stop eating or control what or how much they are eating. Bulimia also involves inappropriate compensatory behavior to prevent weight gain, such as self-induced vomiting; misuse of laxatives, diuretics, enemas, or other medications; fasting; and/or excessive exercise. As with anorexia, people with bulimia base their self-worth on their body shape and weight.

A third eating disorder category is designated as "eating disorder not otherwise specified" (eating disorder NOS). This diagnosis includes disorders of eating that do not fully meet the criteria for anorexia or bulimia. This includes females who meet all of the criteria for anorexia nervosa, but who still have regular menses, or, despite significant weight loss, the person's current weight is in the normal range. It also encompasses people who meet all of the criteria for bulimia nervosa except that binging and purging occur too infrequently to meet the criteria for bulimia nervosa. It also involves the regular use of purging by an individual of normal body weight after eating small amounts of food (such as self-induced vomiting after eating two cookies). Some people repeatedly chew and spit out large amounts of food, while others may have recurrent episodes of binge eating in the absence of purging.

INCIDENCE AND PREVALENCE

Disordered eating may be a bit of a misnomer, given that only 15 percent of the population has normal eating habits and/or no preoccupation with weight or shape. It appears that abnormal eating is actually normal in our society. About 70 percent of the population is preoccupied with weight and body image. In fact, 70 percent of high school age females diet. Approximately 5 percent of college women have mild forms of anorexia and 20 percent of college women experience transient bulimic symptoms.[5]

Using strict criteria for eating disorders, 1 percent of women have anorexia nervosa while about 4 percent of women have bulimia nervosa. Eating disorders are more prevalent in women than in men. In patients who seek treatment at clinics, the ratio of women to men is about 10:1. However, if you take a general population sample, the estimates are closer to 3:1 for anorexia nervosa and bulimia nervosa. For young men, there is a pressure to be both thin and muscular. About 17 percent of male high school wrestlers meet short-term criteria for an eating disorder.[6, 7, 8]

Eating disorders are more common in the United States, Canada, Europe, Australia, New Zealand, and South Africa than in other parts of the world. Rates are increasing in Japan and China. In the United States, the highest rates of eating disorders are for Caucasians, while African American women are more likely to develop bulimia or purge.[9]

Why Eating Disorders Occur

There are various biological, psychological, and societal factors that predispose some people to develop an eating disorder over others.

Biological factors include having a biological relative with an eating disorder, obesity, or a mood disorder, such as depression or bipolar disorder. Genetic studies suggest a link between certain genes and eating disorders. Studies involving twins support the genetic link for eating disorders. In fact, if one twin has an eating disorder, an identical twin is three times more likely to also have an eating disorder than a non-identical twin.

Psychological factors include a history of abuse, including sexual, physical, as well as emotional abuse. Any type of trauma, in fact, including witnessing violence, may increase one's sense of anxiety and wish to be in control. This can fuel the beginnings of an eating disorder.

A number of social factors influence the development of an eating disorder. The most important of these factors is a high value of thinness in a particular culture. Researchers at Massachusetts General Hospital studied two samples of Fijian schoolgirls before and after they were exposed to Western television. Before television, eating disorder symptoms were rare among these girls. However, after television exposure, key indicators of disordered eating were significantly more common. Information from the girls' narratives revealed an interest in weight loss as a means of modeling themselves after television characters. The study suggested that television can have a negative impact on societal attitudes and behaviors concerning food.[10]

When Do Eating Disorders Occur?

Eating disorders are three times more prevalent in women than men and have their onset most often in the teen years. Risk factors for developing an eating disorder in adolescence include having an early puberty, as well as being obese around the time of puberty. For some women, the eating disorder may be a response to a feeling that their body betrayed them in puberty. For other women, the eating disorder may have been an effort to avoid puberty altogether.

Anorexia may be associated with a higher social class, although bulimia tends to be independent of social class. Someone who moves from a rural to an urban setting has an increased chance of having an eating disorder. In males, there is an increased incidence of eating disorders in those with homosexual orientation, which may have to do with a higher value in gay culture placed on thinness and muscularity.

Additional activities that kids and adults engage in that predispose them to having eating disorders include ballet, modeling, gymnastics, figure skating, jockeying, running, crew team, and wrestling. In fact, ballet students are at a seven times higher risk for developing an eating disorder than the average person.

CASE STUDY

Janet—Failure to Grow

JANET WAS A SIXTEEN-YEAR-OLD girl who had been a dancer since the age of three. She enjoyed tap dancing and ballet, but she also dabbled in other dance disciplines, such as jazz and modern. Like many of the other children in her classes, Janet was thin, but unlike her peers, Janet had made no weight or height gains since age twelve. She rarely ate meals with her family, instead devoting the time to hours of extra dance practice on top of her already rigorous dance classes. She never began menstruating, and in the last two years, she had three stress fractures in her ankles and feet. After her most recent fracture, her doctor checked her weight and noted that she met the criteria for anorexia nervosa.

DISCUSSION

Janet's case is not rare. While she did not lose any weight at all, she failed to make appropriate weight gains with each progressing year. After four years, this left her far behind the weight she was supposed to be at age sixteen, resulting in anorexia. Her family did not notice she was not eating as much as a growing teen should, as she was always off at school, dance classes, or with friends. They thought the extra dance practice just showed her motivation for the activity, until the doctor mentioned anorexia. It is often easy, especially during growth periods where development can be so uneven, to miss the early warning signs that teens are not eating as they should to maintain a healthy weight.

WARNING SIGNS AND PROBLEM AREAS

How can you tell whether your child has an eating disorder? Often it is hard to tell, because people, especially teens, with anorexia and bulimia tend to hide their symptoms. They do this for a number of reasons. People with eating disorders sometimes see their behavior, thoughts, and attitudes as acceptable and consistent with whom they want to be as a person. This behavior is called ego-syntonic, since the person lacks insight into their behavior being disordered or "off-the-mark" in any way.

Teens with eating disorders may even realize they have a problem and that their behaviors are not helpful, but they may be too ashamed or embarrassed to tell anyone about the symptoms. They may also fear they will be made to gain weight if others find out about the disorder. This is particularly true for adolescents who are often already in a struggle with their parents for control and autonomy. They assume that if their parents find out about their eating issues, they will be forced in some manner to eat according to their parents' wishes.

CASE STUDY

Carl

CARL WAS A FIFTEEN-YEAR-OLD wrestler in the lightweight class who wanted to lose weight so he could wrestle at a lower weight class. Carl thought that if he lost ten pounds, he would have a better chance of beating the kids in the lower featherweight class. Carl started by cutting out all food with high fat content and lost weight. He then decided to become a vegetarian, which resulted in further weight loss. After losing ten pounds and winning a couple of wrestling matches, he decided to become a vegan in an effort to lose even more weight.

As Carl's obsession with his weight progressed, he started to take diuretics and laxatives to shed pounds quickly before weigh-ins at wrestling matches. After losing another eight pounds, he became tired and weak and started to lose all of his matches, even in practice. Carl was not able to lift as much weight at the gym, and he was having trouble concentrating in school—his grades were falling. Carl's wrestling coach noticed the changes and called his parents about his concern.

Carl did not start out with a plan to develop anorexia, but that is where he ended up. He was trying to achieve an ideal weight for optimal performance at wrestling, but he ended up entering a cycle of dieting and weight loss that he could not control. This case exhibits how coaches and teachers, as well as families and friends, must keep an eye out for kids who struggle with eating disorders.

The most important component of treatment for Carl was nutritional counseling. Carl met with a nutritionist who specialized in eating disorders and athletes. The nutritionist directed him toward foods his body needed to improve his weight and performance, and they were able to make plans for working exercise back into his routine. Once Carl was in a healthy weight range, the nutritionist recommended healthy amounts of exercise that would maximize his athletic performance. By the following year, Carl was at a healthy weight and back on the wrestling team, winning more matches than he did before the eating disorder.

SYMPTOMS OF A DEVELOPING EATING DISORDER

People with anorexia nervosa usually exhibit rapid and severe weight loss. This occurs through dieting (restricting types and amounts of food), and it may include excessive exercise and calorie counting. There is an extreme focus on body image and appearance. The rapid and severe weight loss may result in symptoms of weakness, dizziness, and intolerance to cold temperatures.

People with bulimia nervosa may exhibit knuckle abrasion from self-induced vomiting, acid reflux disease, loss of dental enamel (often noted by their dentist), as well as parotid and salivary gland enlargement. This looks like puffy cheeks or chipmunk cheeks. The parotid glands are just below the sideburns on the side of the jaw. A parent may notice trips to the bathroom after meals or even find vomit in garbage cans, outdoor bushes, or even bags hidden around the house.

We address the symptoms for those with an eating disorder NOS in the case study and discussion on the following page.

CASE STUDY

Kendra

THOUGH SEVENTEEN-YEAR-OLD Kendra was one of the most popular girls in her school and was considered very attractive by her peers, she was convinced that she appeared "fat" and was obsessed with her negative body image. One day, Kendra was in the girls' bathroom with a friend, who filled her in on the concept of purging, in other words, vomiting after meals, so she would not absorb the calories. To Kendra, this seemed like the perfect solution. She began vomiting into zipper-lock bags after meals and concealing them under her bed. She arrived for treatment after her father discovered more than forty bags hidden under her bed. Kendra had developed a serious eating disorder.

DISCUSSION

Kendra was very upset that her father found the bags under her bed. She was embarrassed and ashamed that she had an eating disorder. She also worried that people would try to make her give up her eating disorder, now that they knew she had one.

Since Kendra purged by vomiting, but did not exhibit binge eating, she met diagnostic criteria for an eating disorder (eating disorder NOS), but not bulimia or anorexia. Initially Kendra's insurance was reluctant to pay for weekly therapy because Kendra was at a healthy weight and did not have either anorexia or bulimia. However, after her primary care doctor detected abnormalities in Kendra's electrolytes (low potassium and high bicarbonate levels), her insurance agreed to pay for the treatment.

Kendra worked with a cognitive behavioral therapist (CBT) who specialized in eating disorders. They worked together to determine events and feelings that would trigger her urges to purge. They developed healthier coping strategies so that Kendra could tolerate and cope with anxiety, anger, sadness, and frustration. She used techniques such as journaling (writing about her feelings and urges to purge) and distraction (reading, watching television, and walking), and she learned to seek support from others when she was having a hard time. After seven months,

Kendra still had occasional urges to purge, but she was able to success-fully work against these urges and not purge.

Purging is an attempt to get rid of unwanted food intake, whether it is after a binge or after even after a small amount of eating. There are a number of ways that people purge, the most common method being self-induced vomiting, thereby directly removing the food that was just consumed. Sometimes people use ipecac syrup to help them throw up. Ipecac is supposed to be used only for accidental poisonings. If used more frequently, such as for bulimia, it can cause heart damage in addition to the damage caused by the eating disorder. Ipecac is directly toxic to the heart and dangerous.

Teens often use diet pills to help them lose weight. Most diet pills contain combinations of stimulants and caffeine, which tend to reduce ap-petite and subsequently weight. These medications often have side effects of increased heart rate and blood pressure, as well as symptoms of anxiety. The most dangerous of these medications is ephedrine, which can cause cardiac arrhythmias and death. This medication has been removed from the market, but some teens still seem to find it through the Internet.

Other teens use laxatives as a purging method, but they do not result in any true lasting weight loss. They do result in a release of feces and wa-ter, which looks like quick weight loss on the scale. However, this water weight is gained back eventually, and chronic use of laxatives can cause permanent bowel damage.

Still other teens abuse diuretics. These drugs also cause water loss, except it is through action on the kidneys. This causes increased urina-tion and a short-lasting decrease in weight. However, this too is just a loss of water weight, so the body will quickly gain it back.

Some teens abuse exercise to control their weight. While some amount of exercise can be healthy, many people with eating disorders exercise to a point that it becomes unhealthy.

EATING DISORDER OR MEDICAL PROBLEM?

A parent may wonder, Is my child losing weight because he or she is sick? What if this is not an eating disorder, but a medical problem? Some medical problems do cause weight loss, such as gastrointestinal illnesses, endocrine disorders, thyroid problems, and cancer. However, medical causes of weight loss are not accompanied by a fear of gaining weight and a distorted body image. These are telltale signs of an eating disorder. Other serious indications of an eating disorder include the loss of body fat and muscle, which are the most obvious signs of anorexia.

The best place to look for signs of an eating disorder is the heart. When people are starving, their body will start to eat its own muscles, including the heart muscle. This results in a smaller and weaker heart. This may cause a heart rate that is too slow (bradycardia) as well as low blood pressure (hypotension), swelling in the legs (edema), irregular heart beats (arrhythmias), heart murmurs, and low exercise tolerance. Most of the deaths from eating disorders are thought to result from either heart problems or suicide.

Thus, if a medical professional suspects that weight-loss symptoms may be due to other causes, he or she should evaluate for these accordingly.

CASE STUDY

John

JOHN, A JUNIOR IN HIGH SCHOOL, had always been a bright student. He earned straight A's through his freshman year before developing an eating disorder the summer before sophomore year. Due to teasing from his peers, John thought he was overweight, and he was determined to lose a large amount of weight by restricting his food intake and throwing himself into an intense exercise program. As John began to lose weight, he hid the loss beneath layers of baggy clothing.

When John's sophomore year performance earned him grades of B's and C's, his parents asked for testing to see whether he had a learning problem. The testing showed that John was struggling with attention and concentration problems, as well as difficulties with his short-term memory. He was prescribed Ritalin by his primary care doctor for suspected attention deficit disorder (ADD). The Ritalin reduced John's appetite (a common side effect) and resulted in additional weight loss over the next year at school. As his grades continued to plummet, John became worried that he would not get into a competitive college; he finally admitted to his parents that he had an eating disorder.

When the brain is not getting enough food, it does not function correctly. Kids with eating disorders often develop problems with their concentration and memory, resulting in school difficulties with falling grades. If these troubles are misdiagnosed and ADD and stimulants are prescribed, the eating disorder often worsens.

Stopping the Ritalin was not the only solution for John. He also required intensive individual and family therapy, in addition to working with his family doctor and a nutritionist. As John's eating disorder and health improved, so did his school performance. It is important to note, however, that medications prescribed to treat John's concentration problems worsened the physical and physiological aspects of his eating disorder, placing him at increased risk for potentially serious cardiac complications.

EATING DISORDERS' ADDITIONAL EFFECTS ON THE BODY

As noted, the brains of people with eating disorders do not get enough food. On brain scans, the size of the brain is often reduced, which is called atrophy. In addition, fluid-filled spaces (the ventricles) increase in size, while the brain tissue (cortical mass) shrinks. Outward symptoms of these brain changes include poor attention, concentration, and memory, as well as trouble with more concrete thinking. At times, these difficulties will result in falling school grades or even seizures.

When the body does not have enough nutrition, it cannot make enough red or white blood cells. The red blood cells transport the oxygen from the lungs to the rest of the body. A reduction in red blood cells, called anemia, may contribute to weakness and low energy. The white blood cells fight infections, so reductions in these cells make the body more susceptible to infections.

The digestive system also changes in people with eating disorders. Because the body is not getting enough food, or vomiting is eliminating the food, it reacts by slowing down. There is a delay in stomach emptying, and the entire gastrointestinal system decreases its rate, resulting in chronic constipation.

Accompanying the symptoms noted above are changes in hormones. These hormonal changes may cause the loss of a period (amenorrhea), loss of interest in sex, loss of bone mineral (osteopenia or osteoporosis), thyroid abnormalities, and body hair growth, called lanugo. Lanugo is the fine hair that covers the body on most babies. This hair reappears on people with anorexia because of hormonal changes. This may be the body's effort to provide insulation to help maintain a consistent body temperature when normal body fat has disappeared.

EATING DISORDER OUTCOMES

The outcome of an eating disorder depends largely upon which disorder the person is struggling with.

Anorexia Outcomes

A number of outcome studies have been done with patients who have anorexia nervosa. One study followed fifty-one people with anorexia for ten years. Half of the people in this study had little or no formal treatment for their eating disorder. After ten years, 6 percent still met the full criteria for anorexia nervosa, 27 percent had a persistent eating disorder, and 12 percent had experienced a period of bulimia during the intervening ten years. About 50 percent received an assessment of poor psychological functioning at ten years, as determined by psychological rating scales.[11] These numbers are not very promising.

Generally speaking, about 40 percent of people with eating disorders will recover completely, 35 percent will improve, 20 percent will develop a chronic eating disorder, and 5 percent of patients with anorexia die from the disease. In longer-range studies, however, the death rate may be as high as 20 percent (one person out of every five) for someone who has chronic anorexia. As noted earlier, most cases of death are from cardiac arrest and suicide.

Factors that suggest a better outcome for teens with anorexia include the following.

- Treatment by an outpatient team experienced with eating disorders

- Few or no other psychiatric disorders

- Beginning treatment with a less-severe decrease in weight and a short duration of illness

- Having the onset of the symptoms in the mid-teen years

- If in an intensive treatment program, such as inpatient or residential care, being discharged at a healthy weight

Bulimia Outcomes

For people with bulimia, the outcome research shows slightly more promising outcomes than for those with anorexia. In one study that followed people with bulimia for about eleven years, 11 percent still met criteria for bulimia nervosa, but 70 percent were in full or partial remission.

A different study followed the natural course of bulimia in women over a five-year period. The 102 women studied were between the ages of

THE MOST EFFECTIVE TREATMENTS FOR EATING DISORDERS

Treatments for all eating disorders have certain basic goals. The broadest goals are to stop all abnormal eating behavior and attain and sustain a normal body weight.

- Cognitive behavioral therapy (CBT) works to dismantle the cognitive distortions and core beliefs of the eating disorder and replace them with the capacity for emotional and behavioral self-regulation.

- Psychodynamic therapy attempts to uncover the underlying causes of the eating disorder and liberate the person from patterns of behavior that no longer work for them. CBT is more therapist-driven than psychodynamic therapy, in that the therapist tends to lead the sessions. Psychodynamic therapy is more patient-driven, and it works better for patients who prefer less input from their therapists.[14] For eating disorders in particular, however, the best assessment of whether the treatment is working is the reestablishment and maintenance of a healthy weight.

- As treatment progresses toward recovery, there needs to be an added focus on relapse prevention. As people with eating disorders have used their maladaptive behaviors to cope with difficult feelings and situations, it is important to build alternative coping skills that are healthier. Also, anticipating future crises—whether social or work-, school-, or family-related—will reduce the chance of relapsing.

- In addition to treating the eating disorder, patients will need treatment for any other psychiatric disorders they may have. That may include problems with anxiety, depression, bipolar disorder, substance abuse, and other difficulties.

16 and 35. After fifteen months, 31 percent still had the disorder, and at five years, 15 percent still had the disorder.

Factors that suggest a better outcome for adolescents with bulimia include beginning treatment with a shorter duration of illness, beginning treatment at a younger age, and being in a higher social class. Indicators of a poor outcome include a history of drug and alcohol abuse; having a personality disorder, particularly borderline personality disorder; and having low motivation to make changes in the eating disorder symptoms. In addition, obesity prior to the onset of the symptoms suggests a poorer prognosis. [12,13]

• Everyone with an eating disorder needs an outpatient treatment team, including an individual therapist, a nutritionist, primary care doctor, and family therapist for the whole family. The nutritionist will usually develop a recommended meal plan and provide nutritional advice to the person with the eating disorder, as well as to the family. The primary care doctor will monitor for medically concerning conditions arising from the eating disorder. Either the nutritionist or primary care doctor should monitor and chart the patient's height and weight to monitor treatment progress, with specific goals in mind. (Note that it is not unusual for adolescents with eating disorders to experience stunted growth. On rare occasions, they will experience osteoporosis and actually lose height.) Often the patient will not be told the specific weight goal, since that number carries such strong meanings. Instead, they are usually just told whether they are making progress, losing ground, or staying the same. If psychiatric medications are prescribed, then a psychiatrist is usually added to the outpatient team.

• Family therapy is an important component of care for patients up to the age of eighteen, or occasionally through young adulthood. The goal of family therapy is not to point the finger at something the family did to cause the eating disorder. Rather, the focus should be to change family dynamics that make the disorder difficult to treat. For example, not eating together as a family may not have caused someone to have an eating disorder, but eating together as a family may make the disorder easier to treat.

Choose the Right Treatment Setting

Treatment levels for people with eating disorders vary, from inpatient hospitalization to family-based care.

The highest level of care is inpatient medical treatment. This level is appropriate for someone who is medically unstable, with heart, blood pressure, electrolyte, or other irregularities, and needs to be admitted to a medical hospital. At a slightly lower level of care is an inpatient psychiatric unit, which may be appropriate if the patient has a separate psychiatric problem that would require hospitalization on a locked unit, such as suicidal thoughts or manic or psychotic symptoms.

Treatment at a residential facility can take place when someone does not need to be supervised on a locked unit, but still needs twenty-four-hour care. These patients may include teens who need supervision or have severe family conflict.

Partial hospital and day programs typically provide treatment from 9 a.m. through 3 p.m., and evening programs can be helpful for teens and young adults who attend school or work during the day. These work best for people who need more support than just outpatient care, but do not need twenty-four-hour treatment.

A specific family therapy method that is helpful for some adolescents with eating disorders is called the Maudsley approach.[15] This therapy empowers parents to use their skills and creativity to find ways to feed their child the food that he or she needs to return to good health. However, once back to a healthy weight, the teen again resumes the responsibility for his or her own nutrition. While this structure can be helpful for some people with eating disorders, others do not respond well to the loss of control, which may result in further family conflict.

CASE STUDY

Steve

FIFTEEN-YEAR-OLD STEVE started to skip meals after he heard kids at school say he was "ugly." Though he was an average weight for his height, Steve thought he would look better if he were thinner, like celebrities in the magazines.

Steve's family did not notice he was skipping meals, since they usually did not eat together. His mother was a heart surgeon who worked long hours, including weekends on call. Steve's father worked as an investment banker, and he was lucky to be home in time for the evening news.

Steve was often left to fend for himself at breakfast and dinner. On his way out to school in the morning, he would place a small amount of cereal and milk in a bowl and set it in the sink so it looked like he was eating. His parents generally worked late, and they never questioned him when he told them he had already eaten by the time they returned home.

At Steve's next checkup, his pediatrician noticed the weight loss and suspected the onset of an eating disorder. When the pediatrician asked his parents what Steve was eating, they realized that they did not really ever see him eat.

DISCUSSION

When eating disorders are caught early, sometimes small changes can disrupt the downward spiral of symptoms. Steve and his parents met with a nutritionist and a family therapist to help him get back on track with eating. His mother started to eat breakfast with him each morning, and his father came home from work early to eat dinner with him. If Steve was not following his meal plan, which was set by his nutritionist, his parents put limits on his television and computer time. They also had Steve eat lunch with a teacher at school for the first two months of treatment, until he was eating more consistently.

The structure and supervision at meals were helpful in treating the eating disorder. Through therapy, Steve's parents realized their lives had been so chaotic that they were not spending quality time with their son. The eating disorder, in the long run, helped Steve's parents to better prioritize work and family time. Both parents started to come home in time for dinner, and they even made time some evenings to play board games or talk as a family. Steve's parents limited his computer time and access, and the family worked to find alternative, more highly interpersonal, forms of activity that their son might enjoy.

In addition to family therapy, support groups for both patients and parents can be helpful. Often these groups provide education about eating disorders, as well as support and guidance for people getting started in treatment or trying to maintain their recovery. Local or national eating disorder organizations can provide similar assistance (see the resource section on page 278).

Close communication between the professionals involved, especially with a younger teen, is essential, and communication with the parents of younger patients should always be part of this process. The team needs to agree on concrete parameters for treatment and plan for a potential transition to more intensive treatment. This may include factors such as weight, binge and purge frequency, exercise limits, or other criteria. For example, if Steve's weight falls below 123 pounds, or if he starts running seven or more miles a day, he will be admitted to an inpatient eating disorders treatment facility.

CASE STUDY

Hilary

HILARY FIRST STARTED DIETING at age twelve. She attended a small school and said kids often teased her because her family was known to be wealthy. Shortly before her thirteenth birthday, Hilary lost a modest amount of weight. Then, her father passed away after a brief battle with brain cancer. In the aftermath, Hilary lost thirty pounds in two months, while severely restricting what she was consuming. She said she felt happy only when she looked at the scale each day and saw how much she lost.

A few months later, Hilary began binging and purging on a nightly basis. A binge would consist of a whole pizza, a box of macaroni and cheese, chips, cookies, and whatever else was in the kitchen. During the day, she would starve herself, curbing her urges to binge eat, as evening approached. She would purge by vomiting and taking laxatives, sometimes consuming an entire box of Ex-Lax at a time. In addition to these eating habits, Hilary ran eight miles and did 500 abdominal crunches per day.

Hilary also reported having a sad mood and trouble with her sleep, low energy, poor concentration, and guilty thoughts about her eating disorder behaviors; she was suffering from depression.

By age fifteen, Hilary had been hospitalized twice due to the consequences of drastic weight loss and repetitive purging. She spent two months in a day treatment program for eating disorders after the second hospitalization. However, Hilary was not compliant with the meals in the program, and she would return home in the evening and continue the restrict-binge-purge cycle. Hilary was prescribed an antidepressant in an attempt to regulate her mood difficulties, sleep issues, energy, and motivation. Though her mood improved, her eating disorder continued.

DISCUSSION

Hilary's enduring behavior around eating suggested that she needed a more intensive level of care. She was admitted to an inpatient eating disorders treatment program, where personnel could supervise her bathroom use and would make sure Hilary completed her full prescribed meal. If Hilary refused to finish a meal, she was given a liquid nutritional supplement by tube feeding. The tube feeding had to happen only once before Hilary decided she would follow the meal plan.

With a few weeks of structured eating, weight restoration, and supervision to prevent purging, Hilary started to make small steps toward taking more responsibility for her eating disorder. She would take passes with her family for meals and was eventually able to transition back to the day program, where she made better use of the treatment this time. Hilary vowed never to return to the inpatient unit and knew she had to make progress with her eating disorder. With Hilary's mood in a better place, she was able to follow through on her plans for recovery.

The Role of Medication in Treatment

For the treatment of anorexia, restoring someone to a healthy weight is the most important treatment. There is no approved medication treatment for low-weight anorexics. For someone who is underweight, food equals medicine.

Weight gain is usually slower with less intensive treatments. In outpatient care, one tries to obtain a weight gain of about one pound per week. In partial hospital treatment, the goal is usually two pounds per week, and a gain of three to four pounds per week can be obtained in residential or inpatient treatment.

MEDICATION FOR ANOREXIA NERVOSA

The use of medications can sometimes be helpful in the treatment of anorexia nervosa. Once someone has attained a healthy weight, fluoxetine (Prozac) may help to prevent a relapse of symptoms. Medications that target other symptoms, such as anxiety or depression, can decrease overwhelming emotional swings and decrease the likelihood of returning to eating disorder behaviors to cope.

There is also some research to suggest that zinc gluconate (Cold-Eeze) or cyproheptadine (Periactin) may be helpful for the treatment of anorexia. However, the studies that support these recommendations are generally weak.

There are anecdotal reports (single case reports, case series of a number of patients) of other medications being helpful for anorexia. Most of these medications fall under the categories that are used to treat anxiety, depression, bipolar disorder, and psychosis. The anti-psychotic medications are of particular interest, since they may potentially treat the distorted thinking underlying the eating disorder. Unfortunately, however, many of the antipsychotic medications have weight gain as a common side effect. While this might sound like a benefit for people with anorexia, it may make them less likely to take the medication.

MEDICATION FOR BULIMIA NERVOSA

From a medication standpoint, fluoxetine (Prozac) showed an improvement in symptoms of bulimia and also improved the remission rate. The U.S. Food and Drug Administration (FDA) has currently approved fluoxetine for the treatment of bulimia.

But the medication might not be necessary at all. For bulimia, there is little outcome difference between fluoxetine and cognitive behavioral therapy (CBT), and no difference between a combination of fluoxetine and CBT, versus CBT alone. In the treatment of bulimia, cognitive behavioral therapy (CBT) has proven to be effective in reducing symptoms, such as binging and purging, and to improve remission rates.[16] Additionally, it can improve attitudes toward weight and body shape.

In research studies, desipramine (Norpramin) and imipramine (Tofranil) improved symptoms of bulimia and produced better remission rates.

Also important to know is that the antidepressant medication buproprion (Wellbutrin) is not recommended for people with bulimia. This medication causes an increase in seizures for people with bulimia.

Medications that may be helpful for the symptom of binge eating include sertraline (Zoloft), fluvoxamine (Luvox), fluoxetine (Prozac), topiramate (Topamax), and sibtramine (Meridia). These may be used to treat both bulimia and binge eating disorder.

HOW AND WHERE TO GET HELP FOR YOUR CHILD

What do you do if you suspect your child has an eating disorder? The first step is to talk with him or her about your concerns. It is sometimes helpful to make notes to remind yourself of important points or to help organize your thoughts in this emotional discussion. It is essential to trust your own observations and suspicions and not to be dissuaded by the adolescent's denial or angry refrain to "Mind your own business . . . I am just fine."

Remember that individuals with eating disorders, especially adolescents, try to hide their illness and maintain control over their eating and weight. They are often unable to even recognize the illness themselves; thus, they may not be intending to be deceptive but have developed a degree of cognitive distortion that leaves them feeling fat and leads them to believe that their maladaptive eating behaviors are normal. In their minds, they are merely compensating for "real" weight issues, not acting unusually and certainly not doing anything that their parents should get involved in.

CASE STUDY

Ashley

ASHLEY'S MOTHER SUSPECTED her daughter had an eating disorder. After speaking with her husband, they decided to broach their concerns with fourteen-year-old Ashley. Together, they prepared the following discussion: "Ashley, your father and I love you and always want the best for you. We are concerned about some things we have noticed about your behavior lately. Oftentimes, large amounts of food disappear from the kitchen and we don't know where it goes. Sometimes we find food wrappers in the garbage in the garage, but other times we find multiple empty food containers in your room. In the last few months, it seems like you eat dinner quickly and then get up to go to the bathroom directly from the table. Last week, Dad found you in the kitchen at 3 a.m. finishing off a new box of cookies, and last night I heard you throwing up in the bathroom. We are worried that you might have an eating disorder."

When confronted by her parents, Ashley screamed and became tearful. She denied any problems with eating and said she was hurt that her parents would accuse her of something so gross.

DISCUSSION

Because of their strong suspicions, and some evidence, Ashley's parents took her to her pediatrician. The doctor did a complete physical exam and had lab work performed. They found a low heart rate, as well as laboratory abnormalities suggestive of purging (elevated amylase, elevated bicarbonate, and low potassium).

When Ashley was confronted with this information, she admitted that she was struggling with binge eating and purging. The eating disorder started six months prior, after Ashley read online that throwing up after meals was a good way to lose weight. After the vomiting started, she felt empty and unsatisfied, which led to binge eating to feel "full." After a few weeks, Ashley felt like the binging and purging were out of control. She did not ask for help or admit to the eating disorder because she was embarrassed and ashamed.

Steps to Getting Help

If you suspect your child has an eating disorder, the first step is a visit to his or her primary care doctor. The physician will check your child's height and weight and make comparisons to past measurements on a standardized growth chart.

If this doctor has followed your child for a long time, he or she will know quickly by the growth chart whether there is cause for concern.

If not, he or she will compare your child's height and weight to age-matched healthy standards, check vital signs, and perform basic laboratory studies.

Eating disorders treatment is highly specialized, so look for outpatient providers with expertise in these disorders. Though it is most important to find an individual therapist with this experience, it can be just as crucial for the other members of your child's treatment team to have similar experience. A complete treatment team consists of a primary care doctor, a nutritionist, an individual therapist, a family therapist, and, if medications are needed, a psychiatrist.

Certain areas of the country have clinics that specialize in eating disorders. They often have complete treatment teams under one roof, which facilitates communication between team members. Eating disorders often involve secrecy, so it is important to have team members on the same page with regard to treatment progress. If the primary care doctor notices weight loss and suspects purging, this needs to be addressed in both family and individual therapy. Also, the nutritionist would need to be in the communication loop. He or she would have the child follow a meal plan during the day to reduce urges to binge and purge in the evening.

The Internet can be a source of both excellent and terrible information on medical and mental health problems. Eating disorders are a perfect example of this. Some of the more helpful websites for this information include those of the National Institute of Mental Health and Medline Plus, as well as others that appear in the resource section of this book (see page 278).

CONCLUSION

Eating disorders are becoming more common, especially among adolescents, in developed and some developing countries. Recognition of symptoms early on is important, since treatment outcomes are improved when the duration of the illness is shorter. Do not be afraid to talk with your child about your concerns regarding his or her eating.

If you suspect your child has an eating disorder, make an appointment with his or her primary care doctor for a checkup to discuss your concerns. If you do not feel your child's doctor is tuned in to a real problem, do not hesitate to consult a specialist in eating disorders.

The minute your child is diagnosed with an eating disorder, aggressively pursue treatment with a complete treatment team. Again, this includes a primary care doctor, a nutritionist, an individual therapist, and a family therapist. If medications might be helpful, your child will also need a psychiatrist.

Most important, try to maintain a healthy relationship toward food and body image in your family. Eat meals together as a family and spend quality time with your children each day. That enjoyable quality time today may prevent years of treatment in the future.

Additionally, while you cannot obliterate the culture that now surrounds developing teens, try to influence their exposure to material that encourages weight loss by commenting on and correcting societal stereotypes about weight that have the potential to lead to problems. A parent can set the tone for what is important, and an overemphasis on looks and thinness can lead to later difficulties. This family involvement extends to monitoring participation in activities as well as exposure. Thus for the teen who is wrestling or doing ballet, for example, do not allow unsafe weight loss to occur in the name of performance enhancement.

Although eating disorders cannot be completely avoided in today's society, they need to be identified and responded to when they occur, and prevention should be practiced as much as possible.

CHAPTER 7

Teens and Delinquency

Ben Molbert, M.D.

Conduct problems among adolescents are often highly variable, difficult to understand and, at times, seemingly purposeless. The inner world of a teen is a complex and ever changing environment that entails immeasurable challenge. The outer appearance of teens and the manner in which they choose to present themselves to the world, including their volitional behaviors, project volumes of information about them to all they encounter. Attempting to understand the full context of teens can lead to understanding their reasons for choosing either adaptive or maladaptive behaviors. Identifying their drives and ambitions in carrying out these behaviors can help parents and other involved parties assist them in making better choices and, ultimately, in maturing in a more desirable way.

The typical conduct problems of adolescence often are magnified in the world of teens battling learning problems, mental illness, substance abuse, and various cultural, environmental, family, and interpersonal difficulties. These youths often become trapped in the juvenile justice system. While this system is in place to provide services and divert teens from developing more criminal behaviors and characteristics, it can be an imperfect system full of intimidation and stress for teens and their families. Susceptible teens may appear to never have a fighting

chance in what can be perceived as an uphill battle to live a "normal"
teenage existence. This chapter will focus on developing an under-
standing of conduct problems and delinquency and how parents and
other responsible adults can help to shape the immediate and near
future of teenagers who face these demands.

PARENTS FACE MANY different forms of difficult behavior from their developing teens. Most of these are a part of normal adolescence and often
will pass over time and as teens gain mastery of managing their immediate environment.

Often teens will not want to be guided through difficult situations
by their parents or other adults, instead preferring to work through the
challenges of adolescence in their own way. Teens can sometimes view
adults who offer too much advice or solutions to their problem as trivial-
izing their struggles. When teens find a way to work through a complex
situation and are fortunate enough to find a satisfying conclusion, it can
be highly rewarding. They may carry not only their own satisfaction, but
may often receive kudos from their family or teachers and the respect of
their peers. In fact, this is the brilliance of developing into a successful
young adult.

Unfortunately, many adolescents are faced with impediments to
having such successes. Most kids truly want to comply with the rules and
limits of their families and communities. They derive a sense of satisfaction when they act in accordance with expected norms. Those teens who
aren't able to meet these expectations may view themselves as "losers"
and begin to devalue themselves. Repeated disappointments can damage an adolescent's self-esteem and lead to negative consequences in
his or her environment and behavioral response. In the absence of close
parental supervision and/or accessible school and community supports,
these failures can often accrue and cause a teen to feel a sense of inef-
fectiveness and hopelessness. A teen may begin to feel he or she can be
proficient only in carrying out negative behaviors. If severe enough, these
behaviors could meet the criteria for a clinical condition that mental
health providers refer to as conduct disorder. At worst, this behavior
could result in intervention of the juvenile court.

CONDUCT DISORDER DEFINED

Conduct disorder is a complicated group of behavioral and emotional problems. People with this disorder have difficulty following rules and behaving in a socially acceptable way. They are commonly viewed as having repetitive and persistent patterns of violating the basic rights of others. Despite effort, or in the absence of effort, they often are unable to conform to major, age-appropriate societal norms. Here are some characteristic behaviors of conduct disorder.

- Frequently being truant from school
- Staying out at night
- Running away from home
- Deceitfulness
- Theft
- Fire setting
- Destroying property
- Sexual promiscuity
- Occasionally, bullying or threatening others, getting into physical fights with or without weapons, or being physically cruel to people or animals

Often these behaviors progress from the home to the community and school. When these behaviors go unchecked, they can often lead to more aggressive and out-of-control actions that may require police and court intervention.

Prevalence rates for conduct disorder range from 1.5 percent to 3.4 percent of children and teens in the United States.[1] However, many of the studies on conduct disorder were done in juvenile justice settings, so they may not be an accurate reflection of all community-based etiology or prevalence.

The onset of conduct disorder can happen anytime from early or middle childhood all the way up into later adolescence. Early onset of the disorder is often associated with a worse prognosis. Behaviors may worsen in severity over time, but this is not always the case, especially if interventions are sought early on. Conduct disorder tends to be more prevalent in youths from lower socioeconomic status, but it occurs in all class settings, schools, and neighborhoods.

Conduct disorder is three to four times more common in boys than girls. Conduct problems may not be as easily detected in girls. Boys tend to engage in more overt forms of misbehavior such as bullying and fighting, while girls often engage in more covert behaviors such as shoplifting and being sexually promiscuous. For roughly half of teens with conduct disorder, it coexists with other forms of mental illness such as mood or anxiety disorders, substance abuse, attention deficit hyperactivity disorder, or learning problems. However, it can also occur as a distinct entity.

FACTORS THAT CONTRIBUTE TO CONDUCT ISSUES

Many factors contribute to the development of conduct disorder. They include the following.

• Biological factors such as genetics and early development can play a part. There is a high genetic correlation for conduct disorder that occurs across genders and tends to cluster in families. Aggression in fathers has been linked with conduct disorder in their sons. There is also a link between mother and daughter antisocial behavior. Biochemical markers believed to be involved with increased aggression include low serotonin levels and increased cortisol levels. Perinatal problems such as low birth weight and injuries occurring during delivery may be associated as well. Neurological problems, including seizure disorders and head injuries occurring from either accidents or abuse, may also be implicated. Early developmental factors include children who have very intense or negative emotional reactions, poor adaptability to change, inflexibility, and resistance to parental discipline.

• Family factors that may lead to recurrent conduct problems include instability in the composition of the family unit, failure of bonding between the parent and child, and the occurrence of family violence. The absence of a parent, mental illness of or substance abuse by parents, the younger age of parents, and conflict between parents can all contribute to development of conduct problems. Early parental rejection, abandonment, neglect, and child abuse all can make significant contributions to deviant behavior. Discordant parenting styles, inadequate limit setting, and lack of parental monitoring or supervision may contribute, as do poor abilities to manage conflict and harsh or inconsistent discipline. Lastly, parents who lack warmth or emotional reciprocity may contribute to the development of more serious conduct problems.

• Cognitive factors include low intelligence, reading problems, and learning disabilities. Few people with conduct disorder have severe retardation, but there are often low-normal or borderline range of IQ scores. Deficits in verbal skills are often present and can account in part for low IQ scores. Language and reading problems may impair teens' abilities to put their thoughts, feelings, and attitudes into words rather than actions. Unrecognized and untreated cognitive dysfunction and learning disabilities can make school a place of frustration rather than gratification and learning. Many behavioral problems by teens can also be accounted for in part by poor judgment, impaired reasoning, and difficulty planning ahead and anticipating consequences. Children with conduct problems tend to quickly and impulsively think of nonverbal, action-oriented solutions to social problems, thus often leading to poor choices.

For many children, teachers are the first adults other than their parents with whom they have extensive contact. School may be their first arena of success or failure. School-based risk factors include low achievement, low aspirations and goals, and lack of commitment to education. Lack of belief in the validity of school rules, peer rejection, social alienation, and association with delinquent peers all can figure into prominent behavioral problems at school.

Disorganized or disruptive school settings may lead to increased conduct problems, as may lack of attachment to the school and teachers, or having parents who have negative attitudes about education. Peer rejection both in the community and at school is also correlated with aggression.

WHEN TO SEEK HELP

Though there is no hallmark sign of when the best time is to seek help for a teen with conduct problems, the best rule of thumb is to seek intervention at the earliest possible opportunity. The first signs of conduct problems may occur early and often they will come out in a sequence of increasing severity with slighter behavioral problems being followed by progressively more severe conduct problems.

The following factors may predict such a progression.

- Early onset
- A greater frequency of disruptive behavior
- A greater variety of types of conduct problems
- A greater range of settings in which they occur
- The presence of mental illness or substance abuse

Sometimes conduct problems resolve on their own; however, the following factors predict the persistence of disruptive behavior.

- Low intelligence
- Severe family dysfunction
- High levels of parental conflict
- Continuing parental neglect or abuse
- Financial disadvantage
- Living in a high-crime neighborhood

While certain factors are not easily remedied, early intervention or treatment may help to reduce the risks.

One of the more frightening situations that can occur for a child and family during a teenager's development is finding one's teenager involved in legal difficulties, police actions, or juvenile court proceedings. While these involvements are certainly not common for most children and teenagers, they can be more prevalent in the lives of those who must also contend with behavioral, educational, and emotional problems. Likewise, people who deal with heavy situational stressors and are in personal crisis may find themselves in circumstances that precipitate legal involvement. Incidents that occur in the community, at home, and at school can all lead to acting-out behaviors and, in some cases, to juvenile court involvement. Navigating the legal system can be both alarming and confusing, and advocating for the best interest of one's child can be a difficult endeavor.

This chapter will describe the conduct problems parents need to be on the alert for and how these behavioral issues can lead, when untreated, to involvement of the juvenile court. It will also seek to provide guidance for teens and families who may find themselves in these circumstances.

LEGAL TERMS OF IMPORTANCE

Certain legal terms will be used in this chapter. Most states define a minor as someone who has not reached the age of legal majority, which is the age when a person can exercise all normal legal rights, including voting. The age of majority in most states is eighteen. This is in contrast to the definition of a juvenile, who is someone who has not reached the age for which a particular state would define him or her as an adult in the criminal justice system. For many states the age at which one is considered to be an adult is younger than eighteen, sometimes as young as fifteen or sixteen.

Many juvenile court proceedings involve status offenses. A status offense is one that juveniles may commit and is considered an offense by virtue of their age and status as juveniles. These offenses often involve juvenile violation of behavioral and academic norms that would not be expected of an adult. Examples might include violating an age-specific curfew in the community, being truant from school, running away from home, or repeatedly refusing to obey the rules of the home or school. These cases frequently come as referrals to the court by parents, school officials, or local law enforcement agencies that attempt to assist a troubled teen in conforming to the lawful expectations of his or her community.

In contrast to a status offense, a delinquent offense is one that a juvenile may commit that would also be considered an adult criminal offense. Examples of these might include assault and battery, breaking and entering, shoplifting, or illegal possession of drugs. Law enforcement agents usually refer these cases to court after a juvenile has been taken into custody under suspicion of engaging in an unlawful act. Many jurisdictions set age parameters on who may be presented to the court as a juvenile offender. For example, in Massachusetts, those between the ages of seven and seventeen may be the subjects of a delinquency petition. Those younger than seven fall under special circumstances and those older than seventeen are handled in the adult court. Many states have youthful offender provisions or mechanisms for direct waiver of an older juvenile into the adult court system. This often involves the court making a decision to handle a juvenile as an adult or transfer his or her case to an adult criminal court based on the severity of the offense or on the seriousness of a prior record.

In contrast to the adult criminal court system, juvenile court proceedings are civil actions and focus more on diversion and early prevention where possible. Juvenile courts are considered non-criminal, although the accused has the same right to counsel and a jury trial as an adult defendant.

Many teens who are involved with the court show a high prevalence of exposure to various types of trauma and other disruptions in psychosocial development. They often experience associated high rates of anxiety disorders, affective disorders (such as untreated depression), substance abuse, learning problems, disruptive behavior disorders, and personality disorders. The court is also apt to look at protective factors that may bode well for the rehabilitation of a teen, such as the ability to relate to others, areas of competence and intelligence, the capacity for high levels of responsibility and self-discipline, a good relationship with at least one parent or other important adult figure, pro-social—as opposed to antisocial—peers, or good work habits. These considerations are part of how the court understands a teen's situation.

The following case studies illustrate how underlying biological predispositions can combine with social factors to create conduct issues. The hope here is to demonstrate how a child's biology can combine with family and other environmental issues to, in certain cases, lead to the development of a conduct disorder by adolescence.

In each case presented, there are factors in the child's history that can and cannot be controlled or altered. For example, intelligence level is a fixed characteristic that combines with temperament and then is further influenced by upbringing. All pertinent issues need to be considered when identifying and then trying to intervene around a behavioral issue, especially when the behaviors appear or worsen during adolescence.

Furthermore, many conduct issues in adolescence end up necessitating the involvement of school administrators, social welfare agencies, the court system, and the use of protective service orders.

Following are several examples of ways in which teens' behaviors may become disruptive and land them in the social service and/or legal arena and how families, the courts, and community agencies may then be able to assist during these difficult times.

Brianna—Developing Conduct Problems

BRIANNA IS A TWELVE-YEAR-OLD who lives at home with her parents and younger brother. She attends seventh grade at a local public high school. She has never been held back or failed, and she is an A–B student. Brianna has had no major behavioral problems at school. There is no family history of mental illness, substance abuse, or medical problems.

In the past year, Brianna's parents noticed that she has been more withdrawn at home. She says little spontaneously to her family and often seems irritated when they ask her questions. Brianna often tells her family to mind their own business and respect her privacy. Her parents describe her as being more moody, and her brother says she is not as nice to him as she used to be. Brianna feels as if they are overreacting and finds her family to be annoying. Her parents are concerned that she is becoming a negative role model for her younger brother.

Brianna has kept up with all of her usual friends, whom her parents feel are good kids. She still enjoys school and is still active in the school drama club. When her parents asked her teachers whether she appeared any different to people at school, they all reported she seemed like "the same old Brianna." This response concerned her parents as they feel she has more of an attitude with them and her younger brother. As Brianna's parents confronted her more on the changes in behavior at home, Brianna became progressively angrier with them. She began to refuse to do household chores and stated her parents should hire a maid if they need help around the house. She started to refuse to come home on time after school, saying she had a right to hang out with her friends and that her parents should just get over it. She also began to refuse going to church with her family, reporting she no longer believed in organized religion and that her parents could not control her beliefs.

DISCUSSION

Behavioral problems that begin in subtle ways at home often do not generalize out into the community or at school. This situation can be frustrating for parents who often assume that the oppositional behavior must be a result of something that they are doing wrong. Many times, behaviors such as those exhibited by Brianna, however, are a normal part of adolescence and a customary part of the teens' quest to separate themselves from their families and establish their own identities.

Some of Brianna's behaviors are provocative and may be designed to elicit negative responses from her parents. It's important to remember that the response that teens receive from their families can alter the course and intensity of their subsequent behaviors.

On the positive side, Brianna maintained some form of a connection with her family and continued to have strong connections at school and with her friends. Her good work habits at school, ability to relate to others, and willingness to maintain ties with her pro-social friends are all indicators of healthy adolescent behavior.

In this type of circumstance, it would serve the teen's parents best to, at least initially, focus on his or her continued success in these arenas rather than on newer and more negative behaviors. There are limits, of course, to what an individual family can handle in terms of disruptive or problematic behaviors in the home. While in this instance, Brianna would not likely require mental health intervention, there are approaches her parents could take to assist her during this time.

Her parents should work on prioritizing those rules of the home that are most important to them and work on a system of setting limits with Brianna. To ensure she follows the most important limits, they may have to make concessions on behaviors that they do not consider as severely problematic. They need to develop a clear system of rules and consequences that can be consistently, fairly, and equitably enforced. Brianna's parents should clearly communicate expectations for behavior and consider a written contract around the most important expectations. Using a consistent system of reinforcement and recognition for meeting expectations may likely help to shape Brianna's future behaviors.

If Brianna did not meet these expectations, then there would need to be enforcement of previously determined consequences. However, parents should avoid imposing sanctions without prior warning. Brianna may better receive disciplinary actions if her parents use progressive discipline, beginning with low-level responses, and carefully choosing the timing of the discipline.

Parents need to remain as calm as possible, even during conflicts. It is a natural tendency for parents to get angry when their child is misbehaving and to want to show them who is boss. These displays of anger often do not work with more oppositional teens and sometimes only reinforce the negative behavior. Parents should pause for a moment and relax before responding to defiant behavior from teens. This allows parents to gain control of their own tempers and consider their next action prior to continuing a confrontation. This behavior often shows the teen that their parents are in control of their own emotions and the situation at large. It also models appropriate anger management in a stressful situation. When parents intervene, they should do so decisively and with steady eye contact, but in a calm and quiet manner.

CASE STUDY

Frank—Mood Problems that Lead to Aggressive Conduct

FRANK IS A FOURTEEN-YEAR-OLD who has spent most of his life being raised by his grandmother in a rural area. He never knew who his father was and his mother passed away of a drug overdose when he was three. Many family members, including his mother, were believed to have had mood problems and drug and alcohol addictions. Frank always had a good relationship with his grandmother and tended to be obedient and thoughtful in his mannerisms around the home. He was very close to his grandfather who had passed away a year ago from a heart attack.

Frank has always been in good health, a good student, and maintained a good group of friends. Shortly after the beginning of his freshman year, however, his grandmother began to notice that his behavior at home was becoming more erratic. For about one week, Frank would sleep only for two or three hours each night, but he looked hyperactive when he would get ready to go to school in the morning. He appeared angry and irritable without a clear reason, and his behavior toward his grandmother became more oppositional. Frank was suspended from school for shouting and cursing loudly at one of his favorite teachers after she had asked him to stop talking to a friend during class.

Upon returning home that afternoon, Frank was highly agitated and yelled at his grandmother. He appeared very tense, talked in a rapid, loud fashion, and was unable to have a rational conversation with his grandmother. At one point, he grabbed a pot from the stove and threw it through the kitchen window.

Out of concern for Frank's condition and safety, his grandmother called the police and reported the incident. Two officers arrived at the home shortly thereafter. Upon seeing the police, Frank ran out the back door and began running through the woods. The officers pursued him on foot and eventually tackled him a hundred yards away from the home. Frank fought with the officers briefly and had to be handcuffed and placed in the back of the police car, where he continued to yell loudly.

The officers returned to the home and questioned Frank's grandmother about the afternoon's events. She described that he had always been a pleasant boy and that something had changed recently. She described the family history of his mother and others having had mood problems and voiced concern that this could somehow be related. The police questioned whether he could have taken any illegal drugs and his grandmother could not say for certain that he had not. The officers debated taking Frank back to the police station, but upon his grandmother's urging, they decided that Frank should be taken to a local emergency room for further evaluation.

While at the emergency room, Frank was found not to be under the influence of drugs or alcohol and was diagnosed as suffering from a manic episode. The decision was made to hospitalize Frank at a local inpatient psychiatric unit for teenagers for further evaluation and treatment. At this time the officers left and no formal charges were filed in connection with the incident at home.

Once in the hospital, it was recognized that Frank was suffering from a mood disorder of the bipolar type and he was placed on a mood stabilizer as well as anti-psychotic medication.

In this particular example, the changes in Frank's behavior and emotional well-being were fairly rapid and pronounced. His grandmother's ability to describe these changes to the police officers helped them understand the context in which his aggressive behaviors occurred.

Officers called to a scene have an obligation to provide for the safety of those involved. Juveniles may be taken into custody, but they do not always have formal charges pressed against them. Given the situation, officers can choose other interventions that may better serve the individual as well as the community. Many teens who have not been previously involved with the law receive warnings in cases that are less dramatic than Frank's. A key factor is the presence and involvement of a parent or other responsible adult who is willing to advocate for the child and ask what steps other than legal action can be employed to help a troubled teen.

It is also important, however, that parents understand that local law enforcement are typically trained in juvenile matters and, as long as no major law violation has occurred, would prefer to see the teen and family get the requisite mental health support.

CASE STUDY

Janet—Underlying Anxiety That Leads to Truancy

JANET IS A TWELVE-YEAR-OLD who lives at home with her parents and two older sisters. They are a close-knit family that places a high priority on education and being active in the local community. There is no family history of mental illness, substance abuse, or medical problems. Janet has always been an A–B student and has had no behavioral problems at school, at home, or in the community.

In the middle of her eighth grade year, Janet began to make multiple visits to the school nurse with complaints of nausea, dizziness, and feeling like her head was pounding. These visits tended to occur in her early morning classes. She described feeling nervous and worried she was having a heart attack or something else was medically wrong with her. On one occasion Janet fainted at school. Her family took her to see her pediatrician, but he couldn't find a medical reason for these episodes. Often Janet would call home and ask for one of her older sisters to come and pick her up from school for the remainder of the day.

As the school year progressed, the visits to the office began to happen on a daily basis. Janet met with a school counselor who communicated to the family that she was probably "faking it" to get out of school. Meetings were held and the process became more adversarial between the school, Janet, and her family. Janet became more anxious about going to school and voiced fear that these attacks would just keep happening. She began to refuse to get out of bed in the morning, telling her parents that between the attacks and the way people at school made her feel, it was unbearable to go. Janet's parents became concerned over her refusal to go to school and made an appointment with a local psychologist. Unfortunately they could not get an appointment for two weeks. Janet's attendance at school continued to be marginal.

Janet's parents received a letter from the local juvenile court indicating that her school had filed a petition for a truancy status offense hearing. Janet and her parents went to the hearing, where school officials were also present. School officials indicated their belief that Janet's family was not being stern enough with her and that if the judge could place her on status probation with a truant officer assigned, it would provide the structure needed to keep Janet in school. Janet's parents described a suspicion that she was developing some form of an emotional or anxiety problem and that they were making efforts to keep her in school and seeking an outside evaluation for her.

The judge considered both arguments and decided to refer Janet for evaluation by one of the psychologists at the juvenile court clinic.

DISCUSSION

After meeting with Janet, her family, and the school counselor, the court clinician gathered further history and obtained a better picture of what had occurred. She diagnosed Janet with panic disorder, a type of anxiety disorder. She indicated in her report to the judge that the recurring situation at school was causing Janet to experience school as an increasingly anxiety-provoking environment, which was leading to more anxiety attacks. She recommended that Janet be referred for an outpatient appointment with a psychiatrist to evaluate for possible medication options to help decrease Janet's anxiety and that Janet keep the previous scheduled appointment to see a therapist in her community.

The judge decided not to order a period of probation, but to reschedule a follow-up hearing in six weeks. At that hearing, school officials reported that Janet's attendance was not perfect but significantly improved. Janet's family said she had been to four appointments with her new therapist and would see a psychiatrist in two weeks for a medication evaluation. The judge decided to dismiss the case from the juvenile court.

This is often the outcome when families and/or school officials file a truancy (sometimes called "stubborn child") petition with the court. These are not criminal complaints, and they do not involve any initial transfer or sharing of custody by the parent with the state, but they can be effective in helping children realize that there will be consequences if their behavior fails to improve. If no behavioral improvement occurs, the judge can then order a period of probation during which the court is there to assist the parents, school, and so on in making sure the child desists from antisocial behaviors and activities and conforms to parental and societal expectations. Often parents are afraid to involve the court system and fear losing control of their parental rights. But unless a child progresses to illegal behaviors or chronically refuses to attend school or follow any rules to maintain their own safety, courts are not interested in taking away parental custody. In fact, these petitions can help families by preventing more dire outcomes, helping the family to receive public assistance in terms of mental health treatment, as well as potentially access publicly funded insurance that covers more intensive psychiatric care.

CASE STUDY

Pam—Social and Family Factors and Promiscuity

PAM IS A FOURTEEN-YEAR-OLD who has been raised by her mother. She does not know her biological father. Pam has a history of educational problems, including difficulties with reading and problems with verbal skills. She was held back once in third grade for not making sufficient academic progress.

Pam's mother struggled with alcohol and cocaine abuse during Pam's early years, and many different boyfriends served as father figures to Pam during her grade school years. At the age of eight, Pam was sexually abused on multiple occasions by one of her mother's boyfriends. Pam did not report this at the time, but it came out years later, when Pam was ten. Pam's mother took her to see a therapist at the time, but Pam was unwilling to discuss the incidents and denied they ever occurred. The therapist advised Pam's mother that Pam was not ready to discuss the possible trauma and recommended she return to treatment at a later time. Pam continued without noticeable problems for the next two years.

When Pam turned twelve, she became more oppositional with her mother at home. She achieved passing grades and exhibited no behavioral problems at school. Her mother attempted to become strict with rules around the home, but this approach seemed to lead only to angrier and more defiant behavior by Pam. Pam's mother tried to get her to attend therapy sessions, but Pam refused. For the next two years, Pam's mother tried various approaches in handling her and attempting to set up reasonable house rules and expectations. These met with little success.

After Pam turned fourteen, her mother learned that kids in the community were talking about Pam having multiple boyfriends and being sexually active with multiple boys. Her mother attempted to discuss this with Pam, but received little cooperation. Attempts to "ground" Pam eventually led to her running away from school in the afternoon and often not coming home until the middle of the night. On many occasions, her mother called the local police and asked them to help in locating her daughter. They often were able to locate Pam in the community and return her to the family home. Officers recommended that Pam's mother go to the local juvenile court and file a petition for a runaway status offense hearing, as this would enable the courts to further assist in the matter.

Pam's mother did finally petition the court for a runaway status offense hearing. At the hearing, Pam was assigned a lawyer to represent her interests. Pam's mother described the mounting problems that they had been experiencing and voiced her concern over not only her daughter's promiscuous behavior, but her own inability to keep her daughter safe while she was out and unsupervised in the community. Pam said little at the hearing.

DISCUSSION

The judge believed Pam was a status offender by virtue of her runaway behavior and placed her on twelve months of probation. She was assigned a probation officer whom she would meet with immediately and then for every month thereafter. Pam and her mother were also instructed that if Pam's runaway behavior continued she might be taken into custody and remanded to juvenile detention for purposes of maintaining her safety. The judge also ordered a mental health evaluation via the juvenile court clinic.

Following a thorough evaluation via a social worker from the juvenile court clinic, it was believed that much of Pam's behavior could be traced to her confusion about her early upbringing and her role in the family. Pam's early abuse and lack of treatment for this may have contributed to a low self-esteem and her developing a style of handling relationships in a fragmented manner. While having multiple relationships made her feel that she was more attractive and valued by guys, it also frequently put her in harm's way and worsened her low self-esteem. Pam resented her mother and blamed her for many of the things that had happened to her in life. These combined feelings led to a conflicted relationship between mother and daughter that only further compounded Pam's difficulty.

The social worker from the juvenile court recommended that Pam begin individual therapy and that she and her mother both attend family therapy sessions as a condition of her probation. The court agreed. Pam followed these recommendations, as she did not want, even for a brief period, to be taken out of her home.

CASE STUDY

Tony—ADHD and Family Problems That Lead to Substance Use

TONY IS A THIRTEEN-YEAR-OLD who was raised mostly by his mother. His father was often absent from the home as he suffered from alcoholism and substance addiction and was frequently incarcerated during Tony's early years. There is an extensive family history of alcohol and substance abuse on both sides of Tony's family. His mother has never had substance abuse problems, but has had a history of post-traumatic stress disorder related to early domestic violence at the hands of Tony's father. Tony's parents divorced when he was nine years old, and the court gave his mother sole legal and physical custody of Tony and his two younger brothers. Tony has had no contact with his father since the divorce.

Tony has a long history of disruptive behavioral problems at home and school. He was diagnosed with attention deficit hyperactivity disorder (ADHD) at age five. For most of Tony's life, he has seen a psychiatrist who treats his ADHD with a stimulant medication, Ritalin, and a therapist whom he sees every other week for supportive therapy. Tony also has a specialized educational plan at school that allows him extra time for test taking and three hours a week of assisted study hall. Tony has never failed or been held back a grade.

Tony is frequently in trouble at school for various oppositional behaviors, but he usually can sit through class without problems. In the past school year, however, he has become truant at least one day every two weeks, has had multiple suspensions for fighting with peers, and is beginning to fail more than half of his classes. School personnel say he has been more hyperactive and impulsive and has had more difficulty following directions in class. They tell his mother that his daily behavior is similar to his behavior on days when he forgets to take his Ritalin.

At home Tony has become increasingly argumentative and isolative. He has been spending more time alone in his room and less time with his mother and two brothers. He is not willing to let his mother come in his room as he used to. At his mother's urging, Tony's therapist has begun seeing Tony once a week. Tony says he feels he is doing fine and that people should just leave him alone. He tells his psychiatrist that his medication must not be working anymore and that he probably needs a higher dosage.

One morning, Tony's mom gets a call from school telling her that Tony had been caught with a small quantity of marijuana while on the school bus. School officials informed her they would not notify the police as he was not on school property at the time, but that they intended to file a habitual school offender status offense petition with the juvenile court given his continued violation of school rules.

Upon Tony's return home, his mother searched his room with him present and found a small amount of marijuana and many of his Ritalin tablets. Tony confesses to her that he has been smoking marijuana daily for most of the past year and that he also uses prescription pain pills and sedatives when he can get them. He has been trading his Ritalin for other drugs with kids at school and drug dealers in the community. His mother, school personnel, and his outpatient treatment team were all unaware of his substance abuse.

On the day of Tony's petition hearing, representatives from the school as well as Tony and his mother were present. Tony was assigned a lawyer to represent his interests. School officials described their concern over Tony's increasing problems in the past year and suggested that probation might provide a level of structure that could assist Tony in complying with the standards of his public school. His mother described similar concerns over the decline in Tony's behavior and her belief that he had a substance abuse problem and needed more help than he was currently getting on an outpatient basis. She also presented the judge with a letter from his therapist asking whether the court could mandate him into some form of substance abuse treatment.

DISCUSSION

A strong association exists between conduct problems and substance abuse.[2] Often the conduct difficulties precede the onset of substance abuse by years. Unfortunately, substance abuse co-occurring with conduct problems may also predict criminality. In this case, Tony's early issues with impulsivity plus a family history of addiction undoubtedly contributed to his adolescent difficulties. In addition to these biological and historical factors, he grew up in a single-parent family, making close supervision more difficult. As behavioral control needed to be reestablished, close monitoring of Tony's drug use as well as awareness and education were the major ingredients for behavioral change. Tony's case was handled through the court system where this type of close monitoring and intervention was best available. These circumstances did not alter Tony's need for ongoing treatment of his ADHD or his mother's need for support and guidance once court involvement ended.

The judge believed Tony was a status offender by virtue of his repeated offenses in the school setting and placed him on twelve months of probation. He assigned Tony to a probation officer with whom he would meet monthly. He also made a condition of his probation random urine toxicology screens. At any time Tony's probation officer requested, Tony would have to go down to the probation office and submit a urine sample. The judge also required Tony to attend a weekly substance abuse class and group therapy for teenagers for three months. In this situation, Tony's mother retained full custody but, if Tony failed to comply, the judge was prepared to place Tony in a juvenile detention facility that included drug treatment.

An alternative outcome in a situation like this, where no criminal complaint has been filed, is to order the state's child welfare agency to become involved by supervising teens in their homes and possibly moving them residentially if delinquency continues in the community.

CASE STUDY

Marshall—Adoption Issues and Conduct Problems

MARSHALL IS A FOURTEEN-YEAR-OLD who was born into the custody of the state social services department. His father was not known and his mother was addicted to cocaine and signed the infant over to state custody at the time of his birth. Little was known about his biological family history. Marshall was raised in a foster home until he was three years old, at which time his current adoptive parents adopted him. He was adopted as an only child and has no known biological brothers or sisters.

Marshall was a happy and content child, but he had noticeable delays in many developmental milestones, including acquisition of language and self-care skills. He participated in early intervention programs and began school at an appropriate age. Marshall was unable to keep up with peers and followed poorly in the classroom. He was eventually diagnosed with mild mental retardation. Marshall was placed on an individualized educational plan and worked well in a smaller classroom. For most of his grade school years, he made continued academic progress. In sixth grade he was able to transition into a half day of regular classes with a half day of specialized instruction.

Marshall's parents considered him to be easygoing and loving, with only occasional behavioral problems at home. He was friendly and had multiple friends at school, at church, and in the neighborhood where he would hang out and play sports. Aside from episodic arguments, he had no real behavioral problems in the community. Marshall's parents always paid close attention to whom he was friends with as they believed Marshall was easily influenced by others and suspected other kids might try to take advantage of him.

When Marshall began high school, he started to speak to his parents about new friends he had made at school. These were teens whom his parents did not know. His parents began to talk to Marshall's other friends, who reported the teens Marshall was referring to were a group of kids from another neighborhood. They described seeing these kids picking on Marshall by encouraging him to misbehave in various ways and then telling him he was cool for doing so. Marshall seemed to enjoy the attention. Despite both his parents and his former group of friends telling him they thought these kids were bad news, Marshall insisted on continuing to hang out with them.

One day Marshall's dad received a call at work to come and pick Marshall up at school as he had been suspended. The principal said Marshall had run through the freshman quad during class and busted out three hallway windows with an aluminum baseball bat. Marshall insisted he had done this at the urging of his friends and that it had not been his idea. Despite this, the school suspended Marshall for three days, his family was asked to pay for the damages, the police were called, and a report for destruction of property was filed.

Marshall was released to the custody of his parents, who brought him home that afternoon. Later that day, the charge was presented to the prosecutor's office and the prosecutor decided to file a delinquency petition with the juvenile court. The initial hearing happened the following week and all parties involved were present. Marshall was appointed an attorney to represent his interests.

DISCUSSION

Marshall is an example of a youngster for whom low cognitive functioning and a history of family-of-origin drug use plus a relatively late adoption all combined to lead to his behavioral difficulty as an adolescent. Teens such as Marshall are often able to form early, pro-social attachments to adult figures such as parents, teachers, or mentors in the community. In the absence of having moral and behavioral models provided to them, they are often willing to turn toward more negative peers as their role models.

While these teens may get into more trouble with these peers, they also find a sense of peer identity that they may not have been able to otherwise establish. Also, more antisocial peers may prey upon youths such as Marshall. They are often able to find others with lower cognitive abilities or learning disabilities and exploit their cognitive deficits. They may use them to carry or hold drugs or weapons or do their bidding in other criminal ways. While this behavior is clearly predatory and takes advantage of another's disability, it is a fairly common occurrence among more street-hardened teens and adults. The court's initial inclination toward issuing a delinquency petition and requesting probation in this case represents an effort to provide monitoring for Marshall and assist him and his family in securing him from the more negative peers at his school.

After hearing the facts of the case, however, the judge decided not to find Marshall delinquent (because the juvenile court is not a criminal court, no one is ever found "guilty"; rather, they are found delinquent or not delinquent) nor did he assign him to probation. He believed Marshall's behavior was likely influenced or manipulated by others who wished to have harm befall him.

The judge did not dismiss the case, however, given the severity of the action involved. It was decided that the case would be continued without a finding. Marshall and his family were informed that the judge would set a follow-up court date in nine months. If Marshall were to be presented to the court for any reason during this nine-month period, the judge would set a new date for the destruction of property charge and likely find Marshall delinquent at that time. If Marshall did not appear in front of the court for the next nine months, the charge would be dismissed at that time.

Roger—Early Onset Chronic, Unexplained Conduct Problems

ROGER IS A SIXTEEN-YEAR-OLD who lives with his mother and is an only child. His father died of lung cancer when he was three years old. There are multiple family members in the area to whom Roger is close. Roger was never a very good student. He had evaluations for learning disabilities and was found to have none. He was failed in third grade and later in ninth grade. When Roger turned sixteen, he dropped out of school and began looking for a GED program in which to enroll.

Roger frequently had behavioral problems in the community and at home. He had been caught shoplifting at an early age, tended to hang out and run the streets in the afternoon, frequently got into fights, and often broke curfew. His mother took him to see therapists on multiple occasions, but he would rarely agree to go to appointments more than once. When he did go he often would not talk. Roger had received various diagnoses through the years, such as major depression, conduct disorder, and adjustment disorder. He never remained in treatment long enough for any of the interventions to make a real difference.

Roger began smoking marijuana and drinking alcohol when he was twelve. Eventually, he smoked marijuana two to three times daily and often drank excessively on the weekend. Roger began using cocaine on the weekends when he was fourteen. Despite Roger's mother's effort to get him to stop using and her efforts to encourage him to attend Alcoholics Anonymous, he refused.

When Roger was fifteen, he was taken into custody along with three friends, all of whom were found to have had marijuana in their possession. Two of his friends were eighteen and their cases were handled in the adult criminal system. As Roger was a juvenile, his case was referred to juvenile court. The prosecutor decided to handle the case informally and did not file a delinquency petition. He decided instead to make a referral to have Roger attend an outpatient drug treatment program in his community. Roger was to attend substance abuse classes daily for ninety days and would meet with a substance abuse counselor weekly.

He would also have urine drug screens done at random times while in the program. Roger complied with the program and successfully completed it at the end of ninety days.

Roger managed to remain clean and sober for most of the next nine months and enrolled in a GED course in his community, which he attended regularly. He had a part-time job at a convenience store during the day. He had been more compliant with his mother's requests at home and things seemed to be improving. However, one afternoon he was arrested with another friend for selling marijuana outside of the convenience store where he worked. Roger was taken into custody and later that day released to his mother's home.

Roger was again referred to the juvenile court and the prosecutor decided to file a petition that alleged Roger was a recurrent offender and should be found delinquent. Roger was represented by a lawyer at his hearing who argued that Roger did not need to be involved in the juvenile court system, but rather needed another chance at outpatient substance abuse treatment.

DISCUSSION

Roger is illustrative of kids we see who have longstanding patterns of antisocial and disobedient behaviors since early childhood without clear, coexisting ADHD, anxiety, or mood issues. Childhood-onset respondents are more likely than adolescence-onset respondents to meet conduct disorder criteria involving aggression against persons, animals, and property before age fifteen, and to endorse more childhood criteria and lifetime violent behaviors.[3] Roger suffered the loss of a parent at a young age and had difficulties in school early on, but these factors alone do not account for all of his later conduct problems. What is the story with youths like Roger who just don't seem to be able to stay out of trouble?

For reasons that are not yet fully understood, some children show low motivation, an inability to respond to environmental expectations for positive social behavior, and a tendency to continually break the rules. These kids are often restless and moody and may not respond to traditional therapy or medication. These are the kids who end up with the label of "antisocial" in childhood and, by adolescence, may have fully developed conduct disorders that may not respond to any efforts except court intervention that provides high structure, clear punishments, and very close supervision.

Adolescents like this often benefit from mentoring programs and alternative school settings that allow for vocational training and the attainment of self-sufficiency. Kids like Roger can be extremely difficult for their families in that, in spite of caring adults and many second chances, they seem destined to end up in the legal system.

In this case, the judge found Roger delinquent on the charges of marijuana possession and distribution and scheduled a disposition hearing. At this hearing, Roger's attorney argued that Roger should be able to live in the community without further legal problems if he was on juvenile probation with court-ordered substance abuse treatment. The judge agreed and decided against commitment to a juvenile detention center. Roger was placed on twelve-month delinquency probation with instructions to check in with his probation officer twice a week. Roger was also ordered to submit a urine toxicology screen twice a month. He was ordered to return to the treatment programs that he had previously attended. He was also ordered to do thirty hours of community service at a location to be determined at a later date. Should Roger fail to meet any of these conditions, he would be presented again to the court to face the possibility of juvenile detention.

CONCLUSIONS

As has been discussed in the prior examples, conduct issues in teens can vary greatly and can often be explained or understood better by developing a greater understanding of the context in which the behaviors occur. The biological underpinnings of mental illness cannot be "cured," but careful diagnosis, monitoring, and treatment of them can lead to a significant decline in associated behavioral problems. Likewise, many environmental, family-based, academic, and social difficulties may grow into minor or severe conduct problems in adolescence. Increases in adult supervision, structuring of the teen's day, after-school programs, work or vocational programs, community- or school-related clubs, organizations, and athletics can all provide useful outlets to help broaden a troubled teen's chances of success.

In the best-case scenario, a developing teen falling into the trap of progressive conduct problems can find assistance in such measures and avoid requiring court involvement. Unfortunately, despite the sincere efforts of both the adults involved in a teen's life and the teen, juvenile court involvement is often necessary.

School personnel, local police, and, where necessary, juvenile court officials focus on the best interests of the child and also on the general protection of society. While this will at times require some intrusion into the academic or family setting, the goal is to assist with the proper development of the adolescent and limit behaviors that may be dangerous to the individual and the community.[4,5]

The juvenile court focuses on providing the least restrictive environment for aiding in the child's growth. This could also be looked at as choosing a course of action that will most assist a teen while also not being overly invasive of the child's or the family's lives. Even when there is only a status offense, courts will try to enlist the aid of school personnel, mental health professionals, probation officers and, where, necessary, state child welfare agencies to try to stop the conduct from escalating into the realm of true legal offenses.

While court involvement can be a complex and anxiety-provoking situation, the best way to ensure that the needs of a child will be met in an effective way is to be an advocate and active participant in the process. Teens who advocate for themselves, families that advocate for their children, schools that encourage their students, and community agencies that support the individual can all be powerful forces.

The juvenile court often first meets a child in the context of having allegedly been involved in aberrant behaviors. Often the court's initial understanding of the child is based only on his or her involvement in that specific context. The active participation of those mentioned above can help define the teen as an individual to the court. It may also help to provide a better understanding of the situation in which a teen may have been referred to the juvenile court, and what the most therapeutic course of action may be.

CHAPTER 8

Technology and Your Teen

Blaise Aguirre, M.D.

"Any person who breaks or destroys machinery in any mill used in the preparing or spinning of wool or cotton or other material for the use of the stocking or lace manufacture, on being lawfully convicted . . . shall suffer death."

———

THIS WAS AN OFFICIAL announcement made in 1812 in response to the Luddites, workers in England who were so upset by the reduction in their wages because of the introduction of new technologies ushered in by the Industrial Revolution that they broke into factories to destroy the machines.

Throughout history, new technologies have threatened some of the population some of the time. Our time is no different, except for the rapidity of technological change. Unlike the Luddites, our response doesn't have to be so fear-based or extreme.

Yet these new technologies potentially threaten our children and teens: Online bullying occurs through rapid dissemination of information, sexual predators lie in wait for our adolescents, video game addictions threaten to destroy families, dangerous information is accessible at the stroke of a few keys, friendships are created without context, and peer groups are formed instantaneously. These are all real and substantial threats to our youth. Easy access to illegal substances and sexual predators lying in wait are also not just personally harmful but illegal as well.

As technology advances, so does the legal response addressing these issues. It is challenging for teens not to accidentally step over the legal and ethical lines of behavior regarding technology, given their impulsivity and emotionality.

Hazing over the Internet, for example, is now a felony in many states. Many of the innumerable teens who cross my threshold at McLean Hospital in Belmont, Massachusetts, are involved in such bullying. They often face suspension hearings for unintended plagiarism and writings or pictures posted in a moment of presumed privacy without a thought to the reality of public domain. Some of them find themselves on the adolescent residential unit at McLean where I am on staff.

THE TRAP OF TECHNOLOGY

As parents, we need to educate ourselves and spend more time with our kids even as they immerse themselves in a digital world they have come to know and yet is often alien to most of us. A walk in the park, a game of cards, a family dinner, and a vacation at the beach away from gadgets allow for a dialogue that is becoming increasingly a thing of the past. Yet without this dialogue, this pause, we are doomed to become more lost and confused. Without the education and established right to communicate and regulate our teens' technology, we relegate ourselves to being unhip and uncool and miss the clues of when their cyberspace activities cross the line from being helpful to being destructive.

What I have done in the following case histories is to take the histories of different adolescents seen at McLean Hospital in Belmont, Massachusetts, and blend them so as to create fictional adolescents. Each epitomizes the type of troubled teen we see seeking treatment on a daily basis.

Do keep in mind, however, that there are many more potential ways of getting into trouble using technology that are not listed and are limited only by the imaginations of our children.

Rachel: Online Sexual Predators

RACHEL WAS AN ATTRACTIVE thirteen-year-old girl who looked older than her age and was referred to our program for treatment by her parents for having sex with a twenty-three-year-old man. She was clearly annoyed at having to see a psychiatrist and said that she did not think it was a problem that she had had sex with him. I asked her how she had met him, and she told me that she had posted a very seductive picture of herself on the website MySpace.com and that the man had communicated with her over some months. They had shared a lot of intimate details and she had told him that she was eighteen and living with very conservative parents. She further offered that she couldn't talk to boys her own age and that other girls didn't like her, so that sometimes she felt lonely.

After a few months, they started to communicate by cell phone and through text messaging. At his suggestion, she had substituted the man's name with the name of a classmate into her list of contacts, just in case her parents wondered who was calling. In fact the patient's mother frequently saw calls coming in for Rachel but simply thought that it was her classmate.

One night Rachel agreed to meet the man for sex. He met her at a friend's house and brought her alcohol, which was the first time she had ever drunk alcohol. After this, they began meeting regularly. Finally she asked that he come around to her house as she had been grounded for truancy. Her parents said that that night they heard her leave her room at around two in the morning and were suspicious a few minutes later when she hadn't returned. They went outside and found her having sex with the man and called the police after a confrontation. The man turned out to be from a town thirty miles away, and he was subsequently arrested for having sex with a minor and providing alcohol to a minor. The girl was very upset at the loss of her friend and threatened to kill herself, at which point she was referred to our clinic.

Rachel appeared with no clinical signs or symptoms of a major psychiatric disorder and yet her behavior had put her at significant risk. She had engaged in unprotected sex with an unknown older male who had provided her with alcohol. The ease with which the dialogue took place online made it very simple to exhibit herself, attract an interested male, and connect with him. This, together with her disguising him from her parents by changing his name on her cell phone, made it easy for her to evade their curiosity. This is not to say that she was not complicit in the whole affair, but that it was made all the easier and alluring by the Internet and wireless technology. Thus, in this example, a young girl's loneliness, impulsivity, and lack of judgment were aided and abetted by technology.

With technology's increased popularity, though, it has also become the subject of lawsuits. Social websites like MySpace.com have been the targets of sexual assault–related lawsuits. For example, a fourteen-year-old girl from Texas filed a $30 million lawsuit in 2006 against MySpace.com, saying she had met a man who assaulted her when she was thirteen. The nineteen-year-old man did not deny having sexual contact with the girl, but he subsequently sued the website, claiming he, too, was a victim because the girl falsely portrayed herself as older than she really was. Even if this instance is primarily the case of one young man being duped, sexual predators are definitely out there, hunting for and grooming their next victims in cyberspace.

ADVICE FOR PARENTS

Parents often feel that their adolescents don't need the same restrictions regarding technology as those employed for their younger kids. However, teenagers are *more* likely to get into trouble online than younger children. Teens are more likely to seek out not only different websites but different relationships. This behavior is in part developmentally normal as they begin to explore the world beyond their confines, and as they believe in their own omnipotence. They are more likely to reach out to others besides their peers, setting themselves up as targets for sexual predators. We have treated adolescents who readily provided personal information online and then arranged sexual encounters through text messaging, instant messaging, or voice mail. In one case an adolescent male arranged for an underage female to have unprotected sex with multiple unknown males.

Predators work hard at grooming adolescent victims to first gain their confidence and trust before eventually arranging a face-to-face meeting. We worked with one young woman who withdrew her savings to leave her state so she could go to Florida to meet up with a man she had met online.

One of the things that attract predators to young people is the screen names or handles that the adolescents use in the online chat rooms.

Screen names that are highly suggestive, sexually explicit, or descriptive of body parts often speak to the degree of sexual interest, and sometimes risk, that an adolescent is willing to take. Teenagers often describe the thrill of the attention paid to them by their online "friends" even if they have no idea who those "friends" are.

Studies have shown that up to 20 percent of teenagers have had some sexual solicitations from an unknown person while online.[1] Talking to anyone, and in particular sharing intimate details, frequently draws us closer to another person and that includes people we have never met. This is especially true for adolescents. The old warning of not talking to strangers doesn't seem to work as well on the Internet, as adolescents frequently feel protected by both their perceived anonymity and at times imagined geographical distance. These factors frequently lead adolescents to let down their guard and share intimate thoughts and feelings.

Parents often think of computers as the only way to get online, but today kids are getting online with their cell phones, personal digital assistants, and video game consoles. One young adolescent I know says that she hardly ever uses her cell phone to talk, preferring to use it to send instant messages or text messages. She told me that she had met a man on the bus and would frequently send him text messages. She showed me a picture of the man she had taken with the phone and we spent the rest of the session exploring the potential dangers of her choices and use of technology. Most families neither know of these solicitations, nor where to report them. The resource section at the end of this book (see page 278) contains some essential online resources for parents and adolescents dealing with these situations.

John—Video/Computer Game Addictions

JOHN WAS AN ADOPTED seventeen-year-old who lived with his father and was referred to us because he had stopped going to school and was spending fifteen to seventeen hours each day playing the Sims Online game. He had two other close friends who were similarly spending a lot of time on the game, but now John was refusing to go to school and came out of his room only for meals. His father acknowledged that John was sleeping and eating well and continuing to connect with his school friends by phone, but that his room was beginning to resemble a cave and that John was otherwise completely isolated from his "real" community. When John's father threatened to remove the computer, John became angry, belligerent, and threatening, at which time his father brought him in for an evaluation.

Despite this history, John appeared to be a bright, likeable young man who said that despite the friends he had, he preferred to live in the world he had created where he could control some of the outcomes. He was much happier living in his Internet community. John was African-American and had been adopted as a child by a white father. As he grew up, he recognized that he didn't quite belong in his father's world, but felt guilty about saying anything. A schoolmate had introduced him to this online world, and it had increasingly become more meaningful than his real world. John denied feeling depressed, but admitted to having intense cravings for the computer, feeling socially isolated from real people, lying to his father about the amount of time he spent on the computer, not spending other time playing basketball, which he had previously enjoyed, and being unable to keep a job for fear that the time away from his game could lead to his losing connection with the action in the game. He also wasn't going to school. We admitted him to our substance abuse unit, as addiction to the Internet is similar addictive behavior as drug addiction, and treated him with our substance abuse curriculum. We worked on a plan with his father to have a more integrated life that included some computer time as well as mandatory school attendance. Finally, his father offered to move to a more racially diverse town, which John strongly supported.

DISCUSSION

It's estimated that 6 percent to 10 percent of the nearly 200 million Internet users' dependence on the Internet is so extreme that it leads to the types of problems seen in drug and alcohol addictions. These problems include isolation, withdrawal, and anger and belligerence when a loved one tries to intervene. People with Internet use so severe that it encroaches into their family life, work, and social activities are now being diagnosed as having an Internet addictive disorder. Some skeptics argue that we are pathologizing everything these days, but the loved ones of such patients say that the Internet use has led those "addicted" to experience mood changes, sleep problems, mood disturbances, and loss of relationships.

The diagnosis can additionally include a broader dependency on digital technology, such as spending hours online each day surfing the Web, playing Internet poker or other games like chess or bridge, instant messaging, blogging, and participating in online chat rooms. An additional Internet obsession that carries not only social and behavioral consequences but financial ones as well is viewing Internet pornography. We have now admitted youths who have spent thousands of dollars on their parents' "borrowed" credit cards surfing these sites to support their addictions.

ADVICE FOR PARENTS

On consultation with my colleague Maressa Hecht Orzack, Ph.D., who founded the computer addiction services at McLean Hospital in Belmont, Massachusetts, cognitive behavioral therapy is the treatment of choice for such patients. Others advocate a self-help approach, such as an Internet addicts anonymous group.

Adolescents with gaming addictions have spend so many hours immersing themselves in the game, slaying evildoers in darkened rooms, that they actually incorporate the powers of their heroes into a distorted self-view. Parents complain bitterly that it is destructive to family unity to be jilted for a computer game. Some parents complain that their children are more interpersonally aggressive, especially after playing a video game with violent themes. Studies have shown that playing violent video games for even only twenty minutes per day desensitizes adolescents to real-world violence—meaning that the adolescent feels less emotionally upset when viewing real-life brutality. This desensitization from exposure is insidious and not necessarily intended by video game makers. If only twenty minutes can lead to such desensitization, imagine what the typical exposure of many hours a day will do.

Hardcore gamers complain that theirs is a harmless pursuit, but just ask the parents who try to curtail their activity. Some of the gamers threaten violence or worse if they are disrupted from their games, and parents end up feeling deeply isolated and neglected by their children. I read a report recently that parents and girlfriends of gaming adolescent boys had formed a self-help group like Al-Anon to deal with the emotions triggered by their gamers!

On a positive note, however, video games have been shown to improve spatial abilities and creativity and help in learning various subjects, applying multiple strategies, and developing critical analyzing techniques. As with anything, gaming *in moderation* is key.

What many of the kids who talk about their hours of gaming describe is feeling an emotional high and an adrenaline rush as a result of their success in defeating an adversary or reaching a new level. Some players feel that they have wasted their efforts if they do not reach the next goal in a game. The desire to then play more and reach higher levels or master more complex tasks is rewarded with every success. When the player does this, he or she is once again rewarded with the psychological high. In some ways, it is similar to following your favorite sports team in a game. The rush of excitement is clear when your team scores, but it's limited by the time of play of the game. Addicted gamers have no such time constraints, and when an outside force like a parent tries to prevent further play, problems arise.

In this area as in others, the advice to parents is clear: You need to set time limits and other clear parameters early, before adolescence, about just what types and how much Internet and video gaming you will tolerate in your household. Establish rules about homework first, public placement of computers, and so forth well before teenage rebelliousness sets in.

CASE STUDY

Susanne—The Internet as a Source of Dangerous Material

SUSANNE WAS A BRIGHT eighteen-year-old who had aced school and yet did not feel that she fit in. All her other friends had boyfriends, but she said that they were just interested in "one thing." Susanne felt increasingly isolated and depressed to the point that she wanted to kill herself. Her suicide plan included not wanting to feel any pain and being completely assured of her death. She ruled out anything that might leave her alive, so using a knife or a gun or crashing the car was out. In just half an hour, using Google, she discovered a formula for calculating a lethal dose of Tylenol and instructions for sewing rocks of a certain weight into her clothes—the latter being useful should she decide to drown herself at the lake near her house. She found many other similar resources and took detailed notes for her suicide plan.

Fortunately, Susanne confided in a close friend, who called Susanne's mother, who in turn searched her room and found the notes. At that point, Susanne was referred to us. She was treated for major depression and referred for ongoing individual, group, and family therapy and continues to do well.

DISCUSSION

The reason that I have included this case study is that online resources for how a teen might commit suicide are comprehensive and easy to find. One teen told me that she knew how she could be certain rather than guess whether a drug would be lethal, or whether a fall would kill her. The sites that discuss suicide are not only chat rooms or blogs but also serious, well-frequented sites, which, although I won't name them here, are easy to find.

National statistics for adolescent suicide are striking. About eleven out of 100,000 fifteen- to nineteen-year-olds will commit suicide. Suicide is the fourth leading cause of death among ten- to -fourteen-year-olds and the third leading cause of death for fifteen- to nineteen-year-olds. What is also terribly concerning is that non-lethal suicide attempts are even more common. Statistics show that about 4 percent of children will try to kill themselves in any given year, and about 1 percent of children who try to kill themselves succeed on their first attempt. Among young people aged ten to fourteen years, the rate has doubled in the past two decades.

Parents need to know that the numbers are real and the potential is not just a statistical blip. They also need to be aware of the signs and symptoms of teen suicide, some of which have been covered in chapter 3. The availability of methods and messages on the Internet about this topic has worsened the problem by increasing access and opportunity. The same holds true for acts or plans of violence toward others; the Internet is full of bomb recipes, renditions of school shootings, and a glorification of, and methods for, carrying out acts of mass destruction. Though teens may have considered these ideas in the past, the ready exposure to graphic, suggestive material involving violence and easy methods for obtaining illegal and dangerous materials have never before presented the opportunity that it does for today's youth.

CASE STUDY

Dianna—The Internet as an Instant Peer Group

DIANNA WAS A FOURTEEN-YEAR-OLD from a well-to-do family who seemed to have everything. Nevertheless, she said that she occasionally felt bored and had spent time online looking for kids who were also bored. She met up with a group of kids via a chat room who told her that cutting was an excellent way to relieve boredom (when we reviewed this further she later felt that emptiness more accurately described her feeling of boredom). Dianna started to cut and felt the relief she had been promised. Techniques, methods, and places on the body to cut were openly discussed as well as ways to minimize the chance of infection.

The cutting continued for more than a year before Dianna's mother found a blood-soaked tissue and razorblade in her bathroom. With great ease, Dianna had found a ready-made community of like-minded, enabling, and supportive individuals online.

DISCUSSION

I use MySpace.com as an example of an online community that poses both great promise and potential danger. It is by no means the only one but by far the largest such website at this writing, though it is becoming popular enough with adults that the teens may soon find another, "cooler" space to be. MySpace.com is not evil; millions of kids and adults connect with each other in very healthy ways on it.[2] Similar websites provide valuable support and ways to socialize. Yet I have found groups of young people interested in cutting, anorexia, the abuse of prescription drugs, and many other destructive topics on the site. Some of the discussions aim to help the kids overcome their despair, but others show people the best way to self-destruct.

As in the previous vignette, the issue here is the ease of information acquisition, and the rapidity with which an adolescent can find a group of like-minded kids who all congregate around a psychological symptom such as depression or a behavior such as cutting. Parents should be aware of changes in their teenager that indicate psychological distress. They also need to be vigilant about how much time their teens spend on the computer and whether this behavior is a substitute for real-life relationships with peers.

CASE STUDY
Michael—Obtaining Illegal Substances Online

Michael arrived for treatment as a sixteen-year-old whose grades had deteriorated from A's and B's to near failing. He had started to act erratically, staying up late at night and seldom getting more than a few hours of sleep. His parents had tolerated his behavior while his grades were good but became concerned with his deterioration at home and school. He had a strong family history of major depression. Michael had been regularly receiving packages in the mail, which he said were purchases on eBay. He told his parents that he was spending his bar mitzvah money.

One evening Michael was particularly agitated, insisting that he was the "Second Coming" and that his parents could not see it. His mother called 911 and he was taken to an emergency room where he was diagnosed as having had a manic break. His mother later searched his room and found multiple bottles of a variety of antidepressants. Michael had established a PayPal account and was paying a middleman to get him the drugs from an unknown source. He had been taking this medication over multiple weeks as a cocktail of drugs to "feel better."

DISCUSSION

I did a search on the computer for the word "Valium" and came up with hundreds of different sites offering Valium. Here is what a typical site said with regard to obtaining a prescription:

"Online consultations are a new concept in health care that utilize the Internet to improve patient access to physician care. The patient does not receive a traditional physical exam by the physician, but rather completes an online questionnaire and communicates with the physician using our secure online communication. A U.S. licensed physician will review the information you have submitted and either approve or decline your request. If approved, the physician will write the prescription and send it to the pharmacy where it will be filled and shipped to you via FedEx."

I then checked out the questionnaire and it was obvious that anyone with even a minimum desire to be seen as having an anxiety disorder could easily research the symptoms online and then complete the questionnaire. Although the drugs allegedly come from authorized pharmacies, it was unclear to me where these were located or how the drugs were ensured to be safe. It would be, in my opinion, completely unethical for a doctor to prescribe a habit-forming benzodiazepine medication, such as Valium, to an unknown patient on the basis of a questionnaire. Further, it is unclear to me how effective the safeguards are to ensure the age of the recipient or that the addressee is in fact the patient.

It is equally striking how little parents know about what their kids are discussing on and possibly procuring from the Web. Once again, the information and material coming to today's teens is from unknown sources and people whose agenda is not always clear. A desperate adolescent boy who wants a bigger body will believe that steroid use is safe if that's what he wants to believe and an online "expert" assures him it is. The daily headlines of elite athletes using steroids and setting records have done little to discourage kids from chasing dangerous anabolic steroids.

Finding information on obtaining other drugs was also easy. For example, I found an online chat room in which there was a discussion of symptoms to tell a doctor to get stimulants such as Adderall or Ritalin. A plethora of websites and chat rooms have made it easy for anyone with an Internet connection to set up an account and start "connecting" with anyone on the other end of a server. Without the information superhighway, it would be harder for a teenager to get easy information on tricking a psychiatrist for prescription amphetamines.

The Internet also allows for a greater degree of anonymity. Kids are able to claim that they are adults, and there is no way for others to verify this. In addition, the people giving advice are often hardly experts or altruistic in their intentions. Their anonymity at times gives them license to make outrageous claims and provide unsanctioned, unsupervised substances to our teens.

CASE STUDY

Abby—Internet Hazing— A New Form of Bullying

ABBY, A POPULAR FOURTEEN-YEAR-OLD, started to hate her former best friend, Mandy. Abby had found a letter from her boyfriend to Mandy saying how much he wanted to be with her. Mandy could not have expected what came next. When she returned to school after the winter holidays she found that none of her old friends wanted to be with her, and she was certain that people were talking about her behind her back. She soon discovered that the word was out—untrue, of course—that she had contracted a venereal disease by sleeping around.

What Abby had done was send a text message about Mandy to another girl whom she knew would spread the rumor. The girl sent the message by an instant message (IM) to a list of friends and soon everyone in the school knew of Mandy's "condition." Mandy was humiliated, became increasingly withdrawn and depressed, and was admitted to the hospital after she refused to go to school with stomachaches and worsening depression. The rumors continued that she had been hospitalized for treatment of her "venereal disease," something that was posted in a school-group chat room message board.

Fortunately in this case Mandy's parents intervened with the school, and after a brief investigation, Abby's vicious attack was exposed. She was forced to write an apology, but the damage had been done, and Mandy's reputation had been tarnished. She eventually transferred to another school.

DISCUSSION

I remember old-fashioned bullying. A tough guy would humiliate a little guy into giving up his lunch money or else being beaten up. Still, in these cases it was between the bully and his victim, and although nonetheless painful to the victim, the antagonist was easily identified and the remedy could be swift if dealt with appropriately.

Internet bullying or hazing has its own idiosyncrasies. First, screen names give these bullies anonymity, and under cover of this anonymity they make their cowardly attacks more outrageous and malicious in their allegations. Kids have been scarred by allegations of drug use, insinuation of sexual indiscretions or sexual orientation, and unrelenting threats of harm. Second, the electronic media has allowed for incredible speed in the spreading of such rumors, making them difficult to trace.[3]

To make matters worse, in many cases even being at home is no reprieve from the bullying, as the adolescents involved are frequently online, and text messages or chat rooms instantaneously perpetuate the rumors. Other methods of "modern" bullying include the sending of embarrassing photos, both real and doctored with Photoshop, to lists of people. In one case, a boy threatened to disclose that his girlfriend's parents were having financial problems if she didn't have sex with him, a

WHAT CAN A PARENT DO?

Surfing the Internet together with younger kids is an easy solution to keeping on top of your children's online activities, but not so with older and frequently more Internet savvy adolescents.

Some parents have resorted to sophisticated software that spies on their kids' activity or that blocks certain sites. Other parents severely restrict computer use or prohibit computer access altogether.

One mother I worked with removed her son's computer and took it to an "expert" who scoured the hard drive and stored correspondence because she strongly suspected that he was having frequent sex and using drugs and bragging about these activities to his friends. When the son found out about this, he went underground and used his friends' computers or the local public library computer to continue his activities. Clearly the issue here was less about the technology than the communication between mother and son. The technology has just made it a little easier to escape parental oversight and get into a plethora of unforeseen difficulties.

Consider the following when it comes to staying technologically savvy and keeping your teens safe.

1. Talk with your teens about your expectations, values, and hopes for them.

Understand that your hopes are not theirs and be reasonable as to how things have changed. Be curious about their needs and desires and remember that most of us weren't saints when we were young. Cut them some slack.

2. As with drugs and other teen problems, talk to them of the dangers and tell them that you are available if they encounter problems online.

Parents can do a lot to make themselves approachable. How they respond when their adolescents share problems with them sets the tone for how the adolescent will consider talking to them in the future. Horror stories rarely work. Predators will tend to groom a potential target, and it is the subtlety that parents need to share with their child.

3. Stay ahead of the curve. Learn as much as you can about the Internet and ask your adolescent to show you cool sites for downloading music or gaming. They will more often than not find it positive to be able to show off their superior surfing skills and know that you are not totally opposed to their computer use.

4. Consider using blocking and filtering software. This is a double-

edged sword. Filtering programs will not protect your adolescent from all online dangers. Some dangerous sites are not blocked, and some safe sites are blocked. Further, many adolescents find ways to get around the filters by either disabling them or using a friend's unfiltered computer. Filters and blocking software are generally more effective for younger children than for teens.

5. Know the games. Some parents learn to play online video games with their kids, which enables them to know what their kids are playing, allows for family time, and permits discussion around the themes involved. The kids often describe a certain pleasure in their parents sharing and usually blundering through these computer activities and also express delight at beating their parents at something they are good at. This kind of sharing of cyberspace activities makes it much more likely that your adolescent will not hide things unnecessarily or worry about your reactions to things that may actually be harmless.

6. Obtain online help. If teens are getting into trouble using these technologies, why not use the technologies to reach them? In some cases, they might be willing to get online help for their tech-related problems. I received 124,000 hits when I typed in "online therapy" as a search term in July 2006.

One of my colleagues recommended a website called HelpHorizons.com that did just that. It offered "a safe and supportive environment in which to learn more about successfully meeting life's challenges." On review of the site it appears to be comprehensive with some well-credentialed clinicians and seems like a legitimate option when face-to-face therapy is either practically impossible (e.g., distance from a therapist) or psychologically impossible (e.g., severe social phobia).

There is the International Society for Mental Health Online, which is devoted to in-depth discussions of clinical work that involves the Internet. Here's how the American Psychiatric Association defines e-therapy.

"E-therapy normally refers to the provision of mental health services online (through the Internet). Related terms include cybertherapy, teletherapy, Internet counseling, online counseling, and so forth. With this relatively new form of treatment, there is considerable debate among mental health practitioners about the efficacy of e-therapy, whether comparisons to traditional psychotherapy are valid, and which types of patients may or may not be treated through e-therapy.

"E-therapy relies upon developing technology-enabling communication between two or more parties over a modem or network connection. Among the most common technological devices utilized in e-therapy services are live (real-time) video conferencing, e-mail, instant messaging, chat rooms, discussion groups through e-mail or website message boards, and file sharing."

Again, due to the propensity for impostors and impersonators, it is essential that parents help teens monitor these sites and get outside information concerning their authenticity. I suppose that the fundamental notion behind professionals who construct and support these sites is that it is often impossible to get an adolescent (especially one hooked in cyberspace) to engage in traditional therapy. In this regard, something may be better than nothing at all in addressing an Internet problem or, to use the vernacular, "if you can't reach them, join them."

7. Monitor computer placement. Although the mobility of laptops has made monitoring the placement of computers more difficult, an open family area is more likely to expose a problem than having a computer in the basement or a less trafficked area of the house. If these placement practices, along with parents knowing usernames and passwords, are established during the preteen years, it will then be easier to maintain these practices during adolescence. Parents may then be able to stay on top of whether their teens change their screen information, talk to them openly and honestly about whether they are hiding anything, and negotiate to have at least some access to their Internet activities.

8. Discern between privacy and secrecy when it comes to adolescents' packages and mail. Although opening your adolescent's mail and packages constitutes a serious breach of privacy and trust in many cases, opening packages together might be one of the ground rules with an adolescent who has serious drug problems. This practice is especially important if the Internet and a carrier service has been the source of your adolescent's procuring of drugs or other illegal substance. These practices and parental rights also become important in cases where unexplained credit card purchases have been made. There might be some period of time, say six months of sobriety, during which the mutual inspection of packages would be agreed upon, prior to a resumption of enhanced privacy once the teen has successfully completed a period of abstinence.

form of cyberspace-blackmail.

The numbers for online bullying are staggering. Somewhere between one in five and one in fifteen kids report having been bullied online.[4] The most common method of bullying is a malicious rumor spread by an instant message, or a direct threat made from another kid and broadcast online. Unfortunately simply blocking the anonymous perpetrator from the recipient list allows the attacker to create a new identity and continue the attack. Text messaging, posting embarrassing pictures or videos, or setting up damaging, defaming websites are also fairly common. One particularly vicious form of bullying is when an attacker sends out a malicious message as if from his or her desired victim, leading to all sorts of social consequences on the unsuspecting victim.

I found many websites (e.g., schoolscandals.com) to be particularly troubling. They encourage kids to "speak your mind" without offering any advice about using restraint, or considering the consequences or potential crimes these postings/messages may lead to. On these sites, I found many posts with kids attacking other kids, posts such as "Such and such is so annoying. People tell me she's a dyke," or "So and so is a dirty whore." What is interesting to me was the number of girls who appeared to be posting about other girls, although given the anonymity, it is hard to tell the real gender of the person doing the posting.

CONCLUSION

In closing, consider the way new technology acts as a conduit to obtain established forms of entertainment, such as music and television.

For example, in the past, adolescents were limited in the ways they could obtain music, including music that contains sexually explicit lyrics. They were limited through the availability of this particular kind of music, the accessibility of stores that carried it, and the intervention of parents. These days, with the easy access to online music, the reach of such music has become universal and indiscriminate in terms of listeners' ages. Younger and younger children are listening to such songs.

A study that appeared in the journal *Pediatrics* in 2006 stated that teenagers who listen to music with explicitly sexual lyrics start having sex sooner than those who listen to other music. Typically, such music depicts men as studs and women as sex objects. The songs tend to have

THE BENEFITS OF TECHNOLOGY FOR TEENS

The purpose of this chapter has been to illustrate some of the problems we have encountered with teens today and how technology can lead to trouble. As technology becomes even more sophisticated, we will undoubtedly have different problems with which to deal. I do however want to briefly mention some of the *benefits* that technology can bring to our adolescents.

Social. For some kids, websites, text and instant messaging, and online gaming are the only ways to stay connected and belong to a group. In some cases, the isolation these kids once felt disappears, and competing with and against others leads to friendship and on-line companionship. One mother, with a son addicted to gaming on the Internet and isolated from family life, invited her son's video game peers to her house once a month for them to get to know each other, which led to a marked improvement with her son.

Educational. Computers and the Internet are compelling for adolescents because of the sounds, images, interconnectivity, and rapidity of information. Access grabs their attention and appeals to the intuitive adolescent quest for novelty and new information. Appropriate software can lead to improved creativity play, can help in the mastery of learning for those with learning disabilities, and in general has given teens worldwide access to research and literature once only available following protracted trips to the library. Adolescents today have more ways to learn and find inspiration than ever before; it just needs to be done in a safe, supervised fashion.

fairly explicit references to sex acts, and are often considered degrading to women.[5]

The number of these types of songs has increased. I see increasingly sophisticated sexual behavior in younger and younger people. When I first started as a staff psychiatrist on our adolescent residential unit at McLean Hospital, I remember being shocked at the graphic and sexually explicit lyrics that the kids knew as they sang along to the music stored on their iPods. Whether early sex and sexually explicit music are definitively correlated I cannot say, however; it is clear that the very young are being exposed to such lyrics and concepts at a much earlier developmental stage than ever before, and that modern technology has made access to such music easier.

One long-term study, which began in the 1970s, shows that the rampant violence on TV appears to make teens more violent.[6] Now while TV is hardly a new technology, it is more accessible than ever before. One young man I spoke to said that while his parents did not allow him to watch excessively violent shows on TV, he used TiVo to watch his favorite shows when they weren't at home.

One of the major culprits in this area is professional wrestling, which depicts an increasing level of violence and gore. A 2006 study showed that children who watch professional wrestling are more likely to carry weapons and get into physical fights.[7] It should be noted that these fights were frequently associated with drugs and alcohol. Interestingly, girls were even more at risk than boys to be aggressive after having watched such shows.

The 1960s were the era of sex, drugs, and rock and roll. The young rebelled against the strait-laced social conventions of their parents. The new millennium is a time of sex, drugs, hip-hop, and fiber optic connections. The young do not so much rebel as network within a network in a constant state of contact where time, space, and geography mean less than in the past. Technology has empowered the youth to bypass both restrictions and protections. Understanding the technology will empower us, their parents, to better join with its promise as well as protect from its dangers.

CHAPTER 9

Voices of Troubled Teens

Cynthia S. Kaplan, Ph.D.

As has been repeated throughout this book, one of the reasons
teens get into trouble is that they often rely on each other too much or
not at all while distancing themselves from the adults in their lives.

*Feeling alone, and sometimes stressed out by the demands of school,
the swirl of friendships, the pressure to succeed, and others' expectations, teens often retreat to an inner sanctum—a private world of
thoughts and feelings that is often inaccessible to others. One advantage
of working so closely with teens, especially those on the path to recovery,
is that you get to actually hear their voices; you are invited, if lucky, into
the inner sanctum of their drives and needs, wishes and fears.*

*They write their "stories" for us, like the ones below, as an initial
step on the road back to feeling and functioning better. Several of them
have allowed us to anonymously share their stories with you. Some
are complete original renditions and others are blended accounts from
several teens.*

*Although these tales may seem startling and even at times surreal,
they are the first-hand accounts of teens who for long periods of time
conducted their lives on two levels—one public and one private. These
adolescents' problems developed gradually, spinning out of control,
until their difficulties became apparent, catching family, friends, and*

teachers by surprise. Thus, they each progressed at some point from having routine difficulties to more serious problems that disrupted their overall functioning and led to dangerous situations and outcomes. No one around them knew when things had become really "bad"—no one but the adolescents themselves and maybe a few close friends.

The secrecy that shrouds adolescence occluded their true identity and left them out of touch with the seriousness of their predicament and out of communication with people who might have been helpful. All of these stories are a reminder to adults of how much lies beneath the surface of teen life, especially these days, and how closely we must listen if we hope to see trouble coming.

———————

STORY #1: BULLYING, SELF-INJURY, AND DEPRESSION

MALE, AGE THIRTEEN: A lot of Americans have seen me. That's me, in the movies—the punk kid who needs to rebel. That's me, in the book—the Goth kid who is slitting his wrists. I'm the kid you hear about, that kid who snaps and kills himself.

But even though everyone has seen me, does that mean they know me? This is what has bothered me my whole life. Nobody ever took the time to really understand me.

It started in third grade. It's the first thing I remember. I had one friend, and he wasn't a very good one. I would [daydream] in class and think I was in a video game. At least that happened until I heard the following from my teacher's mouth: "Principal's office, now." I sat there. That was the first time I ever got a discipline card.

Then came career day—the one day of the year you are supposed to dress up as the occupation you want to become. I made a joke. I said I would dress up as an army man. And then I said I was going to bomb the school and laugh as everybody died. I got a call home (from the school) saying somebody overheard me. I was so ashamed in front of my parents. From then on nobody was ever allowed to dress up as an army man for career day and couldn't make jokes like that without being suspended.

I slowly became more and more aware that I was all alone without anybody. I realized this while doing what I normally did during recess:

sitting in a green plastic tube and talking to myself, usually just stupid rants. You know, stupid stuff like about killing people, designing video games, and taking over the world. Another point of blackness passed, this time about a year long.

Then I met J.D. He was my obsession. I needed him as my friend. [But] kids made fun of me. They were saying I was homosexual. So what! I didn't like girls for about five or six years. I cried every night and came home wearing a feigned smile. Eventually I went to the teacher and told her about the bullies; I then had to meet face-to-face with the bullies. I still talked to myself every day and had black nights (meaning I don't remember them).

Then came the day my whole story really started, the event that changed my life for the worst. My friends and I played soccer and we all had nicknames. "Hey mofo-the-gay-dick-licking-chicken, get that ball you retard." I had to try and deal with that name for about five weeks, but each week the name would get more and more under my very thin skin. The sixth week the kid who made up the name used his horrible creation once again. I was crying my eyes out. "Didn't you hear me mo—" I charged at him, picked him off the ground, and sent his body crashing back down to the earth with all of my force. I ran away crying. Kids begged for me to come back and play with them, that they would give me a new name. I told them that they can go suck it and I walked away.

Another year passed. I don't remember much but my first crush . . . and my first cut. I wondered continually what I had done wrong in my life when I started to get depressed. Three slashes across the back of my hand to repent for all of the many mistakes that I made in my life—it meant whatever you do comes back three times, and that was my payment. Then I cut two overlapping circles onto the back of my hand, which represented the moon. That was in class . . . with five friends and two teachers watching. Nobody noticed, nobody cared. My parents didn't even care. I told them what I had done and their only advice was "Don't do it again."

A summer passed. I found my love for the greatest music of all time that summer: punk rock. I got my first girlfriend within the first month of school. I got really depressed and cut about ten more times. I would bleed and write things down in blood. That made me lose another five or six friends and it made me even more depressed. I would cover home-work with blood. When the teacher asked about it, I told her what it was. I guess they never really cared that much that the papers were coated in blood. Months passed.

The whole grade went on a trip to Washington, D.C. I made a new friend, but in making one, I lost four. This kid was a horrible kid anyways so I ditched him. Kids made fun of me and said I was wearing woman's deodorant. Then there was the day in front of that old house where they make all of the money for the United States. I went up to a kid who had teased me and picked him off of the ground, from his neck. "Shut the f**k up man, I don't use that stuff !" Teachers came and pulled me away and said I needed to take some space. I got in no trouble.

But by the time I was done with the trip I heard one thing chanted [by my peers] about a million times: "Strong and beautiful!" That was what it said on the deodorant tube. It was so excruciatingly painful to just sit there powerless. The teacher responded as if all of it was just "child's play." I cut a few more times.

Time passed. I believed in the rule that to gain something you must lose something of equivalent value. I saw it on a TV show, but I decided that it is very true. That is why I cut: the payment of blood and flesh in exchange for something good to happen.

Anyways, months came and went, just as did the many insulting things people said about me. I tried to kill myself one time. I don't really remember it, but I know I was laughing my head off because I was so happy that I might be dying. It was just another game to me. From there on it was a series of girlfriends, cutting, and suicide attempts. I don't remember much of it.

Summer came and went and school started. My girlfriend dumped me. That pushed me and caused me to try and kill myself. I went to the hospital the next day. I slashed at my wrists at the hospital. I still left four days later. The day after I left I made another attempt. My dad walked in on me and dragged me downstairs by my neck. I came to the hospital four days later. Now I am [here] writing this. I hope I can resume my normal life when I leave here. I probably can with all of the coping that I have learned here and lots of help from my family. Maybe my life will one day again be the kid with the smile on his face.

STORY # 2: MOOD ISSUES, SELF-IMAGE PROBLEMS, AND PLANNED SCHOOL VIOLENCE

FEMALE, AGE SIXTEEN: "Back to school" These three words are some of the worst that a kid can hear after an exciting, fun-filled summer. But for me, "back to school" holds more meaning than almost any other phrase in the English language. It symbolizes the circles that we move in, the repetitiveness of day upon day, trudging back to a place that you do not want to be, but can't escape from. To quote one of my favorite bands, "We're addicted to the things we hate." And for me, that thing was school. I didn't always dislike school. In elementary school, I was always at the top of my class, self-assured, and proud of who I was.

But then puberty hit. And I got bigger. I was always a large kid, but once I started filling out, I began to experience hatred—real, honest-to-God hatred. And who was that hatred directed at—me, of course. I hated myself.

By seventh grade I was still at the top of my class, still admired by all the teachers and kids as a leader, as an inspiration, but there was one small difference. I was not the same positive, resilient kid from elementary school. I was depressed, and eventually that depression evolved into an eating disorder. For a year I struggled with anorexia on top of doing my schoolwork and maintaining my positive image. Eventually a psychiatrist gave me some meds that got me back to a healthy weight, but then the hatred manifested itself in another way.

As I gained weight I became suicidal, convinced that I was a hideous fat blob that did not deserve to walk the earth. I was hospitalized for about a week where I recovered somewhat, and the hatred went temporarily into remission. The summer passed uneventfully, and by early September, it was time; time to go back to school.

At first, I was excited. Who wouldn't be? I've always loved learning, and I was moving on to my first year at high school. Maybe I'd finally meet some intellectual equals. Most of my friends had reached physical, intellectual, and emotional maturity far after me and were not the most stimulating conversationalists.

I was lucky. The very first day of school, my biology teacher partnered me with a girl named Julia. And before long we found that we had a lot in common and, additionally, that we were both dealing with depression.

One day in class, probably late November, early December, something funny happened. I was discussing the movie *Fahrenheit 9/11* with Julia and I asked her if she had seen *Bowling for Columbine*, another documentary film by Michael Moore. I can still remember the overly bright gleam in her eyes when she replied with quiet enthusiasm, "I love that movie." I didn't think much of it at the time. I mean, sure, it was a good movie. But by February, I would be agreeing with her with the same gleam in my eyes.

It started in January, like it always does. I began to get more depressed for no specific reason. Maybe it was the overload of schoolwork, or the fact that my family was too busy to spend much time with me, or maybe it was simply the [lack of daylight]. But I began to spiral downward. I started listening to angry and depressing music, music with more hatred, hatred that was resurfacing in me again slowly. I got a lot of the music from Julia, who had been listening to it since the summer.

And then there was that cold, snowy January morning during mid-year where fate seemed to take a twisted turn. Julia and I both had the period off and were lounging around in the cafeteria talking about this and that when eventually, somehow, our conversation landed on school shootings. I started talking about how I didn't find the kids involved in the Columbine shootings very intelligent. Why would they shoot up their school? Julia immediately countered by saying that they were some of the smartest people she had ever read about, and I was a fool to think they weren't.

"How much have you actually read about them?" I remember her asking. I replied truthfully, "Not much." I became curious. Were they really as smart as Julia was claiming? And why did they shoot up their school? Next thing I knew, Julia and I were at a computer in the school library looking at a purple and black website about the shooting.

The next month was a blur. I became obsessed with Eric Harris and Dylan Klebold, the two Columbine High School students responsible for the shootings, who Julia and I lovingly referred to as REB and VoDkA, the names they had called themselves. At home, I was constantly online reading about them, their journals, the transcripts of their homemade movies. At school Julia and I talked exclusively about them and similar topics, such as our hatred for the school and for the jocks. We drew swastikas and anarchy symbols in the snow.

It was not long before I came to Julia, eyes gleaming with passionate rage and mouth twisted into a superior smirk that seemed to be permanently etched on my face. I asked her if she would like to be a part of our own little Doomsday, just like REB and VoDkA's. It didn't take much to convince her.

From there the obsession, the rage, and the hatred of myself just kept building. I began to cut so I could feel something, or to release the rage that bubbled deep in my stomach. I slept constantly, did not do my homework, and spoke only to Julia. When I was awake at home, I would look up recipes for bombs and types of guns that are good assault weapons. Julia did the same, and we talked and laughed about how amazing those fifteen minutes of destruction would be come senior year.

One Tuesday in biology, I got a message from the office that my parents were picking me up early. I said goodbye to Julia, gathered up my stuff, and headed out, expecting to go see my shrink or something like that.

Oh, how wrong I was.

My parents didn't say much, until we got some ice cream.

"We know," they said. I froze, completely numb. I couldn't believe they had figured out what was going on. I thought my life was over. With all of my careful research and planning, I hadn't given any thought to what might happen if I got caught—except, of course, that it would not be good.

After a few hectic days, I checked into the hospital for acute depression, cutting, and homicidal/suicidal fantasies. Unfortunately, there was another girl from my school there at the same time, and I couldn't talk about the Columbine stuff with any of the kids for obvious reasons. I got some help and support, but it was only from adults.

It was after a few days that the numbness began to wear off and I started to ask questions. When was I going to see Julia again? Would I be able to go back to school? I cried a lot. I desperately wanted to see Julia, even if it meant going back to [high school]. I philosophized so much about it that it became extremely abstract and somewhat delusional. One such journal entry reads:

"You might want to deny it, but I could be you. Look in a f**king mirror. You are the cause of my actions. I am the cause of my actions. We all want to some extent or another to wound, hurt, KILL. Don't you see the f**king glint in your eye? Don't you see that one day, you could just lose f**king control and attack? And I know that. You know that, deep down. Everyone is a f**king psychopath to some extent. And yet, only those of us who are self-aware decide to take that power and control it. That's what makes us gods. Control. We control our power and only let it out when it's necessary. Understanding us—self-awareness—gods. Immortality in the masses. That's what separates us, from the rest of you motherf**kers. We are gods, immortal, and you f**king are not. But re-member kids, that that is the only difference. You are just as violent, just as sexual, and just as black and cold-hearted as me. As VoDkA. As REB. You just have to dig a little deeper into the ground to find the Worms."

This was my expression, and although it sounds extremely disturbing, it's also a lot better on paper when you consider the alternative.

Eventually, I even stopped writing in my journal. I got through my sophomore year and went into the summer with energy, enthusiasm, and believe it or not, happiness. I spent a couple weeks at a fashion program in Boston, got a job, and went to NYC with Julia and two other friends. I seemed to be getting back on track.

But then it was time again to go back to school. And I had a little depressive slump like I always do when school starts. It's an adjustment period, and change takes a toll on me. But within this short time period my obsession with Columbine was rekindled. I started again researching various weapons and laws about how to acquire them. I started looking at maps and attempting to find places where I could detonate bombs with-out anyone hearing the blast.

And lo and behold, my parents caught me again. I was lucky this time, though, because they caught me early enough that I hadn't become com-pletely immersed in my fantasy worlds, and my depression had not taken over my life. I could still function.

And so I came back to the psychiatric facility as a day student, and this time I came back involved and committed and ready to change. Wanting to change. I've become more honest and open than ever before. Many times I've felt like I've had to wear a facade to fit in. And I have a long history of hiding things, like my eating disorder and my obsession with Columbine. But no more. As a matter of fact, recently I spoke to both my outside therapist and my case manager, as well as my parents, that I think perhaps one of the reasons my obsession with Columbine was so intense, especially in freshman year, was that I was either in love with, or extremely romantically attached to, Julia, and I felt so overlooked and ostracized by others.

Of course, I had hidden that for over a year and a half, and it feels amazing to get it off my chest. I feel as though I have nothing left to hide and I can finally start fresh. I will work hard with my therapist and psychiatrist to stabilize my mood and work through the obsession. And hopefully, once I'm stable, I can talk to Julia and tell her my feelings.

It's been a long and bumpy circle that I've been running in. But I've come to realize that "back to school," though it may mean traveling in circles at first, is a pattern that can be eventually broken. Safely. Not by blowing up the school or committing mass murder, [but] by taking a leadership role, and actually going back to the place I was before all this happened. It's all been one big, long, circle, but eventually I will break out of the cycle.

So I'm almost ready. Send me back there. Back to school.

STORY #3: ATTENTION DEFICIT HYPERACTIVITY DISORDER AND DRUG USE

MALE, AGE EIGHTEEN: The funny thing is I am just like everyone else I know in most ways. Yeah, I had my share of troubles growing up. My parents got divorced, and I had to change schools. But so what? That happens to a lot of people. The funny thing is that everyone missed what really made me different. It was only years later that I was diagnosed with attention deficit hyperactivity disorder (ADHD). At first I thought this was just a fancy label for my being a f**kup, but now I know it's true.

The thing about the ADHD that made me so different was that I was so restless, even in elementary school. If I wasn't busy doing schoolwork, I was in the principal's office. My motor was always just spinning so fast that I almost never used to think before I leapt, so to speak. If someone said, "Hey, let's go steal some candy," I was right there. Not because I even wanted the candy or because I had no morals. I just wanted to be one of the group so badly and I also, just plain and simple, am one of the most impulsive people I know. But no one ever really understood that or pointed it out to me except to treat me like I was a "badass," and after a while,

I became a "badass." It just became who I was. I never got medication for my ADHD until way into high school. It is too bad, looking back, that everyone said, "Boys will be boys," when I really needed help. I wanted to stay out of trouble, but trouble just found me and, after a while, I didn't really care anymore.

During high school I started to smoke pot and drink on a regular basis. This led to a lot of trouble with the law, my school, and my family. It started off with things that didn't really scare me; a DUI [driving while under the influence charge] that I was cleared of, some shoplifting, and then a possession of alcohol charge. I would smoke almost every day before school. Eventually, things all caught up with me and I realized I needed a break, some kind of help that would get me back on track with life. So I went to a residental psychiatric program for two weeks, learned a lot about pot and alcohol use, and left with a very optimistic attitude and really sound motivation to stay clean.

Once I got out, I thought I had really learned my lesson about addictions, and everything was going great for a full year. Although I would occasionally smoke marijuana about once a month, sometimes even less, I never craved marijuana, or drank to excess, nor did I use any other substance.

I stayed on the ADHD medication they had given me in the program, and when I was on it I felt like a different person. People could suggest doing things to me, but I would be able to take that extra second to think before I acted. It was like my brain had been slowed down just enough that I was no longer going in warp speed. But unfortunately, everyone still thought of me as a f**kup and tried to involve me in every prank and misdeed that came down the pike. Girls especially thought of me as a wild guy and veered away. I was doing better, but no one really saw me as different. It was like the self-fulfilling prophecy; I seemed destined to be a "bad boy" even though I had actually stopped being one.

But then on Christmas Eve of my senior year, I had emergency surgery for appendicitis, and for the pain I received a script for Vicodin [a narcotic obtained by prescription and used to treat pain]. I held onto the pills myself, as I was confident that I could avoid the temptation to abuse them. I took them for the pain as necessary and never overused. However, a few weeks after I had stopped using and was no longer in pain, I had a fight with my girlfriend, did badly on some schoolwork, and felt overwhelmed by a sudden impulse to take them again, which I did.

Unfortunately by this time, I had stopped taking my ADHD [medication] because I felt I no longer needed [it]. A few days after my supply of Vicodin ran out, and after experiencing minor signs of withdrawal, such as small headaches and minor bone pain, I found out that my friend had a supply of [OxyContin] from his parents. I bought fifty-five of them, and began to take about 40 to 60 milligrams a day. After having them only for a few days, I was caught at school with all of the pills on me. The school called the police department to have me arrested, and I was charged with possession of a class B substance. I was brought to a holding cell in the police department, where I had to wait for five hours until the bail commission[er] showed up to let me post bail. A few days later, I went to my arraignment with my lawyer, where I was then given a probation officer and a time and place where I had to go every week to undergo random drug testing.

I know that I do not want to spend the rest of my life in trouble with the law and having to report to a probation officer weekly, which is one more reason amongst the many that I want to remain clean and sober and go back on my ADHD meds. As much as I hate the thought of it, I guess I am always going to have troubles with being impulsive, and drugs and alcohol are always there, calling to me as a quick fix for helping me feel more relaxed and together. I want so badly to be "normal" but guess I never will be.

After being arrested for [possession of OxyContin] and noticing how badly I wanted the drug when I was in the holding cell, I realized that I was starting to develop what had the potential to be a very bad addiction. I signed myself back into drug treatment to take myself away from the [OxyContin] before I bought more, and to reinforce my urge to stay sober.

When I leave here this time, I plan to find an NA [Narcotics Anonymous] meeting to continue my treatment and sobriety. I will also stay in my family therapy to help me continue to improve my relationship with my parents, as well as start individual therapy again with the same psychologist I used before. Between this stay in the hospital and ongoing support through an NA meeting, I am confident that I will be able to remain sober. At least I hope so as this is no way for an eighteen-year-old to live. If I don't stop now, I will become a criminal. I really don't want that to happen. I would rather accept my diagnosis, deal with my impulses, and lead a normal life. So far I am not doing very well in this department. But I pray to God I don't turn nineteen in [prison].

STORY #4: PROGRESSION OF DRUG AND ALCOHOL USE

FEMALE, AGE SEVENTEEN: I first drank when I was fourteen on [Cape Cod] with my brother and a bunch of his friends who were about the same age as me. I drank beer after beer and didn't think I was feeling a thing. After having five or six beers, I decided I would get up and try to walk around, and this is where I realized that I was very drunk. I couldn't walk straight and my speech was slurred.

I liked the feeling a lot, and I was greatly enjoying myself until I realized that I would have to go home to my parent's house, who up until then thought I was a perfect child and never caught me doing anything wrong before. I didn't want to change this image they had of me, so in a vain effort to cover the smell of beer on my breath, I started to chew the breath mints someone else gave me and to think up excuses for my appearance. Although I think they suspected something was amiss, I was able to slip in to the house and get into bed without having to face them directly.

The next morning, I woke up fairly early and still felt drunk, although I did not have what I understood to be a hangover; I did not feel sick to my stomach, nor did I have a headache, but waking up was more difficult for me than usual.

I continued to drink on weekends for a few years, usually drinking every other weekend or sometimes just once a month. I did this for two years until I was sixteen. It was during that summer I smoked pot for the first time. I had started a new job where everybody that I worked with smoked marijuana on a fairly regular basis. I figured that if people a lot older than me could work successfully and smoke pot at the same time, then it really couldn't be that damaging. I tried it and began to like it so much that I began to smoke every day, pretty much from the first day I used.

Within a week, I was smoking more than once a day. Within the next month, I had tried cough medicine, and from there, I tried everything from heroin to cocaine to all sorts of various hallucinogens.

Dextromorphan, the thing that gets you buzzed in cough medicine, was the first hard drug I had ever tried, and it caused me to [feel] that I could leap tall buildings in a single bound and that I existed on another planet, although it was really only a regular weekend night on Cape Cod. The feeling of a wholly different reality it gave me was one of the most incredible feelings I had ever had. Not knowing what was real, and also feeling that I was in control of determining my own reality was, to me, the feeling of supreme power.

All through the summer, I enjoyed whatever drugs my dealers had available, but luckily they were never able to consistently get cocaine or heroin, because I'm sure I would have developed an addiction to these drugs given enough time. Although I never really had the opportunity to shoot up heroin, I did have the chance to snort it, and the rush of both fanciful entertainment and total apathy toward the responsibilities of real life was incredible.

However, of all the drugs I tried, I found that amphetamines were my favorite. I loved the feeling of invincibility they gave me and the ability to stay up for days and weeks at a time without sleep. I felt that I was able to finish everything I had to get done during the hours when the rest of the world was wasting its time sleeping and being unproductive. Cocaine also served this purpose quite well, as it was such a strong stimulant. I loved the feeling of total detached euphoria it gave me.

Looking back, I realize that these drugs gave me a false sense of power and choice and would give me the sense that I could do as I pleased— from not asking permission to stay out for an extra hour to buying a pack of cigarettes or a six-pack. I would threaten to leave the house and never come back, or swear that I would deliberately hurt myself to get my parents off my back. When I was not on amphetamines, the threats toward my parents would diminish significantly, although they never disappeared completely. It was because of these behaviors that I was diagnosed as being possibly manic, triggering my first stay at a psychiatric program.

Because I was hoping and planning to go back to school and play varsity sports, I knew that I had to stop all my use and did so without much delay. Although I started sophomore year with the best intentions, I began to gradually use amphetamines again and ended up developing a crippling addiction. I was using upward of 300 milligrams a day and would stay awake for a week at a time without sleep.

Finally, one day I was talking to my friend, and we were both completely out of our minds. When I turned around, my friend was on his knees talking to the sky. It was at this point that I realized I had to stop, and that I had a serious problem. I was determined to stop at all costs. I was not expecting any major withdrawal symptoms, as I had never had withdrawal bad enough that it made me start using a substance again. However, this time it was different. I was overcome by the worst depression and lethargy that I have ever felt. But I was determined to not use again, and I didn't. Later on, the depression got the best of me, though, and I tried to take my own life through an overdose of sleeping pills and alcohol.

Because of this incident, I was sent first to an inpatient unit and then to acute residential treatment.

One of my losses due to my drug use is that my parents barely trust me anymore. They don't trust me because of all the lies I told them about my drug use. When I go home I'll be living with my mom, dad, and my brother. I get along with them all pretty well.

Another one of my losses is my record with the courts. In early June, I was driving at night with my boyfriend and another friend when we were pulled over for not having a front license plate. When the officers searched the car they found a gram of marijuana, and because they couldn't tell whom it belonged to, all three of us were charged with possession of [a] class D [substance]. When I went to court, my case was continued without a finding because they had no way of definitely proving it was mine. My aftercare consisted of attending Alcoholics Anonymous and Narcotics Anonymous meetings and basically just going to school and staying away from drugs.

I hope now that I have really learned my lesson, but it is hard to be sure. Drugs and alcohol are everywhere I go. It is easy to say "just change your friends," but it is a really hard thing to do. Am I really different than my friends or have they just not been caught? Do I really have to abstain or can I just use occasionally? Right now a life without getting high seems near to impossible, but losing my family and school and facing another court date all seem worse. So each day I struggle to remind myself that one more slip could spell disaster.

STORY #5: DRUGS AND PROMISCUITY

FEMALES, AGES FIFTEEN TO SEVENTEEN: I first started hanging around kids who smoked pot and drank when I was thirteen [and] that's when I lost my innocence. My parents were clueless, and the more I went to parties where kids were drinking, the more people talked about sex and "hooking up." At first I was embarrassed and thought "never me," but then one night I told my parents I was going one place and ended up going to this guy's house. I drank what he told me was a little vodka, and he ended up feeling me up and then trying to touch me between my legs.

I called my parents once to come get me. I guess it was a cry for help. Unfortunately, they were out to dinner and did not seem at all upset that I had "moved" to someone else's house. I wish they hadn't believed me when I told them, with all my friends standing around, that the boy's parents were home. By the time I called again, I was feeling really high, and they said they were coming but did not seem to know I was in trouble. By the time they pulled up my speech was slurred and I threw up in the car. After that I don't remember much except that the room was spinning, my mom was calling me horrible names, and my little brother was sobbing and telling her to stop.

That's how the trouble in my life started, just that simply. From then on I felt embarrassed in school and rumors got back to me that everyone was saying I had given the boy a blowjob, which was simply not true. My mom and dad are divorced and I lived in fear that she would tell him what happened. I couldn't face my brother, and the shame inside of me just grew and grew. The next party I went to was a month later when I finally was allowed to go out again. Anxious and embarrassed, I drank too much and ended up with a boy I hardly knew, but a cell phone call to my mom convinced her I was just going to sleep at a girlfriend's. By now I was starting to have a reputation I deserved.

I'm now getting treatment for drug and alcohol use. My alcohol and drug use plays a big part in my everyday life. When I was younger, I used to just get high when someone gave me something, and I wasn't planning on going home for a while. Now I look to get high every day. I don't do drugs to really hide from the world or anything, I just like getting messed up because then I don't have to really face what a big hole I've dug for myself. I guess that is a type of hiding. Hide and seek, who can find the real me?

I'm very impulsive when it comes to using and drinking. I have even let people inside my house, [in] my room at 3 in the morning if I can get away with it. I might not even know the person that well, but at that moment I won't care because getting high and having company and fun is more important. When I was fourteen, I ran away for two days, all because I was doing whatever came my way. That's when my parents realized how impulsive I was. Sometimes now I will do some lines or drink, and then make rash decisions to leave at 3 a.m., just like I did the night before I came in here. I did some cocaine, some Xanax, and beer. I woke up with a guy I didn't recognize. How scary is that?

I feel wicked embarrassed about things I've done or said while I was high. Sometimes I'll cry about sad times when I was on drugs with my ex-boyfriend and we were doing stupid things to each other all because we were not in our right minds. Sometimes I'll feel bad about things I did all on my own. I remember one night in tenth grade when we ended up hanging out one night and getting totally trashed. I don't remember how it came about, but a good friend of mine named Brian ended up at my house. Soon afterward, he tried to molest both my best friend and me up in my bedroom. That night left me feeling numb. I lost the comfort of my own room, two friends, and my parents' trust once again. The biggest thing I lost was any temporary happiness and self-esteem that I had managed to gain since the time before and the time before that.

I look back now on when I first started hanging around kids who smoked pot and drank when I was thirteen, and I know for sure that that's when I lost my innocence. It took years for my parents to get the picture that I was in deep trouble. Now many family sessions and programs later, I often wonder if things could have turned out differently. If only I could have seen into the future; if only my parents knew then what they know now. I hated them then for trying to stop me; there are days I hate them now for missing all the signs. If only they had come the first time I had called them. But maybe that is blaming others and avoiding responsibility again. My grandmother even told me one time that I ruined my childhood. How sad to ruin your own childhood!

I have minimized my problems almost the entire time I've been using and having sex—saying to myself things like "it's not that bad," or even denying that it happened, like I'm trying to play tricks on my mind. My worst time is remembering all the sexual things that I did with guys for drugs or fun or both. I felt so gross while I was doing it and really dirty and cheap when I was walking home trying to hide the signs, sucking on candy and spraying perfume all over myself. I tried telling myself for a long time that I wanted to fool around with whomever it was that night and I didn't just do it for the drugs or attention, but I know now that that just wasn't true. I look back and know I really was just being used, and yet I still let them, and no one around me figured it out. At least no one figured it out [who] could help me. I guess now I am just going to have to help myself. I am determined to try, but deep down I know that I may never feel clean again.

STORY #6: MOOD AND ANXIETY ISSUES

FEMALE, AGE FIFTEEN: Ever since I was little, I was always late for things. It soon became a habit that I would awake with extra time to spare but would then get caught up in all the details of leaving for the day. Both my parents worked and I knew that I had to have everything together or else. Organizing became my focus although I never managed to get everything together that I needed, and by the end of elementary school there was a permanent "T" next to my name for tardy.

Fast-forward to sixth grade. It was the year before I headed to junior high and my last year of elementary school. I started to engage in more rituals like closing doors, arranging things continually, and worrying all the time about what was to come. No matter how prepared I was, I started to always expect a bad outcome. In a way it became self-fulfilling; I would get so anxious that I would zone out in school or purposely miss an exam and then have to take it over, only to end up with worse results than I wanted or deserved. Before I knew it, junior high was almost over and I was pretty much an anxious mess, always worrying that I wouldn't measure up. My parents saw me crying and heard my complaints but basically acted as if I should just suck it up.

Graduation came and went as did summer. I was nervous to start at a new school, a new grade, on the other side of town with [kids from] two other towns that I didn't know. We all heard rumors like wildfire about the other kids who were stuck up and how mean the upperclassmen could be. It didn't help that no one could deny these rumors because very few of us had actually met anybody that would be joining us from another town. When the first day came, I had to wake up at six in the morning, which I had done only once before. I was definitely not a morning person, and it had always been hard to wake me up. After the first week, I was hardly sleeping just thinking about the hardships that I imagined waited for me the next day.

In January things worsened. In fact, as it turned out, I never went back to school the first day after winter break. I was supposed to start back Monday morning when a snow day was announced. I was then even more nervous to go on Tuesday, when everyone else was returning. So I just stayed home and let my anxiety get the best of me. I finally did go back that week, but I felt all turned in on myself and felt certain that I would fail at everything. In an attempt to keep me on track, my parents seemed to just turn the pressure up, reminding me of missed assignments, talking to me about college, sports, extracurricular activities. My mind became a blur, and I felt sick to my stomach much of the time.

It was that year I got a psychiatrist who prescribed me anxiety and antidepressant medication: Zoloft. I had never taken daily medicine before and at first I refused to take it. I did not want to become a "guinea pig." Eventually I caved and after the first couple of weeks I felt 75 percent less anxious. It was improvement, but I still could not keep up with things, first dropping basketball, then French club, and finally damping down my classes in general. Dreams of being a superstar vanished, to be replaced by the worst feelings of failure and inferiority one could imagine.

Throughout this chaos my family was mostly supportive. They knew I had to go to school and they never said that I could stay home for fun, which I never wanted to do. "Skipping school" and "staying home" are completely different. My parents hated when I stayed home and I did, too. We all wanted me to get help so I could go back to being the "can do everything" kid I once was. We argued a lot about what was best for me. I never refused completely to go to school; I always just got nervous about getting there. Once I got to school, I would often be fine, more or less; I braved through the day, did the work as best I could, and talked to my friends. But I would get tired, anxious, and go to bed late, sleeping little due to my worries, and then the next morning I wouldn't be able to wake up again. As my mom called it, it was a "vicious circle."

My friends asked questions, but after a while they stopped. They wouldn't ask, they would just know. I'm pretty sure people were talking about me a lot, although I trusted a handful of my friends. It annoyed me when people from my classes I barely even knew, let alone talked to, would come right out and asked me where I had been. Was I sick? Did I have some injury or illness? Did I still intend to try out for sports? The answer was that I did not know. Was I skipping school? No. I had never meant to blow off school to throw a party. The most exciting thing I probably did all day when I did stay home was play computer games and watch "Saved by the Bell."

I understand people were curious, especially teenagers. They're always looking for the new bit of juicy secrets that they could "promise they won't tell anyone" and the next day it would be all anyone could talk about. So what was my answer for when people asked where I'd been or why I wasn't doing anything social or athletic? I'd just make something up. The truth is, by the time it got really bad, I was being tutored in the afternoons for an hour or two a couple times a week to make up work. It's one of the many things that kept me home. Little did these kids know, but the more they talked, the more I missed school, the greater the dread, the more intense the avoidance.

Last year I went to court for the first time and got a lawyer. A CHINS [Child In Need of Services petition] was filed against me for attendance issues. To them [court and school officials, social workers], I needed therapists and family meetings. But to me, no one could help me but myself.

The last time I went to court, like almost every time, people there didn't tell the truth. The probation officer and some of the lawyers said I cried all the time and was depressed. And I almost laughed because that was far from where I was. I've never been suicidal and the only disorder I have is anxiety. I was diagnosed with learning disabilities in math, but that's about it. It's insulting to me and other teens that actually have worse trouble than me when people assume I am different than I am. There is a problem with our society in deciding teens have problems without really listening to them before jumping to wrong conclusions.

In the summer I promised myself that I would go back to school in the fall. And I did. From that first day of school in September until December, I probably missed very few days. I was always on time and did my work. It was fun to see other people be late or absent when I was there.

But then before winter vacation, I got chicken pox and was out for more than a week. I returned to school after that, but I was shaken from the break. I missed more and more days, and dropped all my extra activities again until after Christmas. I went back only one day, the day we all came back: January 4, 2006. When I finally did return full-time to school weeks later, people asked me where I was, and I said I had mono. The perfect solution: It makes you tired and unable to do anything, and you get it for weeks at a time. For me, I'd take mono over anxiety any day. There is really nothing worse than being made to feel crazy because you're anxious.

Since then I've gotten another tutor who comes twice a week for several hours, but I'm still behind. I might have to go to summer school, and I'm praying that I don't have to repeat the grade. I want to go to school next year with all my friends. I want to go to yearbook club again and sing in chorus and play sports. I want to play my clarinet in band and perform in drama. I want to see all my friends and make plans for the weekend. I talk to them online or on the phone every day, but I can really see them only once or twice a week. My close friends don't ask where I am anymore. My excuses are numbered, and so are my days.

In March, when I was in court again on my CHINS [petition] they almost took me away from my parents, saying they were irresponsible and that because they don't make me stare at a wall all day, they were being too flexible. No more computer or "Saved by the Bell" for me. By that I mean because I can't function properly, others feel my parents should be blamed. They didn't know what to do and neither did I. DSS [the Department of Social Services] almost sent me to a punishment program. Anxiety, as I insist, should not be punished. It should be treated.

I was always able to drive by the school and not get stricken with fear. And I've been to the school itself after hours, at times when I wasn't going. The word "school" became a bad thing in my vocabulary. It didn't matter that I loved to learn and my grades were overall good. The anxiety was all in the period of time when I get up and when I had to get to school. But it's easier if I had gone the day before. Then, it is practically nonexistent. But as soon as I built some momentum, something would actually happen to keep me home and then I was back to square one with the anxiety.

I hate anxiety: My pulse goes up and my muscles tighten, and I seem to constantly have a headache. There's no real solution for it, except taking meds and going to therapy and learning coping skills. I will always have a little bit of anxiety. But everyone gets it once in a while. Some things work more than others for different people.

For me, medicine has helped a little. But the thing that eventually helped the most was finding a therapist who stopped treating me like I was spoiled or willful and started to really get that I was anxious. She finally helped me come up with techniques that worked, like conversations I could have with myself, and things that I could picture in my mind to reverse the anxiety. Once I started to see her regularly, things started to get better. I even could call her when I was starting to feel like avoiding something. But I still wish I didn't have anxiety.

In the future, if I ever get by this situation, I want to be a fashion designer. All the thoughts of me being a lawyer were lost when I walked into the courtroom. I want to go to college along with all my friends, and I've never wanted to drop out of school. (It is illegal to drop out under sixteen anyway.) I have goals for myself. I'm more than this school problem. I've never had behavioral problems or caused trouble. I've never done drugs or drinking. Anxiety messes up my brain enough. Every since I was little, I've worried about everything. I'm better now, because I don't lie in bed wondering if I'm going to die, my stomach tying in knots and increasing my sleep deprivation. I never used to be able to watch a scary movie, because I would be terrified at everything for months. I'm improving, though.

Anxiety should not be a label for a person who is otherwise normal. I'm just like everyone else, even though I'm obsessed with fashion, I adore my dog, and I have a thing about being clean. People come to me for advice. They talk to me when they're upset. They see me as being a confident, put-together person most of the time. But really, at the end of the day, we're all the same. In my future, I hope this school situation and all my avoidance [don't] restrict me. Because this is not who I am; inside I am someone nice and capable of lots of things. I just need to get over being scared. I just need the right person to help me to get better.

STORY #7: DEPRESSION AND CUTTING

FEMALE, AGE 18: It's 3 a.m. now, and I know I'm not going to sleep, so I'll write this. This has been one of the many symptoms of my illness, my depression, whatever it is labeled as. I'm going to try to chronicle my depression and tell you my story, which is hard when depression is more of a label than something I feel adequately describes my experience over the last three plus years.

I cut myself. The funny thing is that self-injury preceded my depression, not the other way around. The first time I can remember doing it was sitting on the end of my bed, grinding a nail clipper into my arm, wanting to prove, for no good reason, that I was strong enough to do it. After all, some of my friends were. It didn't work, and I remember going into the bathroom and sitting on the edge of the tub, and picking up a safety razor and sliding it down my skin. To me, in that moment, the pain was unbelievable, but I also felt as if I had accomplished something. I was fourteen, and at that time, it was enough, it was purely a test, and in my mind I had passed it.

When I think back, I don't know if something was wrong already, but I guess someone who would do that just for the sake of doing it isn't too healthy either. Sophomore year came. I had done it a few times since the first time. I don't know what made it change. All I can say was that something did. I'd sit there, in front of my computer, or in my bed, or on the floor and it felt like my head was tipping forward and nothing about me was real. I was floating. I'd float through my classes; I'd float home, and float down to my room. I'd respond but not listen, and laugh but not be happy. When I cut myself, as the blood came out, I was tethering myself back to the real world, planting myself back on the floor again.

I let myself get progressively worse. I didn't do it as an experiment; I did it to feel something. Some people describe depression as being sad all the time, but I'm not a sad person really. My depression is all about not caring, about lacking any real care for myself, or motivation that would stop me from treating myself the way I do. Now I was tired all the time, I'd stay up all night, sleep an hour, then go through school mindlessly. Junior year started and I was at my breaking point. I'd cut myself in the bathroom in school, when I got home I'd do it, I'd do it before bed so I could sleep. I was like on a different wavelength from everyone else, where I didn't care about anyone, and I was barely really living my life. When my mother found out, "it" hit the fan so to speak. I don't think I had cried for months, and I don't think I stopped crying for hours when she made me show her that day.

She put me in therapy, and I started DBT [dialectical behavior therapy; see chapter 4]. Now that I think of it, I think this was a big changing point. I laugh about how little DBT did for me, but when I think of the "me" that I knew before it, and the "me" that was after it, there is change. Before, whatever was wrong with me manifested itself in this dead feeling, this person who never cried and was barely awake. DBT is all about identifying your emotions and dealing with the people around you. When I think of my depression, the one I deal with now, it's no longer about never feeling something, it's about feeling so intensely, about being overwhelmed by dealing with the people around me.

In my head, I have a hard time trying to look objectively at what could have provoked my depression, trying to pick apart what is true and the things that I've read about too much in psychology books. I can look at "the me" I am now, not necessarily a "well" person, but someone who's finally starting to deal with things, and through all the emotional extremes, is at least finding what upsets her.

My father was diagnosed with colon cancer when I was eleven. I still remember the outfits I wore, the gifts people gave him, the smell of the sheets they put on his bed at the hospital. I'm crying as I write this, and I can say it's the one thing that will always set me off. My brother and I would go from school to the hospital all the time. It took a long time for him to get well. The fact that he lived is a miracle in itself, though no one told me at that time that everyone thought he was surely going to die. I don't know if my childhood was somehow stunted. I think that's when I started to do a lot of things on my own, became pretty introverted, and a bit unlike my peers. The whole experience is like this big black spot or something on me. He's fine, but it's something I still can't get over.

When I think of my father, I always keep in mind his experience. "You have to be happy he's here to yell at you." "Don't talk to him that way, you're lucky to have him at all." I hate myself for holding so much anger against him. I hate it. I can remember once I got oil pastels on the carpet. I was so scared. I tried to clean it and even cut it out of the carpet. He came home and half lifted, half pushed me down the stairs. Maybe that's where I got my inability to cry; he'd hit us as punishment, or yell at us in a way that scared me more than anyone else could, but I would not cry, I'd whimper at the most. Balancing the memories I have like that, with the way he loves me, or how I'm "daddy's girl," or how he "lived through cancer to see me and my brother grow up," is one of the hardest things for me to do.

I remember reading somewhere that when a child goes through something violent like that when they're young, they learn to associate love with that anger, and when they get older, and the anger or violence goes away, they hurt themselves instead. I don't know if it's just psychological bull, but it made sense to me. He can still set me off in seconds. When I was put in the hospital, he demanded I be taken out immediately and met with my doctor. I've never cried like that in front of anyone in my life. I'm never going to forget what he said to me, don't know if I can forgive him either, but I still love him to death somehow.

My mother and I, well I don't know, we're the typical mother-daughter pair. Somewhat. I take everything out on her to be honest, but I'm getting better, a lot better at treating her appropriately. She always did the best for me, and maybe it was just because I could get away with it that I took the way I felt/feel out on her.

Depression becomes as addictive as cutting myself. I get addicted to letting myself stay in front of the computer for hours, looking at pictures of other people cut open. I get addicted to letting myself ruminate, and let myself just slide down farther and farther until I get to the point where I'm taking out my "bag of tricks," and opening up a surgery in my bed.

But that's the problem with depression. You get into it, and once you're in, no part of you really is motivated enough to get you out by yourself. There's so much behind you in the past that pushed you into that hole, and someone else has to come in and dig it all out, before you can climb out yourself.

Cutting myself is getting old; there's a point where I am going to get sick of it, there's a point where [I] can't get any worse without becoming completely engulfed by my habit. But the depression, the feelings why I [cut], the way that my family makes me feel, all that is much more new.

I pushed it all away for so long, and I have a lot to deal with still before I feel okay. I can't even really imagine it now, but I have to try. If I don't, I'll end up finding another way to deal with it, something that's probably worse than being a collector of scar tissue.

CHAPTER 10

Parents as Part of the Recovery Process

Sue Mandelbaum-Cohen, LICSW

I first met Jake's mother when she appeared at my office looking weary and shell-shocked. She introduced herself, and I invited her into my office to begin a relationship based on the tragic circumstances of her seventeen-year-old son's attempted suicide. When I asked how she was bearing up, her response was to slump onto the couch and convulse into deep, unrelenting sobs.

After some time, we talked about the events of the past two days, starting with her finding Jake unconscious in his room after ingesting fifty Tylenol tablets. Jake left a note for her, his father, and his fifteen-year-old sister conveying his love for them and contempt for himself, which he felt was unbearable and the reason behind his decision to take his life.

An A student at a highly regarded suburban high school, athletic and attractive, Jake was well liked and appeared competent in all areas. In hindsight, there were subtle signs that suggested mood changes but nothing remarkable or life interfering. He stayed home more after a breakup with a girlfriend but assured everyone he was handling things fine. He missed school a few times and spent more time on the computer, sending instant messages to friends late into the night. Jake's parents were successful professionals who placed the needs of their children above their own, providing all the comforts and emotional support they could to ensure their success. They were an "average family" with no glaring problems that might account for this rupture in their son's life and within the family.

Jake's mother's expression pleaded that I not judge her as a parent who failed her child. She could not appreciate that I neither judged nor blamed her, but rather wholeheartedly appreciated her distress. My goal was to help the family participate in their son's recovery.

BY THE TIME CHILDREN enter psychiatric care, families have been to hell and back. Sometimes there has been an exhaustive journey with a long history of symptomatic behaviors that can rip apart family life and create emotional fallout beyond the collective capacity of families, school officials, and mental health providers to contain. There is emotional hazardous waste everywhere. Or, as in the case above, there is hidden, unanticipated devastation that changes every aspect of life following the often inevitable crisis.

From the parental point of view, the nightmare begins when their child ceases to be reliable, predictable, and responsive to their concerns, requests, or demands. They report feeling like they have become incidental players in the lives of children who injure themselves, contemplate or attempt suicide, obsess about hurting others, act with rage and violence, abuse drugs, or show contempt for their families and themselves.

From the adolescents' point of view, their problems may be prompted by acute stressors such as social rejection, high academic expectations, peer pressures, and so forth or extend into a past filled with maladaptive adjustments to family problems largely outside of their control. These teens have contended with issues that often include adoption, divorce, remarriage, parental drug addiction, illness or death of a family member, and parental job loss. Other teens suffer from the consequences of parental neglect, and physical, sexual, and emotional abuse, and removal from their families followed by multiple placements with foster parents or institutional care. The spectrum of adolescent and family dysfunction cuts a swath wide and deep.

From the outset, the goal of treatment is to clarify the causal factors related to the crisis at hand and hope for a chance to re-involve the family in a more constructive fashion.

Many parents walk through the doors of our unit or an outpatient clinician's office hoping for and anticipating a straightforward resolution of the problems that interfere with their child's healthy functioning. They are often exhausted from the events preceding hospitalization and look to clinicians for hopeful signs of recovery and the return to a family life that is predictable and manageable.

(Note: Some patients who arrive at McLean Hospital come directly from locked, inpatient psychiatric units and step down to the McLean program, which is considered less restrictive. Others come directly from emergency rooms where they are evaluated and screened. They may be brought by the police who are called by parents when children are behaving dangerously either due to self-destructive actions or aggression toward others. Sometimes therapists send patients to emergency rooms when they deem them to be unsafe and at risk for hurting themselves or others.)

What parents do not always anticipate is the role they may be called upon to play in the recovery of their child's crisis. The parent-child relationship may, in fact, become the focus of treatment, which can result in parents feeling judged and blamed. In our efforts to assist children, especially in situations involving family and/or psychosocial issues, it is important to acknowledge parents' despair as they grapple with both their child's fate and their own emotional responses to these difficult circumstances.

Parents need to understand and address what might have gone wrong within the structure, communication pattern, and overall context of the family that might have unwittingly contributed to the adolescent's despair. Families are, thus, a major factor and often necessary participants in a teen's recovery.

THE GOALS OF FAMILY TREATMENT

This dissection of a family system, if you will, opens up the private, hidden realities and hardships confronting children, their siblings, and parents. Feelings of guilt, shame, disappointment, anger, and helplessness coalesce the moment a family crosses the threshold into the purview of professional strangers.

Adolescent psychiatry necessitates active participation by parents. The family is the context and frequently the cauldron in which interpersonal problems bubble over and may scald family members.

A psychosocial assessment views the child in the context of family relationships that affect mood, behavior, and degree of emotional reactivity, attachments, and values. It is also an assessment of social engagement beyond the family, which may include social relationships with peers, academic performance, participation in activities, and level of interest in future goals. Biological predispositions are equally important in assessing the origin of symptoms. Thus, biosocial theory is the engine driving assessments when children enter care. Symptoms are seen as a joint outcome of biological disposition, environmental factors, and the transaction between the two during a child's development into adolescence.

When a youngster appears for treatment with symptoms of major depression, physiologic irregularities in brain chemistry may explain the noticeable changes in mood. However, without exploring environmental and situational realities, only part of the picture will have been illuminated. Not all psychiatric problems are byproducts of environmental pressures and stressors, but many are.

The variables that affect relationships between parents and children are infinite. Children seem most secure when they are not burdened by extreme parental discord and the fear of family disruption, when they feel protected from danger, when financial issues are primarily kept within the parental realm of concern. Kids hate worrying about their parents because they feel helpless when confronted with problems beyond their ability to solve. How can a child fill the emotional void created by an absent parent or maintain equanimity when a marriage ends and parents crucify each other for their marital sins?

Approximately 75 percent of all high school age children face a divorce, remarriage, or other significant disruption in their family lives.

Teenagers with a biological predisposition to mood dysfunction may be more or less vulnerable to these outside forces. It falls to the parents and professionals to then work collaboratively to chart a course to recovery.

ISSUES SURROUNDING DIVORCE

When a fifteen-year-old girl appeared for treatment with symptoms of anxiety, depressed mood, and self-mutilation that involved piercing and cutting herself, she was started on antidepressant medications to ameliorate the physical symptoms. The medication would eventually reduce her physical discomfort; however, adapting to the reality of parents who despised one another was another matter.

When her parents were requested to schedule an appointment together, her mother responded by saying, "Meeting with my husband is like sitting with Osama Bin Laden. I won't do it." Speaking in hyperbole may have nailed her feelings about her ex-husband, but it left her daughter an innocent civilian caught in the crossfire of parental warfare. The patient was also adrift in the sea of bad and worse choices: She ran the risk of disappointing her mother if she expressed sympathy for her father and angering her father if she supported her mother. Harming herself had become a way to relieve the tension generated by the unbearable circumstances of her parents' discordant relationship.

Obviously, the spectrum of behavior for divorced parents is enormous. Many parents are sensitive to the ramifications of "fighting with each other through their children" and endure their situation for the sake of their children. For others, what is best for their child gets buried under the tidal wave of bitterness that can obliterate a parent's common sense and good judgment. Ultimately, everyone pays a terrible price if there is no cessation of parental warfare.

Children generally aspire to maintain family relationships that are supportive and loving despite the status of their divorced parents. Unless there has been violence of an emotional or physical nature, children wish for continued contact and integration into the lives of both parents. Taking sides or fearing betrayal of a parent is the stuff of nightmares for children of acrimonious divorce. When parents appreciate and validate the bind children find themselves in when an ex-spouse is demonized, it can reduce a child's anxiety and foster honest discourse. There are times when the needs of a child must trump everything else. Divorce is only one of many situations when parents are called upon to act unselfishly so that children are unscathed by choices the parents make for themselves. They may inadvertently dismiss the feelings of their child and become defensive about their own behavior. In extreme cases, parents are out of touch with the effects their choices of lifestyle and behaviors have on their children.

Contentious divorces can have devastating effects on children, and there are countless permutations of how this plays out. How biological parents get along with each other can affect the relationships between children and their stepparents. When a child does not feel encumbered by a discordant relationship where obvious animosity between their parents exists, adjusting to the presence of new adults in their lives may be less stressful and free of conflict. Many adolescents describe feeling anxious when they have spent enjoyable time with a stepparent. It can be as simple as that. They fear betrayal of the parent who has been replaced by the stepmother or stepfather.

It can be especially difficult if the extenuating circumstances leading to divorce involve mistreatment of a parent where there is degradation of some kind that a child has either witnessed or is aware of. If there is infidelity, it further complicates a child's feelings toward a parent's attachment to a new partner. When one parent is left more vulnerable by events in the marriage, children are inclined to worry and feel protective of that parent.

Sometimes, like the mother who viewed her ex-husband as a terrorist, a parent remains hateful. She may appreciate her daughter's dilemma but remain fixed in a state of mind she cannot change. In situations like this, clinicians can do their best to acknowledge the distress felt by parents and validate the challenges they face when adapting to changing relationships. Strife between divorced parents is frequently a factor of adolescent disturbances in mood and their poor regulation of emotions and behavior.

CASE STUDY

Sam—Familial Acrimony

SIXTEEN-YEAR-OLD SAM was hospitalized for severe temper outbursts, punching holes in walls at home, abusing his stimulant medication by snorting it, and threatening suicide. He was sullen, irritable, easily provoked, and his speech was rapid and intense.

Sam had little regard for the feelings of others and started swearing when frustrated by the rules of the program. He assumed no one had anything to offer him and that his parents made a big mistake sending him to the hospital. If he wanted to die, it was his right. As his history unfolded, we learned about his longstanding diagnosis of attention deficit hyperactivity disorder and struggle with organizational and attention problems.

Because Sam was bright, he was able to function in school until the past year when he seemed overwhelmed by the challenges of high school. He became more depressed and angry. His parents divorced when he ten. At that time, he displayed signs of depression, met with a therapist for a short time, and was started on antidepressant medications with little positive effect.

Sam lived with his mother and had weekly visitations with his father. He was disdainful toward them both, calling them losers. The divorce had been acrimonious, and Sam's parents always argued about what was in their son's best interest. Dad viewed Mom as too lenient; Mom saw Dad as overbearing and unreasonable. The boy was certain they could not agree on anything because they despised each other and would never give the other the benefit of the doubt. He mocked their efforts to control his behavior, comparing his failures with theirs as parents.

DISCUSSION

It took effort getting Sam's parents to agree to meet together. Sam was correct about their animosity and devaluing manner. Their habit of blaming and pointing fingers occurred automatically, and they made no attempt to shield their son from invectives thrown at one another. As their fighting escalated, so did Sam's anger. His disrespectful attitude toward them echoed their bitter fighting.

However, in this case, the parents were able to appreciate the negative affect their fighting had on their son, determined to cooperate in his behalf, and shield him when their differences were highly charged.

This helped the boy view himself within a context of family relationships that needed to change. Expressions of anger that set a discordant, hostile tone were not his problem alone; he realized he wasn't responsible for his parents' ability to get along. A weight was lifted that enabled him to participate in treatment with his parents in a more controlled and restrained atmosphere. Sam began to feel relief knowing that his parents would address their own problems.

Slowly, and then at a more rapid pace, Sam was able to negotiate with his parents. As their aggression toward one another diminished and they learned conflict resolution skills and modeling more effective coparenting, Sam's improvement paralleled theirs.

Many parents want to put aside their differences, but cannot overcome their entrenched patterns of interacting. We see a lot of parents blaming the other for their child's misfortune. When parents unite for the benefit of the child, however, it truly makes a profound difference.

Challenges of Blended Families

Blended families, which are a social unit consisting of one or two previously married parents, their children from former marriages, and/or offspring from their marriage to one another, can become hotbeds of relational disappointment and conflict, resulting in angry, frustrated family members. Many variables account for this, with a teenager questioning his or her sense of belonging within the new family constellation. Teens who struggle with this arrangement feel competitive with step-siblings they perceive as favored and treated more fairly.

A child who believes his or her family unit is complete bristles when remarriage produces half siblings and creates necessary changes in schedules and time with parents. Under the best of circumstances, these are wonderful events and cause for celebration. However, teens who collapse under the weight of such changes benefit from the opportunity to voice themselves and suggest ways to improve relationships with parents.

The term "blended" may be a misnomer when applied to situations that are neither smooth nor well integrated. All too often, children, parents, stepparents, and step- and half-siblings are in conflict, trying to navigate new relationships tainted by past experiences that involve the demise of the original family. Adults can ease this process when they provide children sufficient opportunity to embrace the change, validate the anxiety evoked by conflicting loyalties, disruptions in their routines necessitating change of living situations and less frequent contact with certain family members.

Even the most resilient teenagers are hard-pressed when called upon to adapt themselves to these changes. Parent-child communication during these times is often very emotional and may quickly deteriorate when feelings are hurt and people feel misunderstood.

Amid all this upheaval, the needs of adolescents change as they grow and develop into adults. Arrangements that worked when they were younger may no longer work now, and renegotiations are necessary so that visitation schedules, for example, are more suited to the present.

Children of divorce may have successfully lived alternately with each parent during the week, but as teenagers, they often prefer one home base with a parent and weekend visits with the other. However, schedules change and unexpected events occur that may interfere with visitation schedules. Unless parents and children can be flexible and tolerant, crises are bound to occur that create resentment and recriminations. Families need to maintain open and direct communication during these times, no matter how difficult. Avoiding and denying issues is not effective. Conversations with a counselor, mediator, or mental health provider may help reduce an escalated disagreement. Either way, the dialogue, along with active support, must continue as kids get older and seek more say in their daily lives.

CASE STUDY

Becky—An Outsider in a Blended Family

BECKY'S PARENTS DIVORCED when she was five years old. Her parents had joint custody, while physical custody was with her mother. She remembers being introduced to her father's girlfriend who later became his wife and her stepmother. After the marriage, they had two daughters, two years apart. When Becky visited their home, it was initially exciting to be with the babies and play the role of big sister. Over time, however, her feelings changed dramatically. The younger girls occupied her father's time, which she resented because they lived with him and had daily contact. She rarely had time alone with him.

By age twelve, Becky felt like an outsider during visits to his home. The den room where she slept was made into a larger bedroom for one of her half sisters and there was no space designated as her own. She was increasingly saddened and diminished by subtle changes, which made her feel displaced and less important to her father.

Complicating matters further was the discomfort Becky experienced with her mother dropping her off at the foot of the driveway and never being asked in by either father or stepmother. There had been no integration of the two families. She lived in parallel universes that never intersected, except when crises began to occur and her parents were forced to be together on her behalf.

Becky was initially hospitalized at age fourteen for overdosing on fifty Tylenol tablets. She wanted to die because her life felt intolerable. She felt worthless in spite of superior grades at school, good peer relationships, athletic skills, and artistic talent. Becky revealed that she had been cutting herself for several months. It helped her relieve stress, counteract feelings of numbness, and distract her from emotional pain.

Initially, Becky could not describe the source of her unhappiness. Ultimately, she identified a chronic and unrelenting sense of loss after the breakup of the family and anger at her parents, particularly her father for failing to recognize her needs and longings. She resented asking him for increased time together. Why had he not understood this up front, without explanation from her? Becky hoped for some inclusion of her mother in this blended arrangement to alleviate disquieting feelings when crossing over into her father's world. Her mother struggled financially as a single parent and Becky worried about her mother's well-being. She had not been able to express these feelings to either parent.

DISCUSSION

In this situation, candid conversations about family relationships rarely took place. Becky worried about reprisals from upset adults if she challenged the status quo. Therefore, her feelings were suppressed rather than risk outcomes far worse, such as parental rejection and the burden of guilt for creating dissension.

Over the course of treatment, Becky was encouraged to raise her grievances with the co-parenting arrangements and talk directly about her diminished sense of importance when competing with two younger half-sisters. She wanted time alone with her father without distractions, even if it was for coffee or dinner once a week. Having a designated space as her own in his home reaffirmed a sense of the belonging she lost when her previous space was usurped. It's a fine line feeling like a visitor versus someone who lives somewhere, even if less often.

In addition, Becky challenged the old ways of family togetherness. In her mind's eye, she imagined the easing of rigid boundaries from childhood that separated the two families of which she was a member. It was time for "the adults to get their acts together" and do what was in the best interest of their children. Many adolescents struggle with this very issue and resent parents who won't or can't resolve their differences to diminish tensions and help create a more desirable family arrangement.

ISSUES SURROUNDING ADOPTION

We see many children who are adopted who struggle with issues of identity when they enter their teens, attempting to reconcile biological realities with their adoptive status.

Being adopted means different things to teenagers than to younger children. Some are grateful at having been raised by loving parents instead of a birth parent who could not provide for them. Others experience a chronic pain of feeling different and out of place and suffer the loss and sorrow of abandonment by a biological parent. The words "You're not my mother," or "You're not my father," pierce the hearts of parents who never anticipated hearing this from a child they loved from the outset.

Adolescents begin the journey of self-discovery by convincing themselves they can navigate their boats without oars, sails, or rudders and without bread or water. As a consequence of this fearlessness, they dismiss adults entirely and rely instead on their chosen "crew." The crew, in their minds, is superior to any adult team they've ever known. Often, the crewmembers look like them. They may have the same skin color, speak a common language, and share cultural rituals that bind them and produce a cohesive group.

Trans-racial and trans-cultural adoptions can, therefore, often further confuse adolescent identity development and result in rebellious, angry, and reckless behavior. In these instances, parents who have often given their all in an effort to help their children "blend" within a community or set of family mores/traditions feel utterly lost as to how to help navigate their adopted teen's complete dislocation.

CASE STUDY

Laura

A SIXTEEN-YEAR-OLD GIRL of Hispanic origin, Laura lived with her adoptive parents in an affluent Boston suburb. She was adopted five days after her birth. She had jet-black hair, deep brown eyes, and olive skin. Her adoptive parents were Irish. Her mother was covered in freckles and had strawberry blonde hair. Her adoptive father died a few years ago.

Laura had been running away from home, going into areas of the city considered unsafe by her mother, smoking marijuana, getting drunk, and had become sexually active without using birth control. She swore obscenities at her mother when angry and repeatedly said she hated her.

The only people Laura felt connected to in her town were "the maids" from a cleaning service, comprising mainly Hispanic women who came to clean the homes of the well-to-do. When Laura threatened suicide rather than return home from running away, her mother sought hospitalization to prevent self-destructive behaviors from occurring further.

DISCUSSION

Many meetings took place to begin unraveling the complex factors entangled in the decline of Laura and her mother's relationship. Doors were slammed, voices raised, obscenities hurled, and tears shed.

Laura still grieved the loss of her adopted father years before, and she dreaded another loss. His untimely death had evoked grief not only for the parents she never knew but also for the other aspects of herself that were lost through adoption: the loss of origins and the loss of a completed sense of herself and of genetic continuity.

Because teenagers are so focused on their appearance, appearing so different from her adoptive mother embarrassed her. For a Hispanic child to be raised by an Irish parent, the obvious physical differences that set them apart can cause extreme self-consciousness. Issues of identity get confused for youngsters who look different from their adoptive parents so they often attempt to associate themselves with the ethnic group of their biological parents. Hence, Laura chose to identify herself with "the maids" she believed to be more like her than people who were affluent and white in her community.

Laura connected the untimely death of her adopted father with chronic anxiety associated with loss. She thought of and wrote about the biological family she had never known, all the time refusing her mother's help in an effort to locate and establish some connection with them. Would she have been better off with them, would she be happier? These are questions Laura continuously asked herself but avoided seeking any answers to. In time, she acknowledged her fear of finding this family and devastating her adopted mother, already widowed by the loss of her husband. It would feel unbearable to her, she admitted, having to "choose." This turmoil externalized into rage at her mother and her subsequent reckless behaviors only reinforced her self-hatred for being the disappointment she was.

This situation resolved eventually in an unexpectedly hopeful way. Some adoptive parents are resentful, hurt, and feel betrayed when a child wants to embark on a search for their biological family. Laura's mother, however, was completely supportive as indicated by past efforts to initiate a search, only to be thwarted by her daughter's objections. The patient was too fearful of trusting her mother's words in light of the loss she suffered when her father died.

Ultimately, the "psychological searching" brought clarity to Laura's feelings about being adopted, which she shared with her mother. They began a collaboration, facing the unknown together, looking to expand rather than disrupt their long-established attachment to each other.

CASE STUDY

Meghan

AN ORTHODOX JEWISH FAMILY adopted Meghan, another youngster of Hispanic origin, when she was a year old. She was adopted from an orphanage in Guatemala. Her early childhood progressed successfully, and she was a beloved member of the family.

In Meghan's twelfth year, radical changes in her behavior started to occur. She was unable to keep up with the rigorous studies at a Jewish day school because of learning disabilities and a growing disenchantment with her parents' expectations. Studying for her Bat Mitzvah became agony. She was uncomfortable with the demands and pressures to learn Hebrew, which began to feel more alien to her. The vast difference between herself and the biological children of her adoptive parents further reinforced her sense of separateness and low self-regard. She believed she did not belong to their orderly, intellectual, accomplished world. Thus, she began behaving in ways entirely antithetical to their values, screaming, "I don't have to listen to you! You're not my real parents!" when she broke a rule of the household.

It went from bad to worse. On the holiest day of the year, Meghan was found in the Temple bathroom performing oral sex on a classmate. Choosing this site and on this holiday symbolized how the meaning of family had degenerated into farce. Feeling that she was totally beyond their control, the family admitted Meghan to our acute residential treatment program and began family meetings as part of the treatment.

DISCUSSION

When children feel alienated, they will push the envelope in anticipation of others forsaking them, leaving them isolated and abandoned as they imagined their ultimate fate to be. An adopted child is apt to act up as a way of coping with intolerable anxiety stemming from insecurity and confusion about identity and belonging.

Meghan finally came to the hospital when her parents lost parental authority and feared for her safety. She ultimately went to a residential school to curtail impulsive behaviors and achieve an understanding of what being adopted meant to her, how it affected her behaviors, and what the future might be with her family. She lacked the motivation and will to find a healthier way of integrating her parents' values with her emerging identity, and her parents were unable to tolerate the degree to which she rebelled.

In this situation, the gulf between Meghan and her parents grew so wide that prolonged separation from the family seemed the only choice to avoid further damage. All attempts to negotiate a family contract had failed. It was a devastating choice these parents felt forced to make, inevitably repeating their child's surrender to other caregivers in the hope her life might be saved. They feared her unwillingness to forgive as a consequence of interpreting their decision as final evidence that she never belonged in their family in the first place, and never would. This was a risk the parents were prepared to take if extended treatment could salvage her connection to them and preserve her safety.

Ultimately, Meghan completed a residential treatment program and moved back home. Her parents supported her wishes to attend a cosmetology program and she continues outpatient therapy.

WHEN FAMILY THERAPY IS NOT ENOUGH

Children who cannot regulate their emotions intimidate parents, make them angry because of their level of disrespect, and can cause feelings of helplessness in the entire family. Their emotional dysregulation can manifest itself in the form of tantrums, intense reactivity, mood instability, both verbal and physical aggression, and disregard for both the rules and the feelings of others. In extreme cases, these children become pariahs across the board—at school, in their communities, and within their families.

The behaviors may be symptomatic of mental illness and/or reactions to parenting styles that shift from leniency to overexertion of authority as a means of attempting to regain parental control. No matter the cause, some teen behaviors become so extreme that parents along with siblings are terrorized. Time and again, families describe walking on eggshells in the presence of such behaviors. It feels to them as if they are "living with a terrorist." They are at a loss to intervene and effect any positive outcome. They try everything from family therapy, anger management groups, and appeals to the court system with the issuance of child supervision orders to calling the police.

Parents fear their teen's behaviors will not remain contained within the family and will escalate to criminal activities and that their adolescent will end up in a juvenile detention program, which is essentially a jail for those under age eighteen. When the teen's behaviors appear random and unpredictable and become chronic, parents' lives are interrupted by unremitting crises, including visits to emergency rooms, extra appointments with mental health providers, court appearances, and frequent meetings with school personnel. Parents exhaust time off from work and worry continually about potential job loss.

The tipping point comes when there is too much collateral damage and parents can no longer tolerate a child's destructive behaviors. There have been one too many holes punched in walls, doors broken, sleepless nights when children fail to return home, abuse of alcohol and drugs, suicidal and self-harming behaviors, and obscenities that hover like stale air and reverberate in the broken hearts of parents.

Deciding that a child cannot live at home is capitulating to realities no parent wants to face. Yet prolonged separation from families can begin a process of renegotiation of rules, limits, and expectations, and it can allow for reflection on what is salvageable in a series of fractured family relationships. Parents mourn the loss of the child they remember and once embraced with a loving heart and without intimidation. They cannot explain how it ever got so bad, so out of control, and beyond all efforts to reverse.

Rather than risk a child ending up on the streets and being subjected to potentially lethal experiences, residential treatment, in its many forms, becomes the only option left to parents. While this is heartbreaking, it can also be life saving.

PARENTS AS PERSONAL ADVOCATES FOR TROUBLED TEENS

Bullying and social rejection may cause a targeted youth to become violent or preoccupied with violence as a means of feeling powerful. Conversely, he or she may become morbidly depressed with thoughts of self-harm and entertain suicide.

The humiliation suffered at the hands of those who tease and bully can be devastating. When children are socially ostracized and become outcasts, they may develop post-traumatic stress disorder, generalized anxiety disorder, and/or major depression.

Independent but coexisting psychiatric conditions such as Asperger's syndrome and other pervasive development disorders make social development very difficult, adding to a child's vulnerability for sadistic, abusive behaviors by others. These are cases in which the child may have a biological vulnerability that cannot withstand pressures from the world beyond family and those who are familiar with their idiosyncrasies. These are cases where the origin of the problem may not include family discord, but the solution certainly requires parental involvement.

Today, more than ever before, large schools exist in large communities made up of disconnected and unrelated individuals who can no longer serve as a support or solace to any given, individual teen. Often, there are no "outside" adults who are even aware that a problem is looming. The teen with an anxiety disorder or other underlying developmental delay or difficulty does not appear with the same disruptive behaviors either to their family or the greater community. Therefore, it is easy for their pain to go unnoticed. It is easy for them to stay under the radar, so to speak, of a busy, working family.

We now know, however, that these anxious, bullied kids can be just the ones who end up exploding, whose anger becomes intolerable to the point that they dwell on destruction of both themselves and their tormentors. These kids desperately need their families to both notice and intercede, to become their advocates as well as their allies. The following is an account, written by a mother about her son and his metamorphosis into a young man unrecognizable to his parents. Only once his personal agonies became revealed did the parents have some insight into the dramatic changes in his mood and behavior and understand how they might mobilize and participate in his recovery.

A Mother's Account

When my twelve-year-old son started spiking his hair, dressing in black, wearing studded bracelets and chains on his pants, and obsessing about the end of the world, I didn't know what to think. He'd always been a bright kid with a charming smile and more friends than he could count. But then his grades dropped. He retreated to his room. He listened all night to punk music with lyrics about death, violence, and anarchy. I thought that this is just the way teenagers act these days.

But then he began drawing on his arms and making little cuts with pencils or paper clips. My husband and I told him to stop, but he didn't. In fact, the scratches only grew deeper. The guidance counselor at school called this "cutting." I'd never heard the term before, but she said that teenagers did this to get rid of pain, and that we needed help.

I took him to his pediatrician, who prescribed Prozac. Then I took him to a therapist who wanted him to "contract for safety," that is, agree that he would not cut again. He wouldn't do it. He said he couldn't stop. From there, things spiraled out of control. Our family had been close. We ate dinner together every night and played board games and hiked on weekends. But now, my son acted as if he hated us. Everything we did, everything we said, turned into a battle—homework, household chores, and practicing his instrument. Even normal conversation ended in screams and slammed doors. This baffled and frustrated us, and I began to feel as if I lived with Sid Vicious.

The next I knew, my son's old friends stopped calling and coming by. They wouldn't sit with him at lunch. They teased and bullied him mercilessly. So he found new friends on the Internet. These kids all considered themselves outcasts. They didn't care for school and liked to live on the edge. Some were having sex and using drugs. Nearly all liked to cut. They made a pact: When one cut, they'd all cut. Between this and a suicide attempt, reported by one of his former friends, my son's therapist insisted that I take him to the emergency room to be screened for safety. I took him. We waited five hours, all the while I wondered, what would be the next step? No one told me what to expect from this "safety check." Finally a psychologist came in and said, "Momma, he's not your baby anymore. Wake up to the real world. He's a teenager."

I was shocked. I had wasted a whole evening to hear this, and I felt more lost and confused than ever. Over the next year, things grew steadily worse. My son wrote messages in blood that said, "I hate myself." He'd stand in the front yard and display an anarchy sign to passing cars. Kids at school made fun of him on chat rooms and websites; he could not escape their humiliating taunts and hurtful invectives. He'd run in and out of the house all day and night, and though we tried grounding him, taking away his telephone and computer privileges, he'd just run away again. We called the police three or four times. They'd find him and bring him home, but it only made him angrier. He'd swear at the police and then do it again. I didn't know what to do. I thought maybe I should send him to a tough love camp or a military school. I even thought I could ship him to my sister's house in Missouri, where he'd be a thousand miles from these so-called friends. I felt scared. I knew if something didn't happen he'd be dead, on drugs, or in the juvenile court system.

Then one night, he came to us and told us that he felt unsafe. His girlfriend had dumped him, and all of his "friends" were mad at him and no longer included him in anything. We spent the next few hours talking, and were shocked when he told us that he had tried to hang himself with a belt in his closet. When it broke, he had come downstairs and took a dozen pills from the medicine cabinet. After this disclosure, I took him back to the emergency room. This time he was hospitalized, and that's when I learned that he had bipolar disorder, anxiety, and a slight touch of Asperger's syndrome.

It took time to find the right medications, but when the doctors did, our old son came back. It was like a miracle. I quit working. I signed up for services from the department of mental health. I monitored his therapy and psychiatric visits more closely, and I insisted that the school district send him to a therapeutic school for adolescents with emotional difficulties. Thus, our family began a new life. We had a teenager with a mental illness. He never asked for this, and it wasn't his fault. But it wasn't my fault either. There's no one to blame. But what was clear was that it was up to us, his parents, to become his greatest advocates.

THE NEED FOR PARENT SUPPORT

Medication and psychological treatment may alleviate acute symptoms of depression, psychosis, mania, impulsivity, inattentiveness, irritability, and suicidal thinking. Children may learn new skills to cope with stressors they face in their lives. But the challenges for families are infinite, and once the process toward healthier, more functional living is initiated, there are no shortcuts.

Once a child is sufficiently stabilized behaviorally and emotionally in order to be safe, there is often still a long road ahead for their parents and families. Parents may need to adjust their schedules, participate in what seems like unending therapy, and suffer the barbs of those who know but are not compassionate, toward the pain the entire family is suffering. Often, initial stabilization of a teen is followed by the need to advocate with school officials, outside agencies, and at times, law enforcement and the courts. Some teens need alternative schooling and even a period of time placed outside the home to recover.

But as with a medical illness, no matter where your child is housed and no matter how large and scary the problem seems, there is no room for losing hope or giving up. Parents' enduring love, support, advocacy, and involvement is still crucial to optimize an adolescent's chances of recovery from emotional problems. Knowing this, parents often are lost in terms of whom to turn to, what is available in terms of services, and how to access the "extras" that are necessary for their child. Beyond direct parent participation in treatment, the role and road for parents as advocates will be detailed in the following chapter written by a member of an organization in Massachusetts, the Parent/Professional Advocacy League, developed and dedicated to just this purpose.

CHAPTER 11

Parents as Advocates for Their Children

Lisa Lambert

As an advocate, I regularly hear from parents who are caught between trying to effectively manage their teen's behavior and navigating an often difficult system to find help. Their experience reminds me of my own. When my son was young, he was moody, often irritable, sometimes withdrawn, and at other times, explosive. I was frequently exhausted, trying to focus on him to figure out what was going on while also looking for answers to help him. My son's pediatrician wanted to "wait and see" and what we "saw" was his anxiety and rages growing worse.

When my son finally began therapy, I still couldn't find other resources out there and had no idea what kind of support he needed at school. "Isn't there a book," I would ask his therapist, "where I can just look on say, page 37, and find out the best thing to do for my son?"

In the midst of this, I moved from the West coast to the East coast and had to look for help all over again. It took sixteen phone calls to finally find a doctor who could see my son right away. This doctor was the first link to other supports in my new community. This experience continues to drive me to both assist other parents find help more quickly and advocate within the mental health system to make the process easier for every family.

––––––––––

AFTER MY SON BEGAN to see the doctor, I realized that I needed more information and called several organizations. One sent me a flyer describing a support group for parents whose children had emotional, behavioral, and mental health needs. I traveled every other week to attend it, learning from more experienced parents and absorbing the strategies others used. Connecting with other parents was wonderful for me; I found that many of us are on the same road and have a great deal of knowledge to share.

Not long after, someone asked me to begin a parent-to-parent support group in my own town. The group was a success from the first week, when eight parents showed up. In subsequent meetings, I would never know in advance who would walk through the door; each parent brought unique concerns about his or her child's mental health needs, behavior, substance abuse issues, or whatever prompted them to come. As one parent would say when introducing himself, "I have three children, two boys and a girl. Let me tell you about the son who brings me to the group." And then he would.

It was wonderful to watch parents who at first felt overwhelmed begin to gather knowledge and develop skills to get the support their children needed. Even more important, families formed a new community, some even attending another's team meeting at school or helping each other through tough days or weeks. Each professional along the way was a source of help, but other parents were walking the same walk and could offer their senses of humor, support, and firsthand experience.

My own experience with my son led me to work as an advocate with the Parent/Professional Advocacy League (PAL) in Massachusetts, but the stories told by other families keep me doing this work year after year. PAL is an organization of parents and professionals who advocate on behalf of children with mental, emotional, or behavioral needs, and with their families. PAL's mission is to make sure that parents can access the support and information they need to best advocate for their child.

WHERE IT BEGINS

Nearly all parents find that their children behave in a troubling way at some point during their adolescence. In fact, most of us watch our children enter the teen years and expect some turbulence. Sometimes these problems are brief or only occur once in a while. But for a number of families, the problems persist for weeks or become much more frequent or serious.

In some cases, someone at school may raise concerns, which can either corroborate your own misgivings or come as a complete surprise. In other instances, a parent notices changes in the way his or her child behaves at home or experiences a persistent worry that simply won't go away. At this point, a parent wonders what to do. Should I contact the school or look for a mental health professional? Or is this a phase my child will grow out of? Many of us decide to wait and see, hoping that our children are indeed "going through a phase." In some cases, however, the severity is such that the need for action is immediate. (See "Know When to Seek Professional Help" on page 44 in chapter 2.) However you come to the realization that there is something worrisome going on with your child, you begin a process of trying to understand what is occurring and how best to respond.

The purpose of this chapter is to explore the process parents go through as they make decisions about seeking treatment for their children. You may begin by wondering what to do or whether doing anything at all is the best choice. You may find yourself in a new arena, learning the vocabulary that goes with it. But you can and should trust how well you know your child, your family, and yourself as you make decisions for all of you.

Why Parents Often Wait Before Seeking Help

Here are some of the reasons why parents may wait before seeking help for their children.

THEY IGNORE THEIR OWN INSTINCTS

The following family's story illustrates this well. Melissa, a mother of three girls, knew that middle school would be academically challenging for her eldest daughter. Her daughter had been diagnosed with a learning disability and had help at school for subjects that involved reading. Melissa watched her daughter begin the new school and perform okay academically. She sighed with relief. The next year, however, her daughter slowly changed. She came home late from seeing friends, not just sometimes, but almost always. She consistently "forgot" her family chores. Her grades began to drop and teachers noted that she was irritable at school. Melissa said, "Where is the child I used to have? It's like I have a stranger in her place." Melissa felt discouraged when her attempts to help her daughter didn't work. She wondered whether doing the wrong thing would make things worse, so she decided to "wait and see."

Adolescents are surrounded by an environment that entertains them, distracts them, and often presents them with risks they are unable to handle. When they are in trouble, their behavior is often the strongest indicator that something is wrong. Some teens abruptly lose interest in their old friends or activities, others become secretive or intensely irritable, and still others start behaving in ways that alarm their parents. Parents are experts on their own children—after all, they have known them all their lives. When a parent has a strong feeling or even a niggling worry that something may be wrong, it's best to pay attention. If that feeling should prove to be correct, there are usually signs you notice in retrospect that now make sense and let you know that you were right to take action.

Here's another family's story. Jennifer, a mother of three girls, was worried when her middle daughter suddenly seemed to change. Her daughter came home one day with a pierced nose, was skipping classes at school, and not complying with her curfew. Jennifer waited several months before seeking help. "I thought she was just adjusting to a new school and trying to fit in with new friends," she explained. "By the time we said, 'Enough,' the whole family was affected by the turmoil."

THEY RECEIVE DISCOURAGEMENT FROM OTHERS AND FEAR POTENTIAL STIGMATIZATION

Relatives are often quick to give advice promoting stricter discipline and insist that the problem is with your "parenting style" and not the teens themselves. They may point out ways in which you are too strict or not strict enough. Grandparents might say that you should have been more of a disciplinarian when your child was younger or that having cell phones, cable television, and access to e-mail has spoiled your child and encouraged "bad" behavior. Families from certain ethnic backgrounds may have cultural expectations for children, which, when gone unmet, form the basis of criticism.

Friends and relatives may also discourage a parent from seeking outside help. Combined with a desire not to stigmatize their child and a lack of confidence in their own judgment, many parents wait and see.

Well-meaning advice is usually offered by people who don't know your child as well as you do and haven't been in the same set of circumstances in their own lives. A friend who has raised a teen without encountering more than the usual difficulties will assume that their style of parenting is the one component you need. As one father noted, "It's not my basic parenting skills that need work, it's learning how to parent this child."

Reminding yourself that you need help for this particular child, just as you would if that child needed treatment for asthma, can help you ignore any unwanted, and unhelpful, advice.

THEY STRUGGLE WITH FEELINGS OF ISOLATION AND SHAME

In addition, when parents survey their friends and neighbors, it usually appears as if no one else has any significant problems with their own children. Other families might be willing to talk about their son's asthma, but they are more reticent about their daughter's therapy for depression. This can lead to a feeling of isolation and a belief that you are on your own. As one parent described it when she first discovered her daughter was anorexic, "You suddenly discover that you now belong to a small, elite group of parents and don't know any of the other members." This can be a scary and emotionally overwhelming experience for the parent who desperately wants his or her own child to be healthy and safe.

THEY DON'T KNOW WHERE TO TURN

It's often confusing to decide where the best starting place to find help is. While many parents have a strong relationship with their children's pediatrician, others see the doctor only once or twice a year. Some have regular contact with their children's teachers (or perhaps the school nurse) and may see this person as someone who can gauge the severity of what is going on. Schools see many students each year and know what is typical at certain ages. Other parents decide that they want to have someone with mental health expertise evaluate their child and contact a psychiatrist or other mental health professional.

Even in the face of much conflicting advice and pressure to "wait and see," it is imperative to pay attention to your intuition where your teen is concerned. Parents rarely look back and wish they had waited a month or more to see whether the problem got better or worse on its own. It is unusual for most of us to wish that we had not paid attention to the small voice within that guides us to seek help.

One mother, who had struggled with her own depression, began to see similar signs in her son. She would worry one day about her son's behavior and the next convince herself that she was "just seeing depression everywhere." Her son had been treated for attention deficit disorder by their pediatrician so she made an appointment with him. She was told that she had reasons to be concerned and her son was referred for an evaluation. "It was such a relief to hear I was right—even though I didn't want to be—from someone who has known my son since he was a baby," she said.

WHERE TO SEEK HELP FOR YOUR CHILD

When seeking help for their children, many parents begin by talking to their pediatrician. This person is the professional who has known your child over time and formed a relationship with both of you. Pediatricians know your child's health history and can determine whether any medical issues might be contributing to your child's problems. Additionally, pediatricians see many children each month and can guide families in determining when their child needs an evaluation or treatment. Pediatricians can be the link to many specialists, including those who can treat teens with mental health disorders and difficult behaviors. For many families, this person is the professional they feel most comfortable with and rely upon.

However, not all pediatricians have expertise in identifying or treating mental health disorders or difficult behaviors. (See chapter 12 for more on this issue.) Some parents have reported that their pediatrician failed to ask about their child's mental health during routine visits and when they have relayed concerns about their child, they did not receive the assistance they needed.[1] This kind of response can cause delays in accessing treatment for your child. It can also create reluctance to bring your concerns up again, at least until they are much more serious.

When talking to your child's pediatrician, emphasize the concerns you have and the troubling behaviors you are seeing in a clear, straightforward way. Many families find it useful to make a short, written list with an additional copy for the doctor to look at and include in the notes about the visit. (This list can begin a file in which you keep all of your child's written records, evaluations, and other paperwork.)

This approach lays out the concerns you have and your child's doctor can more readily identify whether your child needs treatment. It is important not to minimize your concerns or downplay your child's behaviors because this is the information the pediatrician will use to map out next steps.

Since many of the concerns parents describe result from their child's behavior, they worry that these behaviors will be seen as either a result of inadequate parenting or undue anxiety on the parent's part over common adolescent behavior. Unsurprisingly, a parent may often anticipate being blamed or having the problem handed right back to them as a nonmedical issue.

Remember that what you tell your doctor is confidential, and unless life-and-death issues are involved, talking about your concerns will not result in your losing control of the solutions. You are still the parent, and you can use the doctor's suggestions to make your own decisions about what may be in your child's best interest. Without a release of information, your pediatrician cannot even contact the school. So list the problems you see, emphasize your own concerns, and ask for a recommendation for any steps you can take.

Further, insist that the advice be something that meets your needs. One parent who went to see her son's doctor listened to his lengthy discussion of the developmental needs of adolescents but didn't get the clearly framed advice she was looking for. "Doctor," she told the physician, "that was very helpful but not at all useful." Be sure you leave with guidance that is useful to you.

Also, talk with your son or daughter's teachers and other school staff to get a better picture of what is going on during the school day. Some school staff will be eager to discuss your child's needs and any behavior changes that they might have seen. Others might be more reticent, worrying that any needs seen at school will be seen as an issue that should be handled solely by the school instead of a behavioral issue that can be addressed by mental health professionals. Compare notes with the school because teachers and other staff see your child for many hours each day. If a teacher says that all is fine at school, keep in mind that troubling behavior usually shows up at home first.

Some families don't have an ongoing relationship with a pediatrician and may not find the school is able to provide the help they are looking for. If this is the case, gather information by reading, visiting websites that focus on teen behavior or mental health needs, and talking to others. This will help give you a better framework for deciding what to do. If you know parents who have been through something similar with their own children, ask for their advice and listen to what they found helpful. Other families may have a strong relationship with their minister, priest, rabbi, or someone in their religious community.

Some parents may still find that their child's behavior is rapidly escalating and they need to handle an emotional crisis. This may involve taking your child to an emergency room or calling the local police. If you do either one, be sure to stress that this is a psychiatric emergency. Emergency rooms see many types of medical crises, and your child will need to see a mental health specialist. Police officers can interpret adolescent behavior in several ways, and you need to be clear about what kind of help your child needs. Remember you know your child better than anyone and can "frame" why this behavior is a cause for alarm and should not be responded to with force.

The following family's story illustrates this well. Zoe, a mother of a fourteen-year-old girl, was concerned about her daughter's behavior. After transferring into a new school the year before, Angela had made new friends who seemed to party all the time. Angela's grades fell and she often missed curfews. Her mother began calling to find a therapist, but the waits for a new patient were several weeks long. One Friday night, Angela didn't come home at all. Zoe called her daughter on her cell phone, but only got her voice mail. When her daughter hadn't returned home by morning, she called the police. After spending several more daylight hours checking out friends' homes and driving the city's streets, Zoe contacted a local police officer. They strategized and he advised her to call the cell phone carrier to get a record of all the calls her daughter had made in the last twenty-four hours. By calling each of the numbers and tracking her daughter's movement from house to house and party to party, Zoe was able to find her daughter several hours later. Zoe was not only a creative thinker and persistent advocate, but was able to work with a police officer in her city to get help for her daughter.

When Mental Health Intervention Is Recommended

Your child's pediatrician can refer your family to a mental health professional for an evaluation or treatment. Often, however, the pediatrician will give the parent a list of mental health professionals to contact. Many families find themselves tackling this step on their own. The mental health system is often difficult to navigate, and finding timely treatment for your child can be particularly tough. In many locales, there is more demand for mental health professionals who are trained to treat children and adolescents than are available. Some families have found themselves making numerous phone calls just to get the first appointment.

Besides the list your child's pediatrician gives you, families can call their insurer and ask for a list of therapists near their home. Unfortunately, many insurers provide lists that include mental health professionals who treat only adults as well as those who treat children and adolescents, which means making many calls to wade through the list. If a parent cannot find a doctor or therapist with a reasonable effort (similar to the effort required to find an allergist), then call back the health plan and insist its representatives assist you. It's at this point that many parents find themselves becoming an advocate for their children as they work to make the system more responsive to their child's needs.

There are also state agencies designed to address the mental health needs of children. Most states have both protective or child welfare services whose mission it is to provide shelter, placement, tracking, and home-based services for children who have been victims of abuse and/or neglect as well as for those children who are chronically truant and unresponsive to rules and limits designed to keep them safe.

There are other agencies, often falling under the rubric of the state department of mental health, whose mission it is to provide more long-term mental health treatments and supports for children diagnosed with serious emotional disturbance. What this means is that if an acute episode of problematic behavior or decreased or unsafe functioning exceeds the limits of one's private insurance benefits, there are potentially other public resources that a parent can access for additional help.

Most states also have some form of public assistance insurance for children under twenty-one with psychiatric disabilities, but again these resources can be difficult to access and often require linkage with a public agency such as those described above. Here again, the parent is often the key advocate in determining what type of agency support is needed and then advocating for their children to obtain the help they are entitled to. Organizations like PAL have now sprung up across the country, forming a system of support and information that can help parents determine what resources exist in their state and exactly how to contact them.

What to Ask After You Receive a Diagnosis

Once you receive a diagnosis or recommendation from a doctor or therapist, ask questions to be sure that you are both comfortable with and agree with the clinical plan. You need enough information to understand what the doctor or therapist is telling you and enough support to be able to advocate for what your son or daughter may need.

Ask how the behaviors you are describing became translated into the diagnosis you hear today. For many families, the rapid shift from thinking this is "just a phase" to finding out that there needs to be a treatment plan can be a difficult adjustment. For others, there is a sense of relief that now they understand what is going on and that there is a plan of action. They can feel that their concerns are validated.

You may want to have a list of questions in hand to help you understand what kinds of treatment are being considered. Here are some questions you might want to ask:

1. Does my child have a diagnosis? How did you decide on this diagnosis?

2. What specific treatment do you recommend?

3. Are you considering prescribing medication? If so, what medication and how does it fit in with the treatment plan?

4. How long will it take my child to improve?

5. Will you need to be in touch with my child's school?

6. What should I do if things get worse?

7. Will my child get better or be the way she/he was with time?

Mental health diagnoses can change over time, as more information becomes available. Sometimes this is because a single diagnosis does not capture your child's behaviors and symptoms. At other times, your son or daughter may volunteer information that is new to everyone. There may also be a clearer picture as your child gets older. When the diagnosis "morphs" from one you are comfortable with to another that is unfamiliar, many parents are confused and alarmed.

When you are gathering information about your child's mental health or behavioral needs, you may get conflicting interpretations. While it is crucial to have as much information as you can, it is usually best to choose one or two voices to listen to and rely on. One of those voices should be someone with expertise around mental health needs and teens.

Once your child begins seeing a psychiatrist or other mental health professional, listen to how he or she describes what is going on with your child since it will not only help you understand your child better but give you the language to explain it to someone else. The other key person is someone who knows your child very well. This may be a teacher, a relative, or perhaps a friend. That person may know your child and your family well enough to make some helpful observations.

It is important to remember that one of the most valuable assets parents have is their relationship with their son or daughter. It may be strained by the behaviors you are seeing; it may at times appear to be beyond repair. Teens are famous for impulsively expressing how angry they are. They are also well known for stony silences. (See "The Dos and Don'ts of Effective Communication" on page 40 in chapter 2.)

This family's story illustrates this point. Julie's son was angry and often explosive during his adolescence. He was diagnosed with depression and had difficulty with insomnia. She found out that he was drinking when the police found him passed out on a city bus. Yet, through their most difficult times, they managed to talk, often while driving in the car. "We would sit side by side and not look at each other. We knew the trip would end after a certain amount of time and that gave us a kind of built-in safety net," she said. "Yet he shared some of his deepest feelings during those trips and those talks kept us connected."

No matter how wonderful or expert anyone who works with your child is, they will only be part of your life for a finite length of time. Therefore, the parent should be driving the decisions and setting the priorities. Others may provide invaluable advice, support, and treatment, but their role is ultimately that of the advisor, supporter, and treater. You will still be an important part of your child's life in six months, one year, and five years from now. As you line up all the competing demands in life, keep in mind that nourishing your relationship with your teen needs to be a priority.

THE EFFECT OF A TROUBLED TEEN ON THE FAMILY

Children and adolescents don't live by themselves. They are part of a family and that family lives in a community. When one child in a family begins to behave in a risky, harmful, or unusual way, it always has an effect on the other siblings in the family. Parents worry about their other children, but they are often stretched thin by the demands of helping their child with the problems as well as with work and other demands. They might see the other children in the family reacting to the chaos or crisis in the household and hope it is simply a normal reaction, but worry that it is the beginning of a similar problem.

Siblings can have any number of reactions. Some become the "good" child or even a caretaker of their sibling with troubling behaviors. Others complain often and loudly about the unfairness of their own situation and point out how much time and attention goes to their brother or sister. Still others try out their difficult sibling's behaviors, often in a way that is a departure from their own way of dealing with life.

Underneath it all, other siblings often feel a lot of confusing emotion, including guilt. They may believe that they are the only ones who have a brother or sister who constantly loses their temper, acts "weird" or erratically, or even frightens them at times. Many express that they don't know why these things happen to their brother or sister and worry that these changes will also happen to them. Some feel guilty that they themselves are okay, while their sibling struggles each day. With a great deal of attention focused on the teen with problems, the child without problems can also feel neglected.

Some siblings attend the same school as their brother or sister or end up with the same teacher a year or so later. Schools each have their own cultures, and some teachers may expect to see the same problem behaviors that they saw in an older, difficult brother or sister. This is not unlike siblings who follow behind an academically or athletically gifted brother or sister. The sibling may feel compelled to live up to a teacher's expectations or prove them wrong altogether.

Be aware of what your difficult child's sibling is going through; he or she needs information to understand what is going on. The information may not change his or her feelings, but it will provide the words to grasp what's going on and even to explain the situation to friends. Your other children also need time of their own with you and with other family members. Let them vent their feelings and assure them that they are unique and important to you. Tell them that this is not a contagious illness, but rather a problem their brother or sister has that the family is helping to solve. Carving time to spend alone with your other children can help them enormously. Sometimes that one-on-one time can be something as simple as baking cupcakes together or going to a movie that you both enjoy without their brother or sister.

Support for Parents of Troubled Teens

Amid the turmoil of coping, looking for help, and trying to meet your day-to-day obligations, many parents simply roll their eyes when told to be sure to take care of themselves. Although it's important to have time to simply relax or take a respite from the stressful situation you might be living through, support comes in many forms. From the time their children are small, many parents talk to other parents to share their strategies, resources, and feelings. It is a time-honored strategy to share information about teachers, compare notes on a pediatrician, or trade information about community activities. When your child has a behavioral or mental health problem that requires help from a mental health professional or a treatment that is new to you, these strategies are still what works best.

Nearly every community has support organizations to call or connect with. These organizations are almost always the best source of information from other parents and about informal supports. (See the resource section on page 278.) Other parents know what books were most helpful to them, which professionals have received their highest accolades, and what shortcuts there might be to locating what you need. Networking and sharing are how families normalize their own experiences, making them more manageable, and ultimately finding ways to successfully deal with a difficult situation.

Becoming a Different Kind of Parent

Other families and support organizations understand your frustrations and concerns yet can also help you find ways to parent the child you have today. As one parent put it, "You have to be the parent your child needs, not necessarily the one you thought you wanted to be." The skills you need to parent the child who is challenging you each day can often be passed on from other parents who have faced similar parenting challenges.

Sharing experiences with other parents can also offer surprises. When your teen is behaving in a challenging way and you realize that how you have parented has simply not been effective or has not been adequate to "fix" this problem, you can feel overwhelmed by frustration, guilt, or a sense of self-blame. Yet when you sit down in a room of parents whose children have similar behaviors, you may often find that the parents themselves have very different parenting styles. One may have strict rules, another may be quite laissez-faire, and a third might say that she is a "yeller" but doesn't always follow through. It is startling for parents with very different parenting styles to realize that their children have the same symptoms or behaviors.

In the midst of trying to find time for yourself, and learning parenting strategies that are effective, most parents experience a range of emotions. Many are angry with their children and sometimes feel guilty about this. Others say that they are shocked and didn't realize that their children's problems were so serious. Still others want to believe that the difficulties their family is experiencing are temporary and things can go back to the way they were before. This range of emotion is a normal part of adjusting to your child's difficulties and the need to find treatment and services for him or her.

Many parents go through a series of emotions often beginning with shock and denial and encompassing anger, grief, guilt and finally acceptance. These feelings do not come in an orderly fashion but can completely color how you see your son or daughter or appear only briefly. Most parents don't feel angry and then get over it, never to experience it again. Instead they may feel angry again and again and then may find themselves overwhelmed by grief. This is a normal reaction to dealing with your child's problems and can help lead you to a greater understanding, which is the foundation of advocacy.

Many families also notice that when another child in their community has a medical illness, the community supports them. They may bring over casseroles or offer help with carpooling. The family is viewed as the victims of circumstances and in need of support. But when a family is in a crisis because of their child's difficult behaviors, this kind of help and support is rare. You are at home trying to figure out what steps to take next, often dealing with your own difficult emotions. You may be coming to realize that the hopes and dreams you had for your child are unlikely to come to pass but you have yet to form new dreams. Again, networking with families who are having similar experiences can be incredibly helpful.

Two teens with a mood disorder or anxiety will have very similar behaviors. A diagnosis is reached, after all, by carefully listing symptoms and creating a picture of what is going on that is visible. The diagnosis once reached, for example that of a major depression, may have a number of contributing causes. Parenting style has a strong impact on your child, but it doesn't create, by itself, the symptoms of a psychiatric disorder such as depression. On the other hand, learning to parent a child with depression can be like learning a refined skill.

This family's story is illustrative: Laurie noticed that her son, Michael, was irritable and agitated yet seemed unable to do many of the tasks that his younger brother zipped through. Michael was exceptionally bright, yet had erratic progress at school. After watching Michael struggle at school, and disrupt their family life for several years, Laurie took him to a psychiatrist. Michael had clinical depression that was difficult to treat. Each son was required to do several chores each week, including cleaning his room. Michael made either a cursory effort or avoided it altogether. His brother resented that Michael got away with this and Laurie felt strongly that he needed to contribute to the family in some way. After some thought, Laurie decided that she would offer Michael a trade; he would be required to mow the lawn each week and someone else would clean his room. Laurie realized soon afterward that Michael often felt overwhelmed by depression when he was in his room and that had resulted in his inability to thoroughly clean his room. This insight came after some discussion with his therapist when the isolative aspect of "room cleaning" and how this interacted with Michael's depression was identified.

Friction over Different Parenting Styles

Not only can different families who have children with similar diagnoses have markedly different parenting styles, but different adults within the same family often do as well. While these inter-parent differences can lead to friction when parenting a "typical" child, the disagreements can be even more pronounced when the child has behaviors that are concerning or lead them into trouble.

It is even more difficult, for example, to agree on what to do when not everyone in the family agrees that the behavior is a problem. Sometimes one parent will see a concerning behavior as an extreme, but still normal teen behavior. Another relative might see your child as willful or stubborn instead of defiant or out of control. When a parent is able to determine for themselves if a behavior is more intense or more frequent than for a typical child that age, it can be a starting point to talk about what you are observing instead of what you believe.

It is important for parents and close relatives to try and reach some consensus about the existence, nature, and degree of their teen's emotional problem. Without this consensus, mixed messages abound, treatment options are less clear-cut, and additional, damaging conflict complicates an already difficult situation.

Others can be your child's teacher, friend, or therapist, but only you can be the parent. You have a unique and highly influential role in your child's life, though there is certainly a time when that seems far from the truth. You are the person who knows your children's history and strengths. You are the one who lives with them, loves them and is there for them. You are their best advocate. Others bring their expertise, their knowledge and their depth of experience, but parents have no other agenda greater than their child's well-being and a bright future. In the world we live in today, treatment decisions are influenced by managed health care, and educational supports often have to be fought for. The treatments and supports needed by a teen with mental health needs or behavioral problems are usually attained only with advocacy.

Advocating with Your Child's School

Many schools play an important role in the provision of mental health services for students. Your child spends many hours each day at school, and many of his or her challenging behaviors may show up there too. Teachers and school administrators can observe any learning or social/emotional problems that may emerge. School nurses, school psychologists, or social workers are trained to provide medical or mental health services to students.

However, schools today are under a lot of pressure to provide a wide array of services, often with inadequate funding. For your child to receive any services that you believe he or she needs, you need to advocate for them. The first step is being aware of what is available.

There are both federal and state laws that require schools to provide a "free and appropriate" education to any child with disabilities. Some students with emotional or mental health disorders require special education services, in the form of an individualized educational plan (IEP), to make this education possible. If you think your child needs those services, you must first request an evaluation. There is then a series of steps from requesting an evaluation to meeting with your child's team, which usually includes the parent(s), student, teacher, other school staff, evaluator and anyone else who may have expertise, to writing a plan that is outlined in detail in other resources.[2] It is important to become familiar with the steps you need to take and the timelines governing those steps. Many parents find they need to stay in regular contact with the school during this process to ensure it moves along within the legal timelines. There are both federal and state laws stipulating, according to where you reside, the exact educational entitlements that you and your teen are entitled to.

There are also professional advocates and lawyers who specialize in helping families receive special educational services when necessary. Although each state maintains Web-based information regarding these laws and policies, there are some general sites where you can gain valuable information about this process (you might start with your state's department of education home page). Also, each state has a parent training and information center where parents can obtain information about appropriate education and resources for their children. Go to www.taalliance. org/Centers/index.htm to find the center in your state.

Some students with special needs require support services to succeed in school but may not need special education in terms of an IEP. Under a law known as Section 504 (of the Rehabilitation Act of 1973), schools must make the accommodations that are necessary for these students to learn. Again, you must request an evaluation, the school will convene a team of people (including you) to determine whether your child is eligible, and will create a plan under Section 504 if the team agrees on eligibility.

Explore every avenue when looking for resources for your teen. Services your child can receive at school are often a key factor in his or her success. The team of people who work with your son or daughter can offer a better picture of how your child functions in different places during the school day. However, most parents find that they must be proactive in both asking for these services and being sure that they meet their child's needs.

CONCLUSION

Parenting is a challenging job even under the best of circumstances. When your child begins to behave in ways that worry, upset, anger, or maybe even frighten you, the challenge seems enormous. As one parent put it, "Brian was my second child. I had been through the teen years before, and I felt that I knew what I was doing. But I needed a whole new set of skills to get us through those two really rough years [with him]. I needed to become not just the parent I wanted to be, but the parent Brian needed." This mother found that she needed not just ordinary parenting skills, but skills to manage Brian's behavior better. And she needed to learn to advocate at school and even with her insurance company.

For many parents, this is a time to find allies, supporters, and advisors. Understanding what is happening with your child is a first, important step and learning how to get the services he or she needs is crucial. But even the best advocates, and the best parents, need support for themselves and their families. Finding professionals, other parents, and personal supports who can help you learn the skills you need, strategize about the next steps, and help you feel confident about your choices can make the difference between coming through with just a sigh of relief and coming through feeling successful and effective.

CHAPTER 12

Treatments that Work

Joseph Gold, M.D.

You're concerned about your child and not sure whether he or she is just "going through a phase" or needs professional help. How can you tell? Where should you start? If you've become more certain that your adolescent needs help, you'll need to determine exactly what the problem is and what treatment is best. This chapter will focus on the key role of your pediatrician, why a precise diagnosis matters, which types of therapy or medication work best for each particular disorder, and how the psychiatric field is discovering the most effective treatments.

––––––––––

IF YOUR ADOLESCENT is less able to enjoy life or struggles in school or with relationships, then it is time to take action. Start by talking with your child. Together, you will need to define the problem, determine how serious it is, and make a plan to address it.

Should you need outside help, your family's pediatrician is often the best person to begin with. Primary care pediatricians, however, vary markedly in their comfort with and knowledge of mental health disorders and substance abuse. Many of them had little training in these issues at the start of their careers but have since been confronted by the large volume of kids at risk and developed relevant skills.

Historically, pediatricians have used hit-or-miss methods to detect emotional and behavioral difficulties. They have relied on the youth and parent to raise concerns or respond to generic probe questions in candid detail. Certain physical findings may serve as clues to the doctor. For example, significant weight change might lead to questions about depression or anorexia nervosa. Distractibility and fidgetiness could prompt questions about drug abuse or attention deficit disorders.

We now know that these chance methods fail to identify at least half of those kids whose capacity to function at home, in school, or with friends is significantly impaired. In response, better tools have been developed. Brief questionnaires completed in the waiting room or answered verbally in the exam room turn out to be much more effective. Read on for examples of these questionnaires.

SCREENING TOOLS THAT CAN HELP

The Pediatric Symptom Checklist (PSC), created by Michael Jellinek, M.D., and Michael Murphy, Ed.D., is a thirty-five-item survey that you can easily fill out in the five minutes before your child enters the doctor's office. The PSC is designed to detect psychosocial dysfunction—a level of distress and impairment in functioning severe enough to warrant further questions and diagnostic evaluation. It has been extensively field tested and consistently found to pick up problems that impair functioning twice as often as traditional methods. It is available free of charge online at http://psc.partners.org.

The CRAFFT is a six-item set of questions developed by John Knight, M.D., to screen for alcohol and substance abuse. It, too, has been demonstrated to be a sensitive, reliable, and accurate tool by which adolescents can quickly give their pediatrician information that would otherwise go undetected. See page 103 for more information on the CRAFFT.

The PSC and the CRAFFT are examples of formal, brief screening tools that have been broadly endorsed and become increasingly common in community-based primary care pediatric practice. Your child's doctor is not mandated to use these or similar questionnaires, but you have every right to request and encourage their use. In just the past few years, the national organization that accredits pediatrics residency training programs has begun to require recent medical school graduates who are learning to be pediatricians to be taught about behavioral and developmental disorders. This training includes familiarity with screening and diagnostic tools.

Some pediatrics practices are on the cutting edge of medical technology, creating computerized electronic medical records. This has made it possible for a number of them to use online psychosocial dysfunction and substance abuse screening tools and more rigorous diagnostic questionnaire software.

The Child Health and Development Interactive System (CHADIS), created by Barbara Howard, M.D., and her colleagues at Johns Hopkins University in Baltimore, is a more detailed survey that parents can complete on their home computers prior to an office visit. By the time they and their child arrive at the pediatrician, the CHADIS results are available to the doctor, including areas of concern and potential differential diagnoses. Go to www.childhealthcare.org for more information.

These and other new tools have made it possible for some pediatricians to supplement their clinical interviews and assessments to more precisely quantify the severity of a child's problem and begin to define it. Many primary care physicians have also diligently pursued continuing medical education in psychiatric disorders and their treatment.

Your pediatrician ideally has known you for many years and your child since birth. You trust him or her with your confidential worries, and he or she can place your child's issues in a broader context. Armed with the ongoing professional training and new tools described above, pediatricians and pediatric nurse practitioners are often able to detect problems early in their course when interventions are easier and more likely to succeed. They are also now better able to diagnose and remedy the issue or to recognize that it is beyond their area of expertise and refer you to a specialist.

In certain geographic areas, primary care pediatricians are able to access diagnostic, treatment, and resource-finding advice and support by telephone while kids and their parents are still in doctors' offices. In Massachusetts, for example, the state legislature has funded a program called the Massachusetts Child Psychiatry Access Project (MCPAP), which consists of six regional hubs that readily provide child psychiatrists, social workers, and resource-finding care coordinators to consult by telephone and for face-to-face evaluations as needed. This has made it possible for pediatricians to directly treat the psychiatric disorders of many more children and adolescents and triage more complex cases to the few available child psychiatrists. You can find a more detailed description of this program on the project's website, www.mcpap.org.

School-Based Screening

Teachers and school personnel frequently witness certain types of difficulties and can then bring them to your attention or confirm your intuition. Regardless of who first notices the problem, it is essential that teachers and, when indicated, school nurses or adjustment counselors also provide information. These educators can also help you determine whether your child's difficulties are evident in all settings or are "situational." In the latter case, symptoms may be most prominent in school where learning, attention, and relationships with peers may be affected.

Your child's school may also ask your permission to allow him or her to participate in school-wide screening for common mental health problems. Many school systems have generously committed the time and resources to provide screening for depression, suicide risk, and/or substance abuse. Some have used tools like the Signs of Suicide (SOS) developed by Screening for Mental Health Inc. The SOS is designed to detect teenagers at risk for suicide by showing students a video that educates them about depression and suicide, followed by a seven-question survey. Students are then encouraged to seek help for themselves or friends who have screened positively on the SOS.

The Columbia University Teen Screen is designed to perform a similar screening function and in addition can be coupled with a computerized structured diagnostic interview. This sequence of tests, thereby, both identifies youth at risk for suicide and also provides the clinical evaluator with detailed symptomatic data and likely diagnoses. The on-site clinician can then deem whether a full clinical evaluation and treatment are warranted.

Many school personnel have begun to access the Massachusetts General Hospital's related website www.schoolpsychiatry.org. It includes a host of diagnostic tools and scales, narrative descriptions of developmental and psychiatric disorders, and suggested academic adaptations for students with each of these respective diagnoses. The website is, of course, also available to parents and pediatricians. Its diagnostic instruments have proven useful to all of these stakeholders in assessing an individual student's psychiatric diagnosis and related challenges and needs.

Schools have also creatively developed or accessed new curricula designed to raise awareness of mental health and substance abuse disorders. The Adolescent Mental Health and Wellness Curriculum edited by David DeMaso, M.D., and this author is one example. It has modules on stress, depression, and substance abuse that can each be tailored to the culture and trust level of a particular school or classroom. These educational tools are interactive and highly participatory. They help to create an environment in which students are more likely to acknowledge the difficulties they are experiencing, and to reach out for help. This curriculum is available online at www.adolescentwellness.org.

Together these multiple initiatives have increased the likelihood that your child's problem may be detected in school even before you notice it at home. This provides an additional safety net and amplifies the importance of close communication between parents, teachers, school counselors, pediatricians, and mental health professionals.

NEXT STEPS IN DIAGNOSIS AND TREATMENT

Once a problem has been recognized—whether your child brought it up, you noticed it, a teacher reported it, or your pediatrician caught it with a questionnaire—the next step is to define the problem as precisely as possible. In medicine, this is called "making a diagnosis."

A diagnosis in its most complete form should provide a great deal of information, including the following:

- Observable signs and subjective symptoms

- Genetic predisposition

- Environmental factors

- Likely age of onset and natural course over time if left untreated

- Genetic basis for response to each medication or other therapy. (The genes that you inherit from your parents and the changes that can occur to those genes before your birth and during your life can all make you prone to certain diseases and can also make your body ideally suited to respond to particular medicines.)

- How the illness expresses itself and how it can be detected (with blood tests, x-rays, MRIs, electrocardiograms, or other tools)

- Likelihood of response to each type of treatment alone and in combination

- Likely course over time with treatment

- How well one can expect to be able to function and fully participate in life despite the illness

- Hereditary risk for the patient's children

For most psychiatric illnesses, we usually can find answers to only a few of the items listed above. Why is this the case?

To explain, imagine that your daughter wakes up with a sore throat that is worse than the day before and now has a fever of 102°F but no running nose or muscle aches. At the pediatrician's office, she takes a "strep test" that turns out to be "positive" and confirms the diagnosis of "strep throat." The pediatrician has just conveyed a shorthand version of the diagnosis of a throat infection caused by a bacterium called *beta hemolytic streptococcus* that is easily treated by antibiotics such as penicillin. If the "strep test" had been "negative" that would have suggested that the sore throat was caused by a less ominous bacteria or—even more likely—by a virus and that the best treatment would be fluids, rest, and ibuprofen rather than antibiotics.

In other words: There is more than one kind of throat infection. Each has its own distinct cause and related treatment. "Strep throat" is not the same diagnosis or illness as "viral sore throat" or throat infection by a virus.

Psychiatry, on the other hand, is generally not yet ready to separate each diagnosis into meaningful subtypes according to their cause.

In fact, our most current diagnostic approach—as exemplified by the American Psychiatric Association's latest *Diagnostic and Statistical Manual of Psychiatry (DSM-IV)*—is symptom-based and does not depend on causes or sequencing of the problems. That means that diagnosis is based solely on what we can observe or what the patient describes and that the cause of this illness has not yet been discovered and is, therefore, not a criterion in making the diagnosis; and if multiple diagnoses occur at the same time then none explains the other—for example, the patient's ADHD is not caused by his depression.

We use this diagnostic approach as a way to help us to uncover one by one all of the aspects listed above for any diagnosis and, in that way, make psychiatry as scientific as the rest of medicine. We need a solid scientific starting point to anchor us as we piece together these details, so we start with what we know for sure: what the patient can describe and what we can directly observe.

Once we discover that there are multiple causes for what we now call a single psychiatric illness, separate matching treatments will emerge and each current "illness" may be divided into several more meaningful and precise diagnoses. For example, two adolescents may display seemingly identical symptoms of depression with insomnia, poor concentration, and sadness. On closer inspection, however, one may have a family history of depression while the other recently suffered the tragic loss of a loved one. They may require very different treatments. The first may best respond to an antidepressant medication while the grief of the second may respond best to psychotherapy.

We are also beginning to know that certain symptoms can suggest or even predict an adolescent's future diagnosis and outcome. Consider that two teenagers with no recent painful life events may both be diagnosed with depression because of the weight loss, irritable mood, and loss of hope and joy that both of them describe and display. However, only one of them also hears or sees things that no one else can (hallucinations); has begun to move, think, and speak so slowly that he seems about to "grind to a halt"; and expresses irrational ideas that do not respond to logic (in other words, has delusions, such as that everyone can read his mind or that his body is rotting away) that do not respond to any logical attempt to convince him that they are wrong. The boy with these particular additional symptoms is quite likely experiencing a depression that is the first stage of what will eventually become a bipolar illness. His current symptoms predict his future course and also help guide medication selection in the here and now.

As long as we are still discovering the causes of each psychiatric disorder and the meaning of certain symptoms, the approach of *DSM-IV* will be useful, but it brings yet another tradeoff: Your child may be given multiple, accurate diagnoses. What does it mean if your child receives multiple diagnoses? Because of the way that *DSM-IV* is designed, it is common for people whose emotional distress is severe enough to disrupt their capacity to function at school, work, or home to meet the criteria for and receive more than one psychiatric diagnosis at the same time. These are called "comorbid" disorders. Do not be alarmed. Having two disorders does not necessarily mean that your child is more ill or that the prognosis is worse than if he had just one diagnosis. The key issue is that he or she recovers and is able to fully enjoy and succeed in relationships, activities, and schoolwork. For us to best help with that recovery, we need to continue to search for the causes of psychiatric and substance abuse disorders.

Why do all of these concepts about diagnosis matter? Because they will ultimately determine treatment success. When your child is in distress, you want to be able to instantly access the best possible treatment that can quickly and substantially reduce the symptoms, target this exact problem, cause minimal side effects, and, ideally, provide a permanent cure.

A vivid example of the new meaning of precision diagnosis and effective treatment comes from outside of psychiatry: the highly publicized lung cancer drug gefitinib (IRESSA).

The IRESSA Story

Stories about IRESSA appeared in major newspapers and popular scientific magazines[1,2] a few years ago, discussing why a seemingly ineffective treatment for cancer turned out to be a lifesaving cure for a small but specific group of patients.

Think of this as the story of a woman—and many folks like her—who had never smoked a cigarette nor ever been exposed to asbestos or other toxins, yet developed lung cancer. She did not respond to standard chemotherapy and was steadily deteriorating until she received a new drug—IRESSA—as a long shot.

Unexpectedly, it worked. Expectations were low at first because the initial results of IRESSA were poor but intriguing. IRESSA proved to be helpful in a mere 10 percent of lung cancer patients, but when it worked, the results were often dramatic.

After much research, scientists found that IRESSA works best on lung cancers with a specific gene mutation most often seen in females who have never smoked cigarettes. This is because the mutation produces proteins that make these lung cancer cells live longer. IRESSA precisely targets these proteins so that the cancer cells die much sooner.[3,4]

Thus, the mystery was solved. These discoveries explain why IRESSA worked in only 10 percent of all people stricken with lung cancer but would so powerfully help that subgroup. The dramatic response seen in this 10 percent of lung cancer patients, and the higher rate of response in females who never smoked now all make sense.

So the related lessons for adolescent mental health and substance abuse disorders are that anything that we call one disorder—whether medical or psychiatric—may turn out to be a collection of seemingly similar but actually quite distinct illnesses. These distinct subtypes differ in their course and response to treatment in ways that may be determined by genetics.

Our accelerating knowledge of the human genome and genetic diversity holds great promise for psychiatry.[5] It will eventually help us to clarify diagnoses, create new treatments, and permit earlier intervention or even prevention. It will greatly improve our ability to predict an adolescent's response to a medication and whether he or she is likely to experience any particular side effect. Current trial and error methods of finding the right treatment for each unique individual will then be replaced by a more tailored and targeted approach to treatments. Until then, what have we already discovered about treatments for adolescents in distress?

Evidence-Based Treatment in Psychiatry

In December 2003, Jon M. McClellan, M.D., and John Scott Werry, M.D., published "Evidence-Based Treatments in Child and Adolescent Psychiatry: An Inventory"[6] to describe which of our medications and psychotherapy approaches have scientific data showing safety and effectiveness.

Using rigorous scientific testing methods called evidence-based criteria, doctors McClellan and Werry reviewed the published literature in child and adolescent psychiatry and found proof that certain medicines and certain therapies are effective and safe for particular disorders.

Specifically, they found that the "strongest evidence" shows stimulant medication to be most effective in treating attention deficit hyperactivity disorder (ADHD) and antidepressant medicines in treating obsessive compulsive disorder (OCD). They also found "reasonable evidence" that selective serotin reuptake inhibitor (SSRI) antidepressants, such as fluoxetine (Prozac) and sertraline (Zoloft), successfully treat moderate to severe depression and anxiety, and that risperidone antipsychotic medicine (Risperdal) is similarly effective in treating autism, specifically autistic children with self-injurious behaviors.

Their survey of published articles additionally showed that the most effective psychosocial therapies are cognitive behavioral therapy and other behavioral interventions. Next came family-based therapy and system of care interventions, in other words, programs that try to integrate the efforts of all of the significant adults and caregivers in a child's life—parents, extended family, teachers, guidance counselors, pediatricians, child psychiatrists, case managers, social services staff, and clergy—and thereby create a single, unified care plan and set of supports.

Following our discussion of ADHD and OCD, we discuss treatment choices for other psychiatric diagnoses toward the end of this chapter.

Different Treatments for Different Diagnoses

Treatments that work for ADHD and OCD are surprisingly different:

ADHD TREATMENTS

The core symptoms of ADHD include being easily distracted and displaying motoric hyperactivity and a pattern of impulsive actions. These tend to be most evident in school and social situations, where adolescents are expected to sustain attention to tasks that may hold little intrinsic interest and to think before speaking or doing things.

We know that stimulant medicines work quickly and effectively to treat the core symptoms of ADHD. As doctors McClellan and Werry noted in their survey, in almost 6,000 patients combined in the 160 studies reported as of 1996, between 65 percent and 75 percent showed a positive response to stimulants. This is compared to only 5 percent to 30 percent who responded well to a placebo. These are reported trials of a single stimulant medication, most commonly methylphenidate (Ritalin).

In more than half of those youngsters who have ADHD and for whom the first stimulant tried does not work, a different stimulant is likely to be successful.

If two-thirds of students with ADHD show marked improvement in their core symptoms when treated with Ritalin, why don't the other one-third respond? A research group in Mannheim, Germany, found that 10 percent of children carry variants of two specific genes that make them non-responsive to Ritalin as a treatment for ADHD.[7] While this does not account for all non-responders, it goes a long way to uncovering the genetic underpinning of different responses to stimulant medication. For the vast majority of youngsters with ADHD, one stimulant or another is very likely to help.

Two teams, led by Rachel Klein, Ph.D., in New York and Lily Hechtman, M.D., in Montreal, tested these hypotheses[8] in a study in which all the participating children received stimulant medication for the first year. They were also randomly divided into groups. One group received a combination of trainings and therapies, which together constituted what they called multimodal psychosocial therapy (MPT). It included parent training, family and individual therapy, remedial education, and training in academic organization and social skills. Another group received an activities-based, non-specific substitute for MPT, such as structured play sessions.

The most surprising finding was that the group that received the intensive and sophisticated MPT interventions plus medication did not do better than the group that received only the medication. The addition of intensive MPT also did not make it possible to discontinue the medication after the first year.

What the study clearly demonstrated was that the positive effects of Ritalin were so large that they statistically dwarfed any effect of MPT. They have, thereby, proven that stimulants warrant their position as the centerpiece of treatment and educational support programs for youngsters with ADHD.

Therefore, stimulant medication is a treatment that helps the vast majority of youngsters with ADHD improve and continue to do so when used over a period of years. Furthermore, these medicines begin to work within hours of the first dose.

Surely, there are some children who are not thoroughly assessed or accurately diagnosed and who do not have ADHD but are prescribed stimulants. On the other hand, there are certainly students—more often girls than boys—who suffer from moderate to severe attention deficit disorders, whose problems go unrecognized and who do not receive the stimulant treatment they need. The conclusion that stimulants work to relieve the core symptoms of ADHD is predicated on accurate detection and diagnosis.

This is one mental health area in which an increasing majority of pediatricians are well trained, skilled, and able to directly assess and treat the youngster often without requiring a referral to a child psychiatrist. The American Academy of Pediatrics developed assessment and treatment guidelines for ADHD and training modules in this approach for primary care pediatricians. There are more complex scenarios in which the ADHD is accompanied by other troubling feelings and behaviors. In accordance with our current philosophy of diagnosis in psychiatry, these situations commonly lead to multiple comorbid, or concurrent, diagnoses. If your child has this sort of complicated picture, then it may exceed the comfort or skills of your pediatrician and he or she is likely to refer you to a specialist.

OBSESSIVE-COMPULSIVE DISORDER (OCD) TREATMENTS

OCD sharply contrasts with ADHD in several crucial ways, including where best to start in treatment. The age of onset, primary importance of non-medication treatment, and the role of pediatricians are all different for OCD compared to ADHD.

OCD is characterized by unwanted repetitive thoughts and actions. It has two main age ranges of onset, commonly first appearing either during childhood or in young adulthood. The two peaks of initial onset are between ages eight to twelve and twenty to twenty-five. In contrast, ADHD appears before the age of seven, with symptoms often more obvious as academic demands increase and generally persists throughout adolescence and, in some cases, continues into adulthood.

Unlike ADHD, cognitive behavior therapy (CBT), not medication, is the first line of treatment for OCD. Cognitive behavior therapy is based on the notion that our feelings and actions are determined by our thoughts. CBT, therefore, targets our attitudes, beliefs, and misconceptions. If you believe, for example, that any imperfection makes you inadequate, then you are likely to be demoralized by any average or defective trait. That feeling of discouragement and anticipatory fear of performing in an imperfect way may manifest itself as sadness or dread. These, in turn, can progress to debilitating depression and anxiety.

CBT would take aim at this perfectionist belief as the irrational source of inevitable emotional upset. It offers well-defined techniques to block out unwanted thoughts, relax muscles and breathing, develop more logical beliefs and achievable goals, and visualize more successful outcomes. In these ways it provides direct relief of obsessive thoughts. CBT also offers symptom-prevention techniques, coupled with relaxation methods, which pragmatically reduce compulsive behaviors.

Unfortunately, there are not enough CBT-proficient child and adolescent mental health professionals. Despite its proven efficacy in OCD, depression, anxiety, and eating disorders, CBT can be hard to access. Most practitioners of CBT are clinical psychologists and more are being trained. At present, however, the parent of an adolescent may have to seek an alternative to CBT when it is unavailable or an adjunct to CBT when it has yielded only partial relief.

The place for medication treatment in OCD and ranking the treatment options are more complicated questions than in ADHD. Daniel Geller, M.D., and colleagues looked at all of the known literature on medication use and pediatric OCD.[9] Their study showed that five medications in particular are effective in treating OCD: four selective serotonin reuptake inhibitors (SSRIs): fluoxetine (Prozac), fluvoxamine (Luvox), sertraline (Zoloft), and paroxetine (Paxil) and one non-SSRI: clomipramine (Anafranil). Clomipramine proved to be statistically the most effective, and the four SSRIs are all tied for second place.

However, selecting the best medication to prescribe must include other factors and led Dr. Geller et al to recommend SSRIs as the first choice if medications are needed for OCD. This is because clomipramine frequently causes sedation and other mild but bothersome adverse effects, has some risk of cardiac effects, and requires monitoring by electrocardiogram and blood tests. All of these factors can reduce an adolescent's willingness to take the medication as prescribed and could, albeit much less frequently, involve a potentially serious side effect. For all of these reasons, Dr. Geller recommends the SSRI options ideally in combination with CBT. He also notes that there is some evidence that acquisition of CBT skills may reduce the risk of relapse when it comes time to end the medication treatment.

On the combination of CBT and medication for OCD, Scott N. Compton, Ph.D., offers an apt medical analogy to diabetes.[10] For certain forms of diabetes, exercise plus diet reduces the body's need for—or helps its response to—insulin. CBT is the treatment of choice for mild to moderate OCD. Medication should be added when CBT—like diet and exercise for diabetes—has proven not to be enough (or is not available) and when OCD is already causing moderate to severe impairment of functioning.

Your pediatrician is likely to refer you to a clinician skilled in CBT if he knows one. He may not feel able to confidently distinguish OCD from other ritualized habits and to prescribe SSRIs or clomipramine for this. A referral to a child psychiatrist is then timely.

TREATMENT CHOICES FOR OTHER PSYCHIATRIC DIAGNOSES

The contrasting nature of ADHD and OCD serves to emphasize how dogmatic attitudes for or against any one type of psychiatric care can hinder progress. No single type of therapy or medication will prove helpful in all situations. It is only in the meticulous examination of each diagnostic category and its subtypes that we will find what works best.

Beyond OCD, CBT has also been demonstrated to be an effective, evidence-based therapy of anxiety and depressive disorders in children and adolescents to such an extent that some regard it as the preferred initial treatment approach.[11]

In autism and pervasive developmental disorders, applied behavioral analysis and its praise-based relational variant called "positive behavioral support" have a strong body of evidence of effectiveness in promoting pro-social and decreasing dangerous behaviors. In this population, the second-generation antipsychotic medication risperidone has also been shown to reduce violent tantrums and self-injurious habits. Other medications in that category have also shown promise.

Adolescents who have suffered trauma, abuse, and neglect are prone to display poor modulation of their emotions and suddenly act on their dangerous thoughts and urges. Dialectical behavior therapy (DBT) has proven helpful to these youths and others with repeated impulsive and self-endangering behaviors, some of whom go on to develop borderline personality disorders. (Read more about DBT in chapter 4.) Treatment approaches for depression, substance abuse, and developmental disorders are addressed in other chapters of this book.

The Treatment of Adolescents with Depression Study, supported by the National Institute of Mental Health, reported many of its findings in December 2006. This study compared treatment of moderate to severe depression by an SSRI (fluoxetine) alone, CBT alone, both of these combined (fluoxetine plus CBT), and a placebo. The study concluded that the combined treatment was the most superior.[12]

After twelve weeks of treatment, the medication alone and the medication plus CBT both were more effective than CBT alone or the placebo for these seriously ill teenagers. While suicidal behaviors lessened with either CBT or the SSRI alone, the greatest reduction in these behaviors was seen with the combined treatment. There was also some evidence that recovery occurred sooner for those adolescents who had CBT plus the medicine. Again, we are reminded of Dr. Compton's analogy (above) to juvenile-onset diabetes: CBT may be a lot like diet and exercise, preparing the body to better respond to the apt medication.

CONCLUSION

Again, it is not whether a particular therapy or medication works but whether it effectively treats a precisely defined disorder or one of its emerging subtypes that will matter for an individual child.

Your child's pediatrician and teachers can help you begin to determine the nature of the problem your child is facing. Many of them have recently become equipped with improved screening and diagnostic tools to aid you in this process. Many of these same tools are now available to you via the Internet. Together you will know whether the help of a mental health professional is needed to further clarify the diagnosis. With assistance, you will also be able to place the issue within the context of your child's and family's strengths, and to carefully match the diagnosis to a treatment.

Epilogue

Cynthia S. Kaplan, Ph.D., and
Sue Mandelbaum-Cohen, LICSW

AS PART OF THE FINALE to this enterprise of trying to encapsulate our view of the distinctive problems facing today's teens, we asked friends and colleagues to review this manuscript and tell us how well it resonated with their experiences and whether the information was valuable.

Every critic had a unique response. Some thought the book presented too dire a picture of adolescence and cited counter-examples of non-rebellious youth who seemed to have made smooth transitions to adulthood, never getting into trouble or, more importantly, rarely challenging their parents' authority.

However, an overwhelming majority expressed a profound identification with the stories told, responding with their own tales of problems, confusion, misguided responses, and grueling efforts to seek help and regain control of an errant teen. They spoke eloquently of mistaking involvement for understanding, referring to the heightened investment in an adolescent's activities and achievements that now exists in our society, and how easily this can obscure a deficiency in authentic communication and awareness. Although they each felt involved in many areas of their teen's daily life, they nonetheless had, in the midst of working long hours and the rushed trek toward success and solvency, not immediately noticed that a child had lost weight, seemed more sad, or spent hours day after day "unwinding" on the Internet.

Many parents expressed to us the strong sense that they had been too lenient, too indulgent, and at some point, had become a chauffeur, correspondent, and check-writer, abdicating other, more essential aspects of being a parent. Looking back, their real authority and jurisdiction seemed to have eroded amid encroaching work demands, escalating financial needs, and adolescent exploits that were concurrently momentous and incomprehensible. In the incessant rush to keep up with and move on to the next activity, they now noted how precious traditions and times together had been sacrificed, leaving less time for togetherness and meaningful conversation and a lowered communal acceptance that family should serve as the anchor of an adolescent's life.

These comments closely matched our own observations and conclusions are not meant, in any way, to glorify the traditional family unit or practices of yesteryear. Much the opposite—we applaud modern advances in terms of working women, nontraditional lifestyles, and the advancement of both beneficial and effective technologies. We are not suggesting a return to the old, but merely a more useful and proactive response to the new.

VIGILANCE AND EARLY ACTION

The most important take-away message from this endeavor is, therefore, one of both prevention and early intervention. We cannot stop advancement and change, nor would we want to. But it is more imperative than ever that parents stay ahead of the curve and try to anticipate and learn in advance of, or at least alongside, their child. And sometimes, as we've demonstrated, even early action, best intentions, and thoughtful interventions are not enough. Sometimes an adolescent will still, even transiently, run into serious trouble. In those instances, the message contained in these pages is to listen to your own judgment, find help as fast as possible, and then keep participating so as to feel that you, as the parent, are not either powerless or merely part of the problem, but rather critical to the cure.

To help imagine what these ingredients are that can pull a teen back from the edge of despair and destruction, we decided to end by showing you that children can and do recover, though it takes time, compassion, and hard work.

THE PATH TO RECOVERY

The adolescent program at McLean Hospital where many of us work is an acute residential treatment center for teens between the ages of thirteen and nineteen, who stay an average of ten days to two weeks, though some remain longer. The population is diverse, spanning different ethnic and socio-economic backgrounds. Behavioral, relational, and psychopharmacological therapies form the cornerstones of treatment. Residents work in groups with peers and individually with social workers, psychologists, psychiatrists, educators, and mental health counselors to effect change and build mastery over their own lives.

The program emphasizes tolerance, respect for others and oneself, the exercise of self-control to manage emotions and behaviors, and reliance on others to learn skills that were lacking prior to admission, thus undermining the teens' ability to function effectively and with greater autonomy. We offer residents an opportunity to rewind their personal tapes and reshape maladaptive behaviors so that they may successfully return to their families, schools, communities, and activities without further interruptions by hospitalizations, suspensions, and conflict.

This process can be particularly striking for kids like Sara, age fifteen, who shed her long-held secret of past trauma and was able to stop the repetitive reenactment of earlier, abusive relationships, and develop a burgeoning sense of trust and confidence, returning once more to the friendly, constructive child her parents remembered.

A therapeutic community is at its finest when teenagers and families can again bask in hopefulness about their future. While teens may initially resent the rules of a highly structured program, they learn to appreciate the advantages of predictable behavioral consequences, daily routines, and clearly identified staff expectations. In our experience, teenagers benefit from and appreciate adult authority that is communicated with caring, concern for their well-being, and a degree of added irreverence that keeps things real. There is a collective sense of joy when youngsters grow more positive about themselves, are motivated to do better, and display renewed confidence to move forward and relinquish past self-destructive and socially unacceptable behaviors.

Such was the case with Mike, a fifteen-year-old who was admitted after being suspended from school for throwing a tantrum in the principal's office, destroying school property, and threatening to kill himself. Over the course of his treatment, he was started on new medications and talked with his parents about their divorce and his anger at all the disruption that had occurred within his family. His overall mood and ability to control his temper dramatically improved, which then helped him prepare for his meeting with school personnel and participate positively in negotiating the consequences that lay ahead.

Mark, too, was more prepared to face his future following his stay in a therapeutic community with an emphasis on positive peer support. A sixteen-year-old who was suicidal upon admission, Mark had refused to cooperate with his diet and insulin regimen to treat his childhood diabetes. He and his parents were in fierce combat every day about his irresponsible behavior. He had a history of multiple medical hospitalizations related to poor management of the disease. He believed he was living under a death sentence until he met Alexis, a fourteen-year-old in the program with a colostomy due to bowel dysfunction and other medical problems. Her resourcefulness and positive attitude inspired him and led to a series of decisions that propelled him forward in his disease management. Fights with his parents diminished as he assumed more responsibility for his own care and developed a constructive perspective on his life not present before.

When adolescents seize the opportunity to take control of their lives, which includes entering an alliance with their parents, the outcomes can be stunning. When recovery occurs, the participants approach one another in new ways that are satisfying and amazing. This can make returning home a welcome goal.

As a participant in a youngster's progress, grand or subtle, the experience can be inspiring and memorable. And we do not by any means only deal with the dark abyss of adolescent emotional illness and despair. Many patients and their families come for help regarding psychosocial challenges and reconcile in ways no one either imagined or expected. Although copious examples of this come to mind, it never ceases to be a privilege to behold, as we did most recently with Jessica, age sixteen and adopted at birth, who finally acknowledged how hard she had been working to reject her family for fear that they might reject her first. Her parents' gradual acceptance of temperamental and cultural dissimilarities between family members and eventual appreciation of the abandonment experienced by Jessica allowed for a stunning cease-fire and cessation of acting-out that showed all the signs of forming a foundation for long-lasting change. Having the opportunity to be candid, honest, and genuine with each other is an uncommon experience for teens and parents. When this occurs, it feels magical and can make an enormous impact on participant and facilitator alike.

The truth—the one that has not changed with time—is that teens and their parents are desperate to establish connections that were lost or maybe never existed. When sufficient healing takes place, the participants are often able to approach and reach each other in ways not previously possible.

We are privy to the entire gambit, from the horrible and intended harm to the heartbreaking mistake and misstep, and attempt in each instance to make the best recommendations for future treatment—treatment aimed at preserving the gains made initially within the therapeutic community that then hopefully lay a foundation for continued reconciliation and reunification.

We obviously expect, and know, that for most teenagers it does not take a respite in a therapeutic community to restore their equilibrium. For most, it means having their parents anticipate problems early and then act swiftly to establish and maintain authority and remain the guide who every teen needs to get them through what can be a troubling period in their lives. But being a teen guide these days is a harder undertaking than most adults first imagine.

What we want is for parents to know that if home- and school-based interventions are not working, there are those of us out here who can and want to help professionally. And we want parents to know that for most teens there is some group of efforts that will unlock the combination to their difficulties and restore them to a less-troubled emotional place. For most teens, like the ones named above, there is an intervention that will work and a journey, albeit difficult, that will lead them toward recovery and a healthier, more promising adulthood.

Resources

CHAPTER 3: ADOLESCENT DEPRESSION

American Academy of Pediatrics
(847) 434-4000
141 Northwest Point Boulevard
Elk Grove Village, IL 60007
www.aap.org/healthtopics/depression.cfm

American Academy of Child and
Adolescent Psychiatry
(202) 966-7300
3615 Wisconsin Avenue, NW
Washington, DC 20016
www.aacap.org

American Association of Suicidology
(202) 237-2280
4201 Connecticut Avenue, NW, Suite 310
Washington, DC 20008
www.suicidology.org

American Foundation for Suicide Prevention
(888) 333-AFSP
(212) 363-3500
120 Wall Street, 22nd Floor
New York, NY 10005
www.afsp.org

American Psychiatric Association
(703) 907-7300
1400 K Street, NW, Suite 501
Washington, DC 20005
www.psych.org

American Psychological Association
(202) 336-5700
750 1st Street, NE
Washington, DC 20002
www.apa.org

Mental Health America (formerly the National Mental Health Association)
(800) 969-6642
1021 Prince Street
Alexandria, VA 22314-2971
www.nmha.org

Parents' Medical Guide
http://schools.lwsd.org/lwhs/counseling/
   teensuicide/index.htm

CHAPTER 4: WHEN YOUR TEEN CUTS

Focus Adolescent Services : www.focusas.
com/SelfInjury.html

CHAPTER 5: TEENS AND SUBSTANCES

National Institute on Drug Abuse
(301) 443-1124
6001 Executive Boulevard, Room 5213
Bethesda, MD 20892-9561
www.nida.nih.gov

National Institute on Drug Abuse for Teens
http://teens.drugabuse.gov

National Center on Addiction and Substance Abuse at Columbia University
(212) 841-5200
633 Third Avenue, 19th Floor
New York, NY 10017-6706
www.casacolumbia.org

The Partnership for a Drug-Free America
(212) 922-1560
405 Lexington Avenue, Suite 1601
New York, NY 10174
www.drugfree.org

CHAPTER 6: WHEN YOUR TEEN'S EATING BECOMES A PROBLEM

National Eating Disorders Association
(800) 931-2237
603 Stewart Street, Suite 803
Seattle, WA 98101
www.edap.org

Something Fishy
www.something-fishy.org

CHAPTER 7: TEENS AND DELINQUENCY

U.S. Department of Justice, Office of Juvenile Justice and Delinquency Prevention
(202) 307-5911
810 Seventh Street NW
Washington, DC 20531

Juvenile Justice Clearinghouse
National Criminal Justice Reference Service
(800) 851-3420
P.O. Box 6000
Rockville, MD 20849–6000
http://ojjdp.ncjrs.org/index.html

National Center for Juvenile Justice
(412) 227-6950
3700 South Water Street, Suite 200
Pittsburgh, PA 15203
www.ncjj.org

Youth Law Center
(415) 543-3379
200 Pine Street, Suite 300
San Francisco, CA 94104
http://ylc.org

Cyberbullying: Mobilizing educators,
parents, students, and others to combat
online social cruelty
www.cyberbully.org

CHAPTER 8: TECHNOLOGY AND YOUR TEEN

American Academy of Pediatrics
www.aap.org/advocacy/releases/
   jstmtevc.htm

National Center for Missing and
Exploited Children
Charles B. Wang International Children's
   Building
24-hour hotline: (800) THE-LOST (800-
   843-5678)
(703) 274-3900
699 Prince Street
Alexandria, Virginia 22314-3175
www.missingkids.com

NetSmartz
http://www.netsmartz.org

CHAPTER 11: PARENTS AS ADVOCATES FOR THEIR CHILDREN

Parent/Professional Advocacy League
(617) 542-7860
59 Temple Place, Suite 664
Boston, MA 02111
www.ppal.net/whoispal.html

New York University Child Study Center
(212) 263-6622
577 First Avenue
New York, NY 10016
www.aboutourkids.org

National Institute of Mental Health
(866) 615-6464 (toll-free)
(866) 415-8051 (TTY toll-free)
6001 Executive Boulevard, Room 8184,
   MSC 9663
Bethesda, MD 20892-9663
www.nimh.nih.gov

Federation of Families for Children's
Mental Health
(240) 403-1901
9605 Medical Center Drive, Suite 280
Rockville, MD 20850
www.ffcmh.org

Substance Abuse and Mental Health
Services Administration,
National Mental Health Information Center
(800) 789-2647
P.O. Box 42557
Washington, DC 20015
www.mentalhealth.org

WrightsLaw
www.wrightslaw.com

CHAPTER 12: TREATMENTS THAT WORK

Pediatric Symptom Checklist
http://psc.partners.org

CRAFFT Substance Abuse Questionnaire
www.childrenshospital.org
(Type "CRAFFT" into the search function.)

Child Health and Development Interactive
System (CHADIS)
www.childhealthcare.org.

Massachusetts Child Psychiatry Access
Project
www.mcpap.org

Massachusetts General Hospital School
Psychiatry Program
www.schoolpsychiatry.org

Adolescent Mental Health and Wellness
Curriculum
www.adolescentwellness.org

References

INTRODUCTION

1. National Center for Health Statistics. "Health, United States, 2005." *www.cdc.gov/nchs/data/hus/hus05.pdf#046.*

2. J. Eckenrode, D. Silverman, J. Whitlock. "Self-Injurious Behaviors in a College Population," *Pediatrics,* June 2006, Vol. 117, No. 6, pp. 939–1948.

CHAPTER 1: THE MODERN ADOLESCENT'S WORLD

1. T.M. McGuinness. "Marriage, Divorce, and Children," *Journal of Psychosocial Nursing and Mental Health Services,* 2006, 44(2): 17–20.

2. U.S. Census Bureau. "Current Population Survey, 2003, Annual Social and Economic Survey (table C-3)." Washington, DC: U.S. Department of Commerce, Economics, and Statistics Administration, 2003.

3. U.S. Census Bureau. "Current Population Reports: America's families and living arrangements, 2003." Washington, DC: U.S. Department of Commerce, Economics and Statistics Administration, 2004.

4. J. Wallerstein, J. Lewis, and S. Blakeslee. *The Unexpected Legacy of Divorce: A 25-Year Landmark Study.* New York: Hyperion, 2000.

5. P. Amato and B. Keith. "Parental Divorce and the Well-Being of Children: A Meta-Analysis," *Psychological Bulletin,* 1991, 10: 26–46.

6. P. Amato. "Children of divorce in the 1990s: An update of the Amato and Keith (1991) meta-analysis 2001," *Journal of Family Psychology,* 15: 355–370.

7. Deborah Belle. *The After-School Lives of Children: Alone and With Others While Parents Work.* Mahwah, N.J.: Lawrence Erlbaum Associates, 1999.

8. Emil Parker, Deputy Assistant Secretary for Policy and External Affairs, Administration for Children and Families; Department of Health and Human Services. "Statement on After School Programs before the Congressional Children's Caucus," October 28, 1999, (www.hhs.gov/asl/testify/t991028b.html).

9. National Institute on Drug Abuse, "InfoFacts," www.nida.nih.gov/infofacts/HSYouthtrends.html (accessed October 20, 2006).

10. National Institute on Drug Abuse. "National Survey Results on Drug Use from Monitoring the Future Study, 1975–2002." NIH Publication No. 03-5374, April, 2003.

11. Walt Howe. "A Brief History of the Internet (Updated 7 Aug 2006)" The Internet Learning Tree. Downloaded (http://www.walthowe.com/navnet/history.html).

12. B. Wells and J. Twenge. "Changes in Young People's Sexual Behavior and Attitudes, 1943–1999: A Cross-Temporal Meta-Analysis," *Review of General Psychology,* 2005, 9 (3): 249–261.

13. Steven C. Martino, Ph.D.; Rebecca L. Collins, Ph.D.; Marc N. Elliott, Ph.D.; Amy Strachman, M.A.; David E. Kanouse, Ph.D.; and Sandra H. Berry, M.A. "Exposure to Degrading Versus Nondegrading Music Lyrics and Sexual Behavior Among Youth," *Pediatrics*, August 2006, Vol. 118 No. 2: e430–e441.

14. Denise D. Hallfors et al., "Adolescent Depression and Suicide Risk: Association with Sex and Drug Behavior," *American Journal of Preventive Medicine*, 2004, 27, no. 3: 224–231.

15. College Board. "Education Pays 2005: The Benefits of Higher Education for Individuals and Society." www.collegeboard.com/prod_downloads/press/cost05/education_pays_05.pdf (accessed October 17, 2006).

16. Judith Herman. *Trauma and Recovery*. New York, Basic Books: 1997.

CHAPTER 2: AN OVERVIEW OF ADOLESCENT DEVELOPMENT

1. M. Lezak. *Neuropsychological Assessment*. New York: Oxford University Press, 2004.

2. J. Piaget. *The Construction of Reality in the Child*. New York: Basic Books, 1954.

3. Elkind, D. *Child Development and Education: A Piagetian Perspective*. New York: Oxford University Press; 1976.

4. S. Durston, H.E. Hulshoff, B.J. Casey, et al. "Anatomical MRI of the Developing Human Brain: What Have We Learned?" *J American Academy of Child and Adolescent Psychiatry*, 2001, 40(9): 1012–1020.

5. J.L. Rapoport, J.N. Giedd, J. Blumenthal, et al. "Progressive Cortical Change During Adolescence in Childhood-Onset Schizophrenia. A Longitudinal Magnetic Resonance Imaging Study," *Archives of General Psychiatry*, 1999, 56: 649–654.

6. D.A. Yurgelun-Todd, W.D. Killgore, C.B. Cintron. "Cognitive Correlates of Medial Temporal Lobe Development across Adolescence: A Magnetic Resonance Imaging Study," *Perceptual and Motor Skills*, 2003, 96: 3–17.

7. I.M. Rosso, A.D. Young, L.A. Femia, and D. A. Yurgelun-Todd. "Cognitive and Emotional Components of Frontal Lobe Functioning in Childhood and Adolescence," *Annals of the New York Academy of Sciences*, 2004, 1021: 355–62.

8. A.A. Baird, S.A. Gruber, D.A. Fein, et al. "Functional Magnetic Resonance Imaging of Facial Affect Recognition in Children and Adolescents," *Journal of the American Academy of Child and Adolescent Psychiatry*, 1999, 38(2): 195–199.

9. D.A. Yurgelun-Todd, W.D. Killgore, C.B. Cintron. "Cognitive Correlates of Medial Temporal Lobe Development across Adolescence: A Magnetic Resonance Imaging Study," *Perceptual and Motor Skills*, 2003, 96: 3–17.

10. E.T. Rolls. *The Brain and Emotion*. Oxford: Oxford University Press, 1999.

11. H. Eichenbaum and N.J. Cohen. *From Conditioning to Conscious Recollection: Memory Systems of the Brain*. New York: Oxford University Press, 2001.

12. M. Dimitrov, J. Grafman, and C. Hollnagel. "The Effects of Frontal Lobe Damage on Everyday Problem Solving," *Cortex*, 1996, 32: 357–366.

13. M. Lezak. *Neuropsychological Assessment*. New York: Oxford University Press, 2004.

14. Elkind, D. *Child Development and Education: A Piagetian Perspective*. New York: Oxford University Press; 1976.

15. *Diagnostic and Statistical Manual of Mental Disorders, 4th ed. Text Revision.* Washington, DC: American Psychiatric Association, 2000.

CHAPTER 3: ADOLESCENT DEPRESSION

1. P. McGettigan, G.K. Isbister, I.M. Whyte, N. Rappaport, D.A. Brent, and B. Birmaher. "Adolescent Depression," *New England Journal of Medicine,* 2003, 348: 473–474.

2. B. Vitiello and S. Swedo. "Antidepressant Medications in Children," *New England Journal of Medicine,* Apr 8, 350(15): 1489–91.

3. J. Angst, F. Angst, and H.H. Stassen. "Suicide Risk in Patients with Major Depressive Disorder," *Journal of Clinical Psychiatry,* 1999, 60(supp. 2): 57–62.

4. D. Shaffer, M.S. Gould, P. Fisher, P. Trautment, D. Moreau, M. Kleinman, and M. Flory. "Psychiatric Diagnosis in Child and Adolescent Suicide," *Archives of General Psychiatry,* 1996: 53, 339–348.

5. S.D. Pine, E. Cohen, P. Cohen, J. Brook. "Adolescent Depressive Symptoms as Predictors of Adult Depression: Moodiness or Mood Disorder?" *American Journal of Psychiatry,* 1999, 156: 133–135.

CHAPTER 4: WHEN YOUR TEEN CUTS

1. E. Loyd, M.L. Kelley, and T. Hope. "Self-Mutilation in a Community Sample of Adolescents: Descriptive Characteristics and Provisional Prevalence Rates." Paper presented at the Annual Meeting of the Society for Behavioral Medicine, New Orleans, Louisiana, April 1997.

2. Laurie MacAniff Zila and Mark S. Kiselica. "Understanding and Counseling Self-Mutilation in Female Adolescents and young adults," *Journal of Counseling and Development,* Winter 2001, Volume 79, Number 1: 46–52.

3. J.H. Rathus and A.L. Miller. "Dialetical Behavior Therapy Adapted for Suicidal Adolescents," *Suicide and Life-Threatening Behavior,* 2002, 32: 146–147.

4. Matthew Knock and Mitchell Prinstein. "A Functional Approach to the Assessment of Self-Mutilative Behavior," *Journal of Consulting and Clinical Psychology,* 2004, 885–890.

5. M. Linehan. *Cognitive-Behavioral Treatment for Borderline Personality Disorder.* New York: The Guilford Press, 1993.

CHAPTER 5: TEENS AND SUBSTANCES

1. John R. Knight, et al. "Validity of the CRAFFT Substance Abuse Screening Test Among Adolescent Clinic Patients," *Archives of Pediatrics and Adolescent Medicine,"* 2002, 156: 607–614.

2. Lance Dodes, M.D. *The Heart of Addiction: A New Approach to Understanding and Managing Alcoholism and Other Addictive Behaviors.* New York: HarperCollins Publishers, 2002.

3. Nancy Darling. "Parenting Style and Its Correlates," *ERIC Digest,* March 1999, (www.ericdigests.org/1999-4/parenting.htm).

4. National Institute on Drug Abuse. "Inhalant Abuse," *Research Report, rev. 2005,* (http://www.drugabuse.gov/ResearchReports/Inhalants/Inhalants2.html#patterns).

5. National Institute on Drug Abuse. "Chronic Solvent Abusers Have More Brain Abnormalities and Cognitive Impairments Than Cocaine Abusers," *Research Findings,* Vol 17, No. 4, (http://www.drugabuse.gov/NIDA_notes/NNVol17N4/Chronic.html).

6. National Institute on Drug Abuse. "What Is the Extent and Impact of Tobacco Use?" *Research Report,* (http://www.drugabuse.gov/ResearchReports/Nicotine/nicotine2. html#impact).

7. American Cancer Society. "Children and Teen Tobacco Use," 2006, http://www.cancer. (org/docroot/PED/content/PED_10_2X_Child_and_Teen_Tobacco_Use. asp?sitearea=PED).

8. National Institute on Alcohol Abuse and Alcoholism. "Underage Drinking," *Alcohol Alert No. 67,* January 2006.

9. National Institute on Alcohol Abuse and Alcoholism. Report, April 2003.

10. National Highway Traffic Safety Administration. Drugs and Human Performance Fact Sheet. U.S. Department of Transportation Report No. DOT HS 809 725, Washington, DC, 2004.

11. National Center on Addiction and Substance Abuse. "National Survey of American Attitudes on Substance Abuse XI: Teens and Parents," August 2006.

12. National Institute on Drug Abuse. "Monitoring the Future Study, 2005."

13. National Institute on Drug Abuse. "Monitoring the Future Study, 2004."

CHAPTER 6: WHEN YOUR TEEN'S EATING BECOMES A PROBLEM

1. E. Schlosser. *Fast Food Nation: The Dark Side of the All-American Meal.* New York: Houghton Mifflin, 2001.

2. A. Becker, R. Burwell, et al. "Eating Behaviors and Attitudes Following Prolonged Exposure to Television Among Ethnic Fijian Adolescent Girls," *British Journal of Psychiatry,* 2002, 180: 509–514.

3. J.L. Hudson, et al. "The Prevalence and Correlates of Eating Disorders in the National Comorbidity Survey Replication," *Biological Psychiatry,* February 1, 2007, 61(3): 348–58.

4. D.E. Pawluck and K.M. Gorey. "Secular Trends in the Incidence of Anorexia Nervosa: Integrative Review of Population Based Studies," *International Journal of Eating Disorders,* May 1998, 23(4): 347–53.

5. Benjamin Sadock and Virginia Sadock, eds. *Kaplan and Sadock's Comprehensive Textbook of Psychiatry,* 8th Edition, Philadelphia, PA: Lippincott, Williams and Wilkins, 2005.

6. Ibid.

7. D.E. Pawluck and K.M. Gorey. "Secular Trends in the Incidence of Anorexia Nervosa: Integrative Review of Population Based Studies," *International Journal of Eating Disorders,* May 1998, 23(4): 347–53.

8. J.L. Hudson, et al. "The Prevalence and Correlates of Eating Disorders in the National Comorbidity Survey Replication," *Biological Psychiatry,* February 1, 2007, 61(3): 348–58.

9. M. Crago M, et al. "Eating Disturbances Among American Minority Groups: A Review," *International Journal of Eating Disorders,* April 1996, 19(3): 239–48.

10. A. Becker, R. Burwell, et al. "Eating Behaviors and Attitudes Following Prolonged Exposure to Television Among Ethnic Fijian Adolescent Girls," *British Journal of Psychiatry,* 2002, 180: 509–514.

11. H.C. Steinhausen. "Ten-Year Follow-Up of Adolescent-Onset Anorexia Nervosa: Psychiatric Disorders and Overall Functioning Scales." *Journal of Child Psychology and*

Psychiatry, 2001, 42: 613–622.

12. P.K. Keel, et al. "The Long-Term Impact of Treatment in Women Diagnosed with Bulimia Nervosa." *International Journal of Eating Disorders,* 2002, 31: 151–158.

13. C. Fairburn, et al. "The Natural Course of Bulimia Nervosa and Binge Eating Disorder in Young Women." *Archives in General Psychiatry,* 2000, 57: 659–665.

14. C. Dare C, et al. "Psychological Therapies for Adults with Anorexia Nervosa. Randomised Controlled Trial of Out-Patient Treatments." *British Journal of Psychiatry,* 2001, 178: 216–221.

15. J. Lock, D. Le Grange, W.S. Agras, and C. Dare. *Treatment Manual for Anorexia Nervosa: A Family-Based Approach.* New York: The Guilford Press, 2001.

16. G. Wilson, et al. *Handbook of Treatment for Eating Disorders.* New York: The Guilford Press, 1997.

CHAPTER 7: TEENS AND DELINQUENCY

1. U.S. Department of Health and Human Services. "Mental Health: A Report of the Surgeon General." Rockville, MD: U.S. Department of Health and Human Services, 1999.

2. S. Hoyt and D.G. Scherer. "Female Juvenile Delinquency: Misunderstood by the Juvenile Justice System, Neglected by Social Science," *Law and Human Behavior,* February 1998, 22(1): 81–107.

3. T.M. Button, S.H. Rhee, J.K. Hewitt, S.E. Young, R.P. Corley, and M.C. Stallings. "The Role of Conduct Disorder in Explaining the Comorbidity Between Alcohol and Illicit Drug Dependence in Adolescence," *Drug and Alcohol Dependence,* September 7, 2006, 87(1): 46–53.

4. S. Mannuzza, R.G. Klein, H. Abikoff, J.L. Moulton 3rd. "Significance of Childhood Conduct Problems to Later Development of Conduct Disorder Among Children with ADHD: A Prospective Follow-Up Study," *Journal of Abnormal Child Psychology,"* 2004, Oct; 32(5): 565–73.

5. R.B. Goldstein, B.F. Grant, W.J. Ruan, S.M. Smith, and T.D. Saha. "Antisocial Personality Disorder with Childhood- vs. Adolescence-Onset Conduct Disorder: Results from the National Epidemiologic Survey on Alcohol and Related Conditions," *The Journal of Nervous and Mental Disease,* 2006 Sep, 194(9): 667–75.

CHAPTER 8: TECHNOLOGY AND YOUR TEEN

1. M. Wittig. "Sexual Predators: Teach Kids Safe Internet Use," *Milwaukee Journal Sentinel,* August 29, 2005.

2. P.M. Valkenburg, J. Peter, and A.P. Schouten. "Friend Networking Sites and Their Relationship to Adolescents' Well-Being and Social Self-Esteem," *Cyberpsychology and Behavior,* October 2006, 9(5): 584–90.

3. R. Brough and J. Sills. "Multimedia Bullying Using a Website," *Archives of Disease in Childhood,* February 2006, 91(2): 202.

4. Ibid.

5. S.C. Martino, R.L. Collins, M.N. Elliott, A.Strachman, D.E. Kanouse, and S.H. Berry. "Exposure to Degrading Versus Nondegrading Music Lyrics and Sexual Behavior Among Youth," *Pediatrics,* August 2006, Vol. 118 No. 2: e430–e441.

6. L.R. Huesmann, J. Moise-Titus, C.L. Podolski, and L.D. Eron. "Longitudinal Relations Between Children's Exposure to TV Violence and Their Aggressive and Violent Behavior in Young Adulthood: 1977–1992," *Developmental Psychology*, 2003, 39(2): 201–21.

7. R.H. DuRant, H. Champion, and M. Wolfson. "The Relationship Between Watching Professional Wrestling on Television and Engaging in Date Fighting Among High School Students," *Pediatrics*, 2006, Vol. 118 No. 2: e265–e272.

CHAPTER 11: PARENTS AS ADVOCATES

1. Manisses Communications Group. "New Center Seeks to Improve Results in Children's M.H," *Mental Health Weekly*, May 22, 2000.

2. U.S. Department of Education, Office of Special Education Programs. "Building the Legacy: IDEA 2004." (accessed February 27, 2007) (http://idea.ed.gov/explore/view).

CHAPTER 12: TREATMENTS THAT WORK

1. J.D. Minna, et al. "A Bull's Eye for Targeted Lung Cancer Therapy." *Science*, 2004, 304: 1458–1461.

2. R. Sordella, et al. "Gefitinib–Sensitizing EGFR Mutations in Lung Cancer Activate Anti–Apoptotic Pathways," *Science*, 2004, 305: 1163–1167.

3. J.G. Paez, et al. "EGFR Mutations in Lung Cancer: Correlation with Clinical Response to Gefitinib Therapy," *Science*, 2004, 304: 1497–1500.

4. T.J. Lynch, et al. "Activating Mutations in the Epidermal Growth Factor Receptor Underlying Responsiveness to Non-Small-Cell Lung Cancer to Gefitinib," *New England Journal of Medicine*, 2004, 350: 2129.

5. A.K. Malhotra, et al. "Pharmacogenetics of Psychotropic Drug Response," *American Journal of Psychiatry*, 2004, 161: 780–796.

6. J.M. McClellan and J.S. Werry. "Evidence-Based Treatments in Child and Adolescent Psychiatry: An Inventory," *Journal of the American Academy of Child and Adolescent Psychiatry* 2003, 42: 1388–1400.

7. G. Seeger, et al. "Marker Gene Polymorphisms in Hyperkinetic Disorders: Predictors of Clinical Response to Treatment with Methylphenidate?" *Neuroscience Letters* 2001, 313: 45–48.

8. H. Abikoff, et al. "Symptomatic Improvement in Children with ADHD Treated with Long-Term Methylphenidate and Multimodal Psychosocial Treatment," *Journal of the American Academy of Child and Adolescent Psychiatry*, 2004, 43: 802–811.

9. D.A. Geller, et al. "Which SSRI? A Meta-Analysis of Pharmacotherapy Trials in Pediatric Obsessive-Compulsive Disorder," *American Journal of Psychiatry*, 2004, 160: 1919–1928.

10. S.N. Compton, et al. "Cognitive-Behavioral Psychotherapy for Anxiety and Depressive Disorders in Children and Adolescents: An Evidence-Based Medicine Review," *Journal of the American Academy of Child and Adolescent Psychiatry*, 2004, 43: 930–959.

11. Ibid.

12. J. March, S. Silva, B. Vitiello, and the TADS Team. "The Treatment for Adolescents with Depression Study (TADS): Methods and Message at 12 Weeks," *Journal of the American Academy of Child and Adolescent Psychiatry*, 2006, 45:12: 1393–1403.

Acknowledgments

Cynthia S. Kaplan, Ph.D.

FIRST AND FOREMOST, I want to thank my coeditors, Drs. Blaise Aguirre and Michael Rater, who were instrumental in both the development and medical oversight of this text. They are friends as well as colleagues, and it is my privilege to work beside them on a daily basis and to share ideas, interventions, and a deep love for the work we do.

A special thanks goes as well to all the chapter contributors, most of whom we know personally and all of whom we admire for their expertise and devotion to patient care and family advocacy and for their determined efforts to improve the emotional lives of children and adolescents. They are Drs. Roya Ostovar, Ken Sklar, Michael Hollander, Ben Molbert, Richard Falzone, Thomas Weigel, and Joseph Gold; Ms. Sue Mandelbaum-Cohen; and Ms. Lisa Lambert. They each worked long hours and gave generously of their time and wisdom to complete this undertaking.

We would all also like to gratefully acknowledge McLean Hospital and Partner's Psychiatry for their endless support of child and adolescent programming. Without this institutional support, it would not have been possible to bring together this impressive collection of talented, diverse, and well-trained professionals, who are each committed to the betterment of child mental health. Nor would it be possible to deliver state-of-the-art clinical care and to provide therapeutic settings where children and families can find answers to some of the complex challenges of adolescent development and behavior.

And then, most important, there are each and every one of the children and families who have passed through our programs and whom we have had the pleasure of getting to know and help. It is a perpetual honor to take part in a child's recovery from emotional illness and to behold the courage, curiosity, and determination essential for healing. This book is, more than anything, our "thank you" to the scores of teens who have allowed us to share in their inner lives, told us their stories, and from whom we have learned the majority of what we now know. They have our gratitude and deep respect, and they are the true inspiration behind this effort to ensure, as many have requested, that their suffering not have "occurred in silence or been in vain." It is our hope and theirs that this project will help avert difficulties and perhaps shorten another child's path to recovery.

An especially significant thanks also goes to our editor, Cara Connors, who has worked extraordinarily hard to bring this project to completion. Coming aboard relatively late in the game, she brought cohesion and a standard of excellence to the collected thoughts of the many contributors, which is not an easy job for anyone to undertake. With persistence and a finely honed ability to stay focused on the key elements and message of the book, she was a delight to work with and clearly made a substantive improvement in the final product.

Thank you, too, to all of the folks who provided input at various stages of the book.

Finally, a personal thanks to my husband, who worked untiringly as unofficial editor, amateur critic, technological assistant, and emotional cheerleader to help me bring this project to the finish line. And last but far from least, thanks to my four children, who taught me many invaluable lessons about how simultaneously precious and precarious teen parenting can be. These lessons have added immeasurably to both my overall professional development and to this current undertaking.

Contributors

Richard L. Falzone, M.D., graduated from the University of Texas, Southwestern Medical School, in 2000. He completed his adult psychiatry residency training and his child and adolescent fellowship training at Massachusetts General Hospital and McLean Hospital in Belmont, Massachusetts. Dr. Falzone is on staff at McLean Hospital in the child outpatient clinic where he practices medication management and conducts the weekly teen dual diagnosis recovery group. He sees young people and adults for psychotherapy and medication management in his private practice in Melrose, Massachusetts. He also runs an outpatient opiate recovery program as part of his private practice.

Joseph Gold, M.D., has worked as a child psychiatrist for the past twenty-five years. He is the chief medical officer, chief of clinical quality, and the clinical director of the Child and Adolescent Program for McLean Hospital in Belmont, Massachusetts, and the director of community child psychiatry services for Partners Psychiatry and Mental Health in Massachusetts. Dr. Gold has devoted his career to the creation and operation of clinical programs and special education schools for youths and their families and to the coordination of care between mental health professionals, parents, teachers, and primary care pediatricians. He is also the medical codirector of the Massachusetts Child Psychiatry Access Project, cochairman of the Massachusetts Chapter of the American Academy of Pediatrics Task Force on Child Mental Health, and a member of the Massachusetts Commission on Child Mental Health. Dr. Gold is board certified in both adult and child and adolescent psychiatry and has a special interest in outcome measures, evidence-based care, and quality improvement initiatives.

Michael Hollander, Ph.D., has been a senior affiliate at Two Brattle Center in Cambridge, Massachusetts, since its inception. He has treated adolescents for more than twenty years and developed an expertise in individual and group therapies, including the use of dialectical behavior therapy with teenagers. He has a strong interest in understanding and treating adolescents who engage in self-injurious behavior. Dr. Hollander received his Ph.D. in counseling psychology from Michigan State University in 1979. He completed a two-year post-doctoral fellowship in adolescent psychology at McLean Hospital in Belmont, Massachusetts, and Harvard Medical School in 1981, at which time he joined the staff at McLean. He is on the teaching faculty in the department of child psychiatry at Massachusetts General Hospital, and he is an instructor in psychology in the department of psychiatry of the Harvard Medical School. He is a trainer for Behavioral Tech, LLC, and is the psychological consultant to the Willow Hill School in Sudbury, Massachusetts.

Lisa Lambert is the assistant director of the Parent/Professional Advocacy League (PAL), the Massachusetts state organization of the Federation of Families for Children's Mental Health. She has worked at PAL for almost fifteen years, during which she coauthored a crisis guide for parents, wrote numerous policy papers, and worked to get family stories in the media. She advocates for systems change to improve the mental health system for children and serves on several boards. She grew up in Massachusetts and attended Mt. Holyoke College, where she received her bachelor's degree.

Sue Mandelbaum-Cohen, LICSW, received her bachelor's degree from Queens College of the City University of New York and her master's degree in social work from Hunter College School of Social Work. She performed her advanced clinical training at the William Alanson White Institute and Nathan Ackerman Family Therapy Institute in New York City. She has worked with children, adolescents, and families for more than twenty years at Westboro State Hospital, the Lawrence Schiff Day Treatment Center, and Pembroke Hospital, all in Massachusetts. Ms. Mandelbaum-Cohen has worked at McLean Hospital in Belmont, Massachusetts, as coordinator of the Adolescent Residential Treatment Program for the past six years and has undergone dialectical behavior training therapy.

Ben Molbert, M.D., attended medical school at the Louisiana State University Medical Center in Shreveport. His post-graduate training included internship and general psychiatry residency via the Stanford University Medical Center Department of Psychiatry and Behavioral Sciences. Dr. Molbert completed his child psychiatry residency at the Harvard Medical School/Massachusetts General Hospital/McLean Hospital Child and Adolescent Psychiatry Residency Training Program. He then completed the Harvard Medical School Forensic Psychiatry Fellowship via the Massachusetts General Hospital Department of Psychiatry and the Law. Dr. Molbert is currently the medical director for the McLean Southeast Adolescent Acute Residential Treatment Program in Brockton, Massachusetts. He holds an academic appointment as an instructor in psychiatry through Harvard Medical School.

Roya Ostovar, Ph.D., is a child clinical neuropsychologist with a subspecialty in neurodevelopmental disorders and psychiatric disorders of childhood and adolescence. Dr. Ostovar specializes in testing and assessing children, from birth to young adulthood, for diagnostic and treatment purposes. Dr. Ostovar is the director of the Center for Neurodevelopmental Services at McLean Hospital in Belmont, Massachusetts, is on the faculty at Harvard Medical School, and has a private practice in Belmont.

Ken Sklar, LICSW, Ed.D., received his master's degree in psychiatric social work from the University of Wisconsin in Madison and his doctorate in counseling psychology from Boston University. Dr. Sklar has held senior administrative positions both as the administrative director of psychiatry at Boston Regional Medical Center and at North Shore Medical Center in Massachusetts. Dr. Sklar is currently the corporate director of Partners Psychiatry in Boston. Dr. Sklar has been a national health care consultant for psychiatry departments at academic medical centers. Dr. Sklar has maintained a private practice for the past twenty-five years, working with adolescents and their families and specializing in the areas of depression and substance abuse.

Thomas J. Weigel, M.D., is a child and adolescent psychiatrist at the Klarman Eating Disorders Center at McLean Hospital in Belmont, Massachusetts, and a clinical instructor in psychiatry at Harvard Medical School. He completed medical school at the University of Wisconsin, a general psychiatry residency at Massachusetts General Hospital/Harvard Medical School, and a two-year child and adolescent psychiatry fellowship at Children's Hospital/Harvard Medical School. Dr. Weigel is a diplomate of the American Board of Psychiatry and Neurology and has training in psychoanalysis through the Boston Psychoanalytic Society and Institute. He has maintained a private practice for the past seven years, specializing in psychopharmacology.

Index